MÉMOIRES
FOR THE INSTRUCTION OF THE
DAUPHIN

V. Vaillant ad vivum faciebat cum Privilegio Regis   P. Van schuppen sculpebat. 1660.

LOUIS XIV
KING OF FRANCE AND OF NAVARRE

MÉMOIRES
FOR THE
INSTRUCTION
OF THE
DAUPHIN

Introduction, Translation & Notes by PAUL SONNINO

The Free Press : New York
Collier-Macmillan Limited : London

THE FREE PRESS
A DIVISION OF THE MACMILLAN COMPANY
866 THIRD AVENUE
NEW YORK, NEW YORK 10022

COLLIER-MACMILLAN CANADA LTD., TORONTO, ONTARIO

Library of Congress Catalog Card Number: 70–81669

PRINTED IN THE UNITED STATES OF AMERICA

printing number
1   2   3   4   5   6   7   8   9   10

CONTENTS

INTRODUCTORY

INTRODUCTION

LOUIS XIV was an earnest person who did not find it necessary to examine himself very closely. Reared by a loving mother, furnished with a practical education by Mazarin and by the royal tutor, Bishop Péréfixe, the young King readily accepted the world as an eminently sensible place. That futile revolt of the *parlements* and of the great nobles, the Fronde, may have caused him to reflect on the merits of absolute monarchy, but, by the same token, it failed to stir in him either a hatred for the nobility or an obsessive fear of revolution. If he learned how to deceive, as in the arrest of the Princes de Condé and de Conti, the experience did not necessarily turn him into a compulsive dissimulator. When he was studying the history of France, the very name of do-nothing kings and of mayors of the palace would distress him, and he selected his vigorous grandfather, Henry IV, for emulation. Yet Louis dutifully married the Spanish Infanta, Maria Theresa, and managed to balance patience against an increasing confidence in his own capacities until March 9, 1661, when Cardinal Mazarin's death inaugurated the personal reign.

The King's approach to life was to be conceded if not applauded by all his intimates during the early years when he was his own master. Still, there was a challenge in testing himself, and his relationships, under the new conditions. He desired to be a model son, dutifully submitting to Anne of Austria's occasional reproaches in private, while exacting, in return, her total abstention from political intrigue. To all who demonstrated their friendship and loyalty, he was eager to reciprocate abundantly. He was hard put to contain his youthful and warm-blooded passions, but he intended to keep them from interfering with the craft of kingship. Louis had succumbed to Mlle. de La Vallière prior to November, 1661, when the Dauphin was born. In 1662, the affair became public knowledge, but he persisted in confining it within his self-imposed limits. Time was to bring increased assurance. The year 1665, marked by the serious illness of his mother, presaged a new emancipation. He had also to consider his son's education, and he himself was approaching a milestone on the road to maturity. He would reach his thirtieth year in 1667.

The King's notions on government were also to be applied rather successfully during the formative stages of his own administration. Louis aspired to restore the French monarchy to its natural perfection.

This meant affording his people the respite of peace, re-establishing the crown's financial stability, relegating the *parlements* and great nobles to their proper functions, and ridding the Church of its Jansenist trouble-makers. These tasks proceeded apace, save for the last, which ran into numerous stumbling blocks. The restoration of order, however, was merely the basis for more glorious excursions into the realms of foreign policy and war. Even during the period of domestic reform, occasions for international prestige, such as avenging insults to French ambassadors in London and at the Holy See, or for territorial acquisition, such as the treaties for Lorraine and for Dunkirk, seemed to arouse the greatest enthusiasm in him. In 1662, the King proudly adopted the sun disk as his emblem, but, once again, the year 1665 stands out. That year, Philip IV of Spain died, leaving his disintegrating monarchy virtually defenseless. For the time being, an Anglo-Dutch war restricted Louis' freedom of action, but the Sun King could still view the advent of his thirtieth year as coinciding with a new and higher stage in the evolution of his designs.

Such a man is not a questioner but a justifier. He cannot be expected to produce confessions in the grand manner, but, rather, descriptions of his calling and how he had mastered it. Louis began early to prepare his vindications. On the very first day of the personal reign, he summoned his secretary, President Rose, and dictated to him the deathbed counsels of Cardinal Mazarin.[1] The matters brought up by the Cardinal, relating mainly to domestic order and to the need for personal rule, were to find their way into the King's own *Mémoires*. Late in 1662, moreover, Louis' financial expert, J. B. Colbert, attempted to secure a historian for the King's personal service. It may not be pure coincidence that in March, 1663, a certain President de Périgny emerged from obscurity to become a *lecteur du roi*. Nevertheless, it was Colbert who, shortly thereafter, assumed the task of chronicling the reign. In April, he began to keep a journal that he subsequently extended into historical notes covering the years 1661 to 1664.[2] The work centered on Louis, stressing his intelligence, dedication, and admirable qualities. It described the domestic and international situations when he assumed personal control, outlined, in the spirit of Mazarin's counsels, the major policy decisions, and diligently recorded the principal events of the reign. But the year 1665, so

1. Published in *Lettres, instructions, et mémoires de Colbert,* ed. Pierre Clément (Paris, 1861–1882), I, 535–536. See also the slightly different version in the French Ministry of Foreign Affairs archives, Mémoires et Documents, *Espagne* 64, ff. 103–106.

2. Bibliothèque Nationale, Manuscrit Clairambault 485, pp. 1–56 [pub. in *Lettres, instructions, et mémoires de Colbert, op. cit.,* VI, 462–490]. See the more complete copy in the Foreign Affairs archives, Mémoires et Documents, *France* 296, pp. 1–94.

central in other respects, also saw Colbert's efforts assume a different character. At that time, he constructed a two-part document intended specifically for the King's own *Mémoires*.[3] In the first section, which analyzes the international scene when Louis began the personal reign, the King speaks in the first person and addresses himself to his son. The moment was at hand for a preliminary accounting in anticipation of much greater triumphs.

Early in 1666, the personal and the political united to introduce the new setting. On the one hand, Anne of Austria died; on the other, Louis intervened in the Anglo-Dutch war. Almost immediately thereafter, we encounter the King giving direct attention to his *Mémoires*. He began to keep brief notes, or *feuilles,* on current events. Periodically, he transmitted these to Périgny, who emerges at this point as his principal collaborator, for insertion into a work book, or *registre*. The *feuilles* and the more extensive *registre* contain both events and reflections. Périgny used the *registre* as his principal source in drafting short segments of text, which he would later present for Louis' scrutiny. In this manner, *Mémoires* for 1666 gradually took shape, and the *Mémoires* assumed the form of contemporary history teaching by example.

That same year found the King, fully emancipated, squabbling with his brother, the Duke d'Orléans. But he may also have sought to find a new authority in the judgment of history by consulting such works as Machiavelli's *Prince* and the *Discourses on the First Ten Books of Titus Livy*. The *registre* contains specific references to these two works, and the entire *Mémoires* not merely demonstrate a knowledge of history, but they emerge as an implicit commentary on that frequently misunderstood Italian thinker.

Meanwhile, Colbert's previous work was applied by Périgny to the compilation of texts for the years 1661 and 1662. He also labored on portions of a text for 1665. Although these are now partly or totally lost, it is clear that they described the condition of France and of Europe at the beginning of the personal reign, Louis' assumption of power, his policies, and his experiences. The emphasis was on administrative, financial, and judicial matters, along with some consideration of religious, foreign, and military affairs. The King's confidence in Périgny may be weighed by the fact that in September, 1666, he designated this little-known man as tutor to the Dauphin.

In 1667, Louis appeared to break off his affair with Mlle. de La Vallière and to center his attentions on the long anticipated war against Spain. But the *feuilles* and the *registre* thrived on the War of Devolution.

3. Published in *Lettres, instructions, et mémoires de Colbert, op. cit.,* II, CCXII–CCXVII.

The King's thoughts were echoed by Périgny, who began the first full text for 1666 with the words, "In the first part of these *mémoires*, which contains nearly five years, I have described to you in what manner I had conducted myself during the peace, and in this second one, I intend to show you how I have acted in war." [4] He was to prepare two such texts and a revision for 1662. Although the year 1668 saw the *feuilles* and the *registre* abandoned, Périgny worked on three texts for 1667 and one for 1668. Then, around 1669 or 1670, came a revision for 1661 as well as a third text for 1666.

These efforts were interrupted by Périgny's death in September, 1670, but even then, Louis showed no intention of putting aside his *Mémoires*. The King quickly found a new collaborator in Paul Pellisson, a former Protestant, who enjoyed some reputation as a penegyrist and historian. Louis and his neophyte assistant undertook a new revision of the *Mémoires* for 1661, in which many additions, reminiscences of youth, evaluations of people, and reflections on religion bear the King's direct imprint. Still another minor revision followed, but the new collaboration proved short-lived. Louis had resumed his *feuilles* in 1670 and 1671, but in subsequent years he turned almost exclusively to the chronicling of his military campaigns.

The King saved these documents with his most personal papers for over forty years, a token of their importance for him. Only in 1714, in the twilight of his reign, did he seem about to destroy them. Instead, he gave the manuscripts to Marshal de Noailles, who subsequently deposited them in the Royal Library. Gradually, the documents have come to light. In 1767, the abbé d'Olivet issued a corrupted segment of Pellisson's revision for 1661, naming Pellisson as the author.[5] Two editions that appeared in 1806, however, are of considerably greater value. The first, that of Gain-Montagnac, relied on the manuscripts and trumpeted Louis XIV as the writer.[6] The second, the Grouvelle edition, is unsurpassed in its choice of texts.[7] The editor possessed copies that are now lost, such as a last section of the *Mémoires* for 1661 and the revision of the *Mémoires* for 1662. Grouvelle believed that the King had labored alone between 1666 and 1670 and was only later assisted by Pellisson.

This progress could not withstand the onslaught of nineteenth-century criticism. To Charles Dreyss belongs the credit for discovering

4. Bibliothèque Nationale, *Manuscrit Français* 6732, f. 180.

5. *Recueil d'opuscules littéraires tirés d'un cabinet d'Orléans et publiés par un anonyme* [Abbé J. d'Olivet] (Amsterdam, 1767).

6. *Mémoires de Louis XIV écrits par lui-même*, ed. J. L. M. de Gain-Montagnac (Paris, 1806), 2 vols. in 1.

7. *Oeuvres de Louis XIV*, ed. Ph. A. Grouvelle (Paris, 1806), 6 vols.

the collaboration of Périgny. To him also attaches the stigma, in his edition of the *Mémoires*,[8] of having misled posterity for over a hundred years. Dreyss used all the scholarly apparatus of his age to advance the implausible and demonstrably wrong thesis that the second part of the *Mémoires*, the texts for 1666 to 1668, was written prior to the earliest texts for 1661 and 1662. The first part, he claimed, had been a mere afterthought, corrupted, moreover, by the futile efforts of the incompetent Pellisson. We find him condemning the work and the style of his own hero, Périgny, on the mistaken belief that it was Pellisson's. The edition seems to concern itself with everything except Louis.

Nevertheless, Dreyss' conclusions have matched brilliantly both the monarchist suspicion that great kings are beyond literature and the republican conviction that willful tyrants live only on borrowed thoughts. Longnon's recent and readable editions, therefore, have been greeted with hostility, or at best sullenly ignored.[9]

*

In view of the scarcity of Louis' handwriting on the manuscripts, however, it is understandable that questions should arise regarding the authorship of the *Mémoires*. The *feuilles,* in the King's own hand, are undoubtedly authentic, and it is evident that Louis transmitted information to Périgny for insertion into the *registre*. But what of the reflections and the references to Machiavelli's works, and what of the actual texts in which statements are amplified, changed, and even eliminated?

Some of the reflections are ascribable to the King, others are avowedly Périgny's, although there are still more, such as the Machiavelli notations, whose precise authorship is still uncertain. Yet we may recall the circumstances that made Louis turn to history. He studied, say the *Mémoires* for 1666, "even the most remote times."[10] The *Prince* and the *Discourses* offer just the approach to statecraft and warfare, along with verdicts on historical figures, that might have aroused the King's enthusiasm. The author, moreover, draws heavily from classical antiquity. Louis missed Machiavelli's point repeatedly, as might be expected of an inexperienced reader with strong preconceptions. The King inadvertently or deliberately distorted this inveterate republican and religious utilitarian in order to exalt absolute monarchy and the true

8. *Mémoires de Louis XIV*, ed. C. Dreyss (Paris, 1860), 2 vols.

9. *Mémoires pour les années 1661 et 1666*, ed. J. Longnon (Paris, 1923), and *Mémoires de Louis XIV*, ed. J. Longnon (Paris, 1927). The correct order of composition is demonstrated in Paul Sonnino, "The Dating and Authorship of Louis XIV's *Mémoires,*" *French Historical Studies*, III, 3 (Spring, 1964), 303–337.

10. See p. 216.

faith. Louis, notwithstanding his own moral fervor, also failed to recognize the same quality in Machiavelli. But all the reflections and notations whose authorship is ambiguous appear more trustworthy if one examines the actual texts, which betray the King's presence in a variety of ways.

They point up events that Louis considered worthy of note and of reflection. Late in 1661, in London, a dispute over precedence between the French ambassador and his Spanish counterpart, Baron de Vatteville, had erupted into a street battle between their retainers. Colbert's historical notes, as might be expected, go into some detail on this matter. At the first news, Colbert relates, the King assembled a special council which unanimously advised a policy of moderation. Louis, however, overrode them on the grounds that the occasion was ideal for a significant diplomatic triumph. Indeed, he brought such pressure to bear that Philip IV was obliged to recall Vatteville and to concede a public declaration that Spanish ambassadors would no longer contest precedence with the French. Colbert's account of the council meeting was used in preparing the *Mémoires* for 1661. Had it been repeated verbatim, this would still provide an insight into the King's character. However, in the text, the description is embellished by Louis' highly personal and self-congratulatory reflections on the affair, which include extremely interesting considerations on the relationship between justice, honor, and utility.[11] If Périgny was the author of these reflections, he had managed to grasp the King's policies better than any of his contemporaries.

The documents also show how carefully Louis supervised the preparation of successive texts. In the years 1664 and 1665, the Sorbonne condemned two books that supported the doctrine of papal infallibility. Pope Alexander VII asked the King to have the censures withdrawn, and when Louis refused to comply, the Pope took matters in his own hands. In June, 1665, he issued a bull condemning the Sorbonne. The *Parlement* of Paris thereupon retaliated with a condemnation of the bull. The King appeared to be on the verge of another crisis with the Papacy.

At that point, Cardinal de Retz, the *enfant terrible* of the Fronde, who had been relegated to an aimless existence in Rome, sought to make himself useful. He attempted, in greatest secrecy, to arrange a compromise between the Holy See and the Sorbonne. Louis acceded to the proposal, which had the effect of relaxing tensions, although nothing ever came of it.[12] Thus, on February 14, 1666, the King handed some

---

11. See p. 16 and p. 77.

12. For a full description of this dispute, see Paul Sonnino, *Louis XIV's View of the Papacy (1661–1667)*, (Berkeley and Los Angeles, 1966).

notes to Périgny, from which the collaborator made the following inaccurate entry in the *registre*:

> Order to Cardinal de Retz to settle amicably with the Pope whatever problems there might be with that court; believing that with the great affairs that might arise for me, it was desirable to have its favor.[13]

Louis would never have displayed such confidence in the old rebel. Périgny continued to give the impression that the Cardinal was a plenipotentiary in the first full text of the *Mémoires* for 1666. The King must have carefully scrutinized this text, because the section on Retz was subsequently corrected so as to read:

> Meanwhile, I charged Cardinal de Retz with seeking ways in Rome, where he was, to settle the problems of the Sorbonne, seeing that since he was himself one of its doctors, he would be more likely to find some reasonable solutions.[14]

It is also true that Louis' offhand statements managed to find their way into the texts. Late in 1667, he was back from a successful campaign in the Spanish Low Countries, marred only by the necessity of abandoning the siege of Dendermonde. The exuberant King found an occasion to wax philosophical, and Périgny did not fail to preserve it:

> It is hard to see to everything at once! He who is charged with a private affair often blames the sovereign for not furnishing him with everything that he desired for his purposes. But he does not consider how many things there are to do at once, that it is necessary to take care of all of them, and that whoever would give too abundantly to one, would inevitably be lacking toward the others.
> This is a reflection that the King has made to me, conversing casually today, September 12. It should be placed somewhere in the present or in the following years.
> In the same conversation, on the retreat from Dendermonde, the King indicated to me that he believed it to be his most virtuous action of the entire campaign.[15]

---

13. Bibliothèque Nationale, *Manuscrit Français* 6732, p. 5 [pub. in Dreyss, *op. cit.,* I, 19].

14. Bibliothèque Nationale, *Manuscrit Français* 6733, ff. 300–301. See the second text, p. 164.

15. Bibliothèque Nationale, *Manuscrit Français* 6732, f. 100 [pub. in Dreyss, *op. cit.,* II, 260–261].

Périgny had already completed most of the first full text of the *Mémoires* for 1666, but he found a place there to insert Louis' reflection, with much embellishment.[16] On the other hand, the assertion about Dendermonde appears in the *Mémoires* for 1667, where the King says of the reversal, "I have regarded it as the only action of this campaign in which I had truly put my virtue to the test."[17] This last example reinforces Louis' claim to the many personal statements that are found in the *Mémoires*, and notably, in the closely supervised Pellisson revision for 1661.

The King, therefore, gave Périgny the substance of the *Mémoires*. He may well have reflected on Machiavelli with him and probably chose from Colbert's historical notes what matters were to be inserted. He carefully checked successive texts. We can be confident that it is he who speaks whenever we find expressions of his own feelings. In the *Mémoires* for 1661, he tells his son that he is leaving him "the means to correct history if it should go astray and misunderstand, from not having fully penetrated into my plans and into my motives."[18] What reasons have we to doubt him?

*

Louis' principal concern in his *Mémoires* is with man and the state. He sees human nature as constant, insisting that men are corrupt and naturally bent toward their own particular advantages. All the same, they fall into different categories. Age and temperament affect their behavior. The King speaks with understandable forbearance about youth, "an age when it is usual to love only pleasure."[19] On the other hand, he displays an equally comprehensible impatience with crusty old age. The elderly Chancellor Séguier was "reputed to be lacking in firmness,"[20] and the Count de Brienne, secretary of state, was "old and conceited."[21] Men, of course, also vary in intelligence, but Louis sees social class as creating the most profound character distinctions. The mass of men seek only what is useful and pleasant. They enjoy criticizing what lies beyond their competence and at such times deserve to be ignored. An assembly of bourgeois, the King notes, is "easy to mislead and to intimidate."[22] All this implies that the bourgeoisie, with rare exceptions, should be kept within its established functions. The *Mémoires*, however, present man's condition as an axiom rather than as a cause for censure. Louis prizes humanity for what can be done with it and yearns for its

16. Bibliothèque Nationale, *Manuscrit Français* 6733, f. 288. See the second text, pp. 158–159.

17. See p. 236.   18. See p. 22.   19. P. 63.
20. P. 34.   21. P. 35.   22. Pp. 249–250.

ultimate approbation. He also manifests especially warm sentiments for the nobility. He takes pleasure in their society. He wishes to reserve even the junior army posts for them. The King delights in relating how the Count de La Feuillade came to the defense of his honor against a detractor in Spain.[23] Both Machiavelli and Louis are humanists, but the Italian moralist's admiration for the natural aristocrat gives way in the King to a predilection for the hereditary one.

It should surprise no one that Louis' conception of society is organic and corporate. "All these different conditions," according to him, "are united to each other only by an exchange of reciprocal obligations."[24] The King also points out that "the more exhausted the provinces are by the soldiers or by anything else, the less capable they are of contributing to the other public burdens."[25] Thus "it is a great error for princes to appropriate certain things and certain persons as if they were theirs in a different fashion from the rest of their empire."[26] This attitude, however, serves mainly to justify the paternalistic obtrusiveness in taxation, commercial regulation, and sumptuary laws that manor and town had bequeathed to the monarchy. Indeed, Louis hastens to add that a king should be "the incorruptible judge and common father of all."[27] Louis also displays an immense respect for tradition. True, he believed the laws and institutions of his own time to be corrupt and in need of restoration. Nevertheless, any departure from tradition was the exception and had to be justified by kings, at least in their own minds. "What they seem to do sometimes against the common law," he explains, "is based on reason of state, which is the first of all laws by common consent."[28] Louis reveres another form of tradition in religion, although he saw the Church, too, as suffering from decay. Corruption had been responsible for the spread of Protestantism. It was probably at the root of the current Jansenist difficulties. All this suggests that if gross clerical abuses were eliminated, heresy would gradually vanish and religious unity could be restored. A particular merit of Christianity was that it taught submission to authority. "Those who would inquire into past times," the King reflects learnedly, "will easily see how rare, since the coming of Jesus Christ, have been those ghastly revolutions that occurred so often under paganism."[29] Once more, Machiavelli and Louis agree in their respect for tradition, their consciousness of decay, and their awareness of religion as a political force. Yet the Italian, in the final analysis, is a radical seeking to escape his time. The King is basically a conservative.

23. P. 193. 24. P. 63. 25. P. 154.
26. P. 154. 27. P. 155. 28. Pp. 43–44.
29. P. 245.

Man's inclination toward self-interest would make democracy synonymous with anarchy, and Louis does not even deign to mention this type of popular rule. But the *Mémoires* make his contempt for any form of limited government abundantly clear. The King displays some irritation at the fact that the house of France no longer retains the Imperial title, but he finds consolation in describing the Holy Roman Emperors as, "captains-general of a German republic."[30] On the other hand, Louis feels sympathy for Charles II of England, since "this subjection that makes it necessary for a sovereign to take orders from his people is the worst calamity that can befall a man of our rank."[31] As to popular assemblies, "it is interest alone, whether private or of the state, that guides their conduct."[32] Nor was the Papacy spared this kind of analysis. It was dominated by persons "not born to greatness," and "able to sustain neither the brilliance that adorns it nor the storms that can threaten it."[33] Such reasoning also explains the drawbacks of prime ministers, whose private origins make their positions insecure and introduce personal considerations into their decisions. It follows, therefore, that the most effective government is one in which the supreme authority resides in the person of a hereditary monarch. He alone "has no fortune to establish but that of the state, no acquisition to make except for the monarchy, no authority to strengthen other than that of the laws, no debts to pay besides the public ones, no friends to enrich save his people."[34] Here Machiavelli's subtle republicanism is opposed by the King's unequivocal advocacy of absolute monarchy.

Louis' traditionalism takes nothing away from his hierarchical and authoritarian conception of society. Nor does it prevent him from asserting that "kings are absolute lords and naturally have free and full disposition of all the goods possessed by clergymen as well as by laymen, in order to use them at any time as wise administrators, that is, according to the general need of their state."[35] Tradition, moreover, requires animation if its effects are to persist. "Private individuals," he says, "seem to find a well-beaten path to wisdom by observing the public ordinances . . . the fear of punishment and the hope of reward are constant aids to them in their weakness."[36] It is the function of a king to "play on these great springs"[37] for the common welfare. Machiavelli makes much the same point, but one suspects that Louis also relishes the quasi-providential flavor of adapting vice to the service of virtue. It was all part of "exercising a divine function here below."[38]

30. P. 51.	31. P. 130.	32. P. 196.
33. P. 212.	34. P. 64.	35. P. 165.
36. P. 149.	37. P. 162.	38. P. 133.

Finally, the breadth of a king's perspective permits him to compensate for the special interests of those who advise or appeal to him. This type of motivational arithmetic was almost second nature to Louis. It pervades the *Mémoires* and elucidates his famous statement that "the function of kings consists primarily of using good sense, which always comes naturally and easily."[39] To act rationally, moreover, is to do "as time and circumstances require."[40] Machiavelli, in his even more famous reflections on free will versus fortune, concluded that men are incapable of changing their temperament to fit the times. The King seems to fly in the face of this conclusion by insisting that this is precisely what a capable ruler must do.[41]

Louis' conservatism may well have been abetted by his immense pride in the French monarchy. He lauds the amiable informality that exists between the king and its nobility. The *parlements,* astonishingly, also come in for his praise. "If age is venerable in men," Louis remarks, "it appears all the more so to me in these ancient bodies."[42] He also values the traditional privileges of the Gallican Church, insofar as they protected the monarchy and its church from the incursions of the Holy See. Machiavelli, of course, emphasized the independence of the nobility and the autonomy of the *parlements* in eulogizing the French monarchy. The King could scarcely have done more to distort him.

It is to be expected that when society lacks the proper leadership, state and church should falter. Quite consistently, Louis claims to bear no animosity for the Fronde. Moreover, "in reviewing history, there is hardly an order in the kingdom, nobility, clergy, or third estate that has not fallen at some time or other into terrible lapses from which it has recoiled."[43] Finally, of course, a king who harms his subjects weakens himself. Thus Louis' goal is merely "to reduce all things to their natural and legitimate order,"[44] and "restoring the purity of the laws and the general discipline in my state."[45] Even this, however, was to be undertaken with great caution. When, during a lull in the preparation of the *Mémoires,* Périgny submitted a high-minded proposal for the reform of the clergy, the King's response was to the effect that one had to improve gradually on his times.[46] In occasional moments, Louis does give way to a vision. He looks forward to a day when extreme poverty will be banished from his realm. He notes, in passing, the desirability of integrating areas that are culturally French, such as Artois and Franche-Comté,

39. P. 30.   40. P. 96.   41. Pp. 168–170.
42. P. 43.   43. P. 42.   44. P. 43.
45. P. 142.
46. For Périgny's proposal, see Bibliothèque Nationale, *Manuscrit Français* 6732, ff. 122–123 [pub. in Dreyss, *op. cit.,* II, 490–495]. See Louis' reaction on pp. 105–107.

into the monarchy. Throughout, he expresses confidence that his efforts will be durable and that the Dauphin will never experience disobedience or rebellion. But then, the King recalls that "the most unscrupulous political thinkers, the least affected by principles of equity, of goodness, and of honor seem to have predicted immortality for this state."[47] Louis is still much closer in mentality to Machiavelli than he is to the idea of progress or to modern nationalism.

The King attaches great weight to foreign relations, one of his major concerns. The starting point of his diplomacy was the character and interests of the various powers. With this in mind, he did everything possible, through negotiation and bribery, to keep together those whose interests coincided with his own and to spread confusion elsewhere. In this regard, the *Mémoires* contain the very key to Louis' foreign policy. There he discloses that "the state of the two crowns of France and of Spain is such today and has been such for a long time in the world that it is impossible to raise one without humbling the other, which has almost nothing else to fear."[48] This "essential jealousy" and "permanent enmity"[49] is a matter of self-defense and excuses even the violation of solemn treaties. The Spanish monarchy being a Hapsburg state, moreover, the King seems to encompass the Austrian and Imperial branch of the family in his enmity. This attitude accounts for his constant probing against the Hapsburgs and suggests that he was still aiming at the Spanish Low Countries in 1672, when he launched his invasion of the Dutch Republic.

The Franco-Spanish pendulum dominated and affected all other relations. The English were "the old and irreconcilable enemies of France,"[50] but their sale of Dunkirk and the defects in the structure of their government seemed to preclude the renewal of their menace. The Dutch merchant oligarchs, though old allies of France, desired only "to maintain their commerce and to humble the house of Orange."[51] Their frequent failure to demonstrate the proper gratitude and confidence was only to be expected, but it nevertheless irritated Louis. For Sweden, another old ally, he displays considerably greater forbearance. His interest in Polish affairs rises when he has nothing better to do. The *Mémoires* are virtually silent on the proper relation between France and the Papacy, probably because the King had such poor success in imposing his will upon it.[52] On the other hand, they indicate a most surprising

---

47. P. 101.   48. P. 46.   49. P. 46.
50. P. 93.   51. P. 27.
52. See Paul Sonnino, *Louis XIV's View of the Papacy (1661–1667)*, (Berkeley and Los Angeles, 1966).

approach toward that "uncivilized nation,"[53] the Ottoman Empire. In noting the "distance and the intractable character of this nation,"[54] Louis seems to exclude it from the European state system.

The King also talks much about war. He describes the reviews that he held in preparation for the War of Devolution, taking the occasion to emphasize the importance of military discipline. He lays great stress on providing his soldiers with adequate pay. Louis' aim is to keep peacetime conditions in France from being disrupted by war, since subjects should be left to carry on their labors and pay taxes while a king pursues his military objectives. But the *Mémoires* are hardly a manual of strategy. Louis does point up the uncertainty of sea engagements and shows a predilection for sieges. He provides an enthusiastic account of his successful campaign in the Spanish Low Countries and gives himself the credit for the project of attacking Franche-Comté. But the King never goes beyond such maxims as "the success of a siege almost always depends on the proper choice of attacks."[55]

Louis hardly dispenses kings from human emotions, notwithstanding their special capacities for exercising good sense. He comes back repeatedly in the *Mémoires* to the problem of controlling one's inclinations. He delights in demonstrating how he has restrained his thirst for military glory, what measures he has taken to resist flattery, and the ability to contain his resentment in the interest of policy. The feelings, however, are not criticized in themselves. He regrets the necessity for kings to repress their openness for the sake of secrecy. He confesses his affection for Mlle. de La Vallière, while insisting that such relationships must be kept separate from affairs of state.[56] Nor can he entirely disavow "that secret inclination of most magnanimous souls for arms and for those in this profession."[57] There is, finally, a passion to which he eagerly surrenders, the desire for renown and for glory.

Was Louis engaging in Baroque rhetoric? Or had he sensed, perhaps, that the mass of men and the Church had interests of their own and that the monarchy actually resided in the finances, the court, and the army? Is it possible that despite his grandiose conceptions, an implicit awareness of the limitations to his power stalks his conservatism, here combining, there separating, public good and the desire for personal glory? The *Mémoires* leave one asking whether it is frustration rather than wisdom that makes him combat the same emotions that he cultivates. He seems to require, in order to reconcile state and king, a notion of higher utility based on intangibles. Perhaps this explains Louis' discovery

53. P. 183.   54. P. 186.   55. P. 252.
56. Pp. 246–248.   57. P. 155.

that "the rules of justice and of honor almost always lead to utility itself,"[58] or his assertion about kings that "their constant desire for glory makes them disregard their own interest in many cases."[59]

Just as utility blended into honor, the natural was permeated by the supernatural. Divinity had established the natural order of things. It did not usually tamper with it, "and when It wants to make a king fortunate, powerful, supported, and respected, Its most normal course is to make him wise, clear-sighted, fair, vigilant, and industrious."[60] The order, however, which at every moment brings together an infinite number of circumstances, is itself beyond the manipulation of men. Indeed, "the entire art of politics consists of playing on circumstances,"[61] and moreover, "the caprice of fate, or rather that wise Providence that rules supreme over our interests for purposes beyond our comprehension, chooses sometimes to deflate the pomp of the loftiest men, in order to oblige them, in the midst of their greatest advantages, to recognize the source of all their blessings and to merit, through a continual avowal of their dependence, the assistance necessary for the success of their plans."[62] Machiavelli's Goddess of Fortune seems barely recognizable in the garb of the Virgin Mary!

If Providence facilitates the trend of events, does not God expect the recipient of His assistance to seize the occasion and to carry out the divine purpose? Louis indicates that his very first successes in kingship made him "as deeply struck as I have ever been by the desire to serve Him and to please Him."[63] The *Mémoires* lead one to wonder if there were moments, in the King's later reign, when he might have assumed the obligation of being an instrument of the divine will. After the profitable Treaty of Aix-la-Chapelle, concluded in 1668, he sent an expedition to the relief of Crete against the Turks. After the Treaty of Nijmegen, complemented by the reunion of Strasbourg in 1681—indeed, at the height of his power, he revoked the Edict of Nantes. Louis XIV may have known less about his own future than he transmitted to the reader of his *Mémoires*.

58. P. 77.   59. P. 196.   60. P. 99.
61. P. 99.   62. P. 225.   63. P. 54.

THE TRANSLATION

THE manuscripts of Louis XIV's *Mémoires* may be found in the Bibliothèque Nationale under *Manuscrits Français* 6732, 6733, 6734, 10329, and 10332. These documents, plus the additional copies published by Grouvelle, combine to provide a wide variety of revisions for possible publication. I present the last texts for 1661 and 1662, the second text for 1666, the last text for 1667, and the sole text for 1668, which is exactly the choice made by Grouvelle. However, I have examined the available manuscripts in order to obtain a more accurate reading, and my text for 1666 contains the greatest number of variations from his. I have also completed in brackets [ ] the obvious lacunae in the documents.

Charles Dreyss was the first to publish from the manuscripts a third text for 1666, and Longnon has followed suit. However, I still prefer the second text. It is longer and includes many reflections that were removed from the last revision merely because they were intended for insertion in years that were still to be prepared. Since the King did not want to deprive his son of these reflections, it does not seem reasonable to deprive the reader of them.

I have attempted in this translation to make Louis sound in English as he might have sounded to his contemporaries, now discursive, now pompous, now colloquial, but never clumsy. Thus I have striven for an accurate rendering of his statements, while sometimes slimming down certain phrases that sound much better in classical French than they do in modern English. I have retained the King's very long sentences, while occasionally combining certain very short paragraphs. The spelling of names has been modernized, and the notes are designed to complement the work rather than to compete with it.

I wish to thank John B. Wolf and Andrew Lossky, who have contributed so much to humanizing the portrait of Louis XIV, for their kindness in reading and checking this translation. I acknowledge, of course, full responsibility for its shortcomings.

P. S.

PRINCIPAL EDITIONS
AND THEIR TEXTS

	1661	*1662*	*1666*	*1667*	*1668*
OLIVET 1767	Third (C)				
GAIN-MONTAGNAC 1806	Second (B)		Second (B)	Third (C)	Sole
GROUVELLE 1806	Fourth (D)	Second (B)	Second (B)	Third (C)	Sole
DREYSS 1860	Second (B)	First (A)	Third (C)	Third (C)	Sole
LONGNON 1923	Third (C)		Third (C)		
LONGNON 1927 ff.	Third plus last section of Fourth (C+D)	Second (B)	Third (C)	Third (C)	Sole
SONNINO 1970	Fourth (D)	Second (B)	Second (B)	Third (C)	Sole

FIRST PART

MÉMOIRES
FOR THE INSTRUCTION OF
THE DAUPHIN

1661

FIRST BOOK

Y SON, many excellent reasons have prompted me to go to a considerable effort in the midst of my greatest occupations in order to leave you these *mémoires* of my reign and of my principal actions. I have never believed that kings, feeling as they do all the paternal affections and attachments in themselves, were dispensed from the common and natural obligation of fathers to instruct their children by example and by counsel. On the contrary, it has seemed to me that in this high rank of ours a public duty combined with the private, and that all the respects that are paid to us, all the affluence and brilliance that surround us being nothing but rewards attached by Heaven Itself to the care entrusted in us for people and for states, this care would be insufficient if we did not extend it beyond us by handing down all our insights to our successor.

I have even hoped that for this purpose I could be more useful to you, and consequently to my subjects, than could anyone else in the world. For those who might have greater talents and more experience than I would not have reigned, let alone in France, and I don't hesitate to tell you that the higher the position, the more things it entails that can neither be envisaged nor understood without occupying it.

I have considered, moreover, what I have so often experienced myself: the crowd of people who will press around you, each with his own design; the difficulty that you will have in obtaining sincere advice from them, the entire assurance that you will be able to take in that of a father who will have had no interest but your own, nor any passion except for your greatness.

I am also sometimes flattered by the thought that if the occupations, the pleasures, and the contacts of this world should, as all too often happens, take you away from books and from histories, where alone, however, princes find a thousand truths unmixed with flattery, the reading of these *mémoires* might somehow compensate for all the other reading, always preserving its taste and its quality for you through the friendship and through the respect that you would preserve for me.

I have, finally, given some reflection to the hard and demanding condition of kings in that they owe, so to speak, a public accounting of all their actions to the entire world and to all time, and yet cannot render it to any of their contemporaries without disclosing the secrets of their conduct and neglecting their greatest interests. And having no doubt that the rather great and important things in which I have participated both within and outside my kingdom will one day stimulate the intelligence and the passions of writers in various ways, I shall not be displeased for you to have here the means to correct history if it should go astray and misunderstand, from not having fully penetrated into my plans and into my motives. I shall explain them to you without deception, even in cases where my good intentions may not have been successful, convinced that it befits a small mind, which is usually mistaken, never to admit a mistake, and that those who have enough merit to succeed most often find a certain greatness in recognizing their errors.

I don't know if I must include among mine that of not having initially assumed the personal administration of my state. I have tried, if this is so, to make full amends for it later, and I can definitely assure you that it was neither the result of negligence nor of weakness.

Even from childhood, the very name of do-nothing kings and of mayors of the palace distressed me when it was uttered in my presence. But one must remember the circumstances: terrible disorders throughout the kingdom both before and after my majority; a foreign war in which these domestic troubles had caused France to lose a thousand advantages, a prince of my blood and of great reputation leading the enemy; the state swarming with conspiracies; the *parlements* still in possession and enjoyment of usurped authority; at my court, very little disinterested loyalty, so that those of my subjects who appeared to be the most submissive were as burdensome and as dangerous for me as the most rebellious; a minister reinstated in spite of so many factions, very able and very skillful, who loved me and whom I loved, who had rendered me some great services, but whose ideas and manners were naturally quite different from mine, whom I could, nonetheless, neither contradict nor discredit without perhaps reviving against him, through the false impression of a disgrace, the same storms that had been quieted with such great difficulty;[1] I myself still rather young, major in terms of when kings reach their majority, which the laws of the state have advanced in order to avoid greater misfortunes, but not in terms of when private individuals begin to conduct their affairs freely, conscious merely of the immensity of the burden without having been able to test my own strength, wanting more than anything, even more than life itself, to acquire a great reputation if I could do so, but realizing at the same time that my first moves would either lay its

1. In 1648, just as the Fronde was breaking out, Cardinal Mazarin concluded the advantageous Treaty of Münster (or Westphalia), ending the Thirty Years' War, but France was still at war with Spain. The Cardinal was temporarily in exile in 1651, when the thirteen-year-old Louis reached his majority. After Mazarin's triumphant return, the angry Prince de Condé (M. le Prince) defected to the enemy, who put him in command of their troops.

foundations or would destroy my hopes for it forever, so that I was almost equally pressed and restrained in my aspirations by the same desire for glory.

I did not fail, however, to test myself in secret, reasoning alone and to myself about all events that arose, full of hope and joy whenever I would discover that my first thoughts were the same with which able and experienced people finally concluded, and deeply convinced that I had not been placed and preserved upon the throne with such a strong passion to succeed without being able to find the means. Finally, after some years had passed in this manner, the general peace, my marriage,[2] and the death of Cardinal Mazarin obliged me to stop postponing what I had both wanted and feared for so long.

I began, therefore, to cast my eyes over all the various parts of the state, and not casual eyes, but the eyes of a master, deeply struck at not finding a single one that did not cry out for my attention; yet carefully observing what time and circumstances would permit.

Disorder reigned everywhere. My court, in general, was still quite far removed from the sentiments in which I hope that you will find it. People of quality, accustomed to continual bargaining with a minister who did not mind it, and who had sometimes found it necessary, were always inventing an imaginary right to whatever was to their fancy; no governor of a stronghold who was not difficult to govern; no request that was not mingled with some reproach over the past, or with some veiled threat of future dissatisfaction. Graces exacted and torn rather than awaited, and extorted in consequence of each other, no longer really obligated anyone, merely serving to offend those to whom they were refused.

The finances, which move and activate the whole great body of the monarchy, were so exhausted that there hardly seemed to be any recourse left. Many of the most necessary and imperative expenses for my household and for my own person were either shamefully postponed or were supported solely through credit, to be made up for later. Affluence prevailed, meanwhile, among

2. In 1659, Cardinal Mazarin concluded the profitable Treaty of the Pyrenees with Spain, which entailed the marriage of Louis to the Infanta Maria Theresa, who officially renounced all her rights to the Spanish succession. The King, however, began to exploit these rights at the first opportunity.

the financiers who, on the one hand, covered their irregularities by all kinds of artifices while they uncovered them, on the other, by insolent and brazen luxury, as if they were afraid to leave me ignorant of them.

The Church, aside from its usual troubles, after long disputes over scholastic matters that were admittedly unnecessary for salvation—differences mounting each day with the excitement and the obstinacy of tempers and even mingling constantly with new human interests—was finally threatened openly with a schism by people all the more dangerous since they could have been very useful, of great merit had they been less convinced of it.[3] It was no longer merely a question of some individual theologians in hiding, but of bishops established in their see, capable of drawing the populace after them, of high reputation, of piety indeed worthy of reverence as long as it were accompanied by submission to the opinions of the Church, by mildness, by moderation, and by charity. Cardinal de Retz, Archbishop of Paris, whom well-known reasons of state then prevented me from tolerating, favored this entire rising sect either from inclination or from interest and was favored by it.

The least of the defects in the order of the nobility was the infinite number of usurpers in its midst, without any title or having a title acquired by purchase rather than by service. The tyranny that it exercised over its vassals and over its neighbors in some of my provinces could neither be tolerated nor could it be suppressed without examples of severity and of rigor. The fury of duels, somewhat mitigated since my strict and inflexible enforcement of the latest regulations, already showed through the well-advanced recovery from such a deep-rooted evil that none was beyond remedy.

Justice, which was responsible for reforming all the rest, seemed itself to me as the most difficult to reform. An infinite number of things contributed to this: offices filled by chance and by money rather than by choice and by merit; lack of experience among the

3. The Jansenists. Two popes had condemned Jansen's *Augustinus* and two assemblies of the French clergy had tried to silence his sympathizers by issuing a formulary to be signed by the entire clergy. In 1661, Louis had been all for pressing the Jansenists, but there was concluded a shaky "Peace of the Church" with them in 1668, several years before he prepared this text, so that his attitude here is more benign toward them.

judges, even less learning; the ordinances of my predecessors on age and on service circumvented almost everywhere; chicanery, established through long possession, fertile in schemes against the best laws, and caused primarily by one thing, I mean this excessive number of people delighting in trials and cultivating them as their personal birthright, with no other concern than to prolong and to multiply them. Even my council, instead of regulating the other jurisdictions, all too often confused them through an incredible number of conflicting decisions all given in my name and as if coming from me, which made the disorder even more shameful.

All these evils, or rather, their consequences and their effects, fell primarily upon the lower classes, burdened, moreover, with taxes and pressed by extreme poverty in many areas, disturbed in others by their own idleness since the peace, and especially in need of relief and of employment.

Amidst so many difficulties, some of which seemed virtually insurmountable, three considerations gave me encouragement.

The first, that in these sorts of things, since kings are men and they must deal with men, they cannot possibly achieve perfection, which is far beyond their limited means, but that this impossibility is a poor reason for not doing what one can and this distance for not perpetually pushing forward, which cannot be without utility and without glory.

The second, that in all just and legitimate undertakings, time, action itself, and the aid of Heaven usually break a thousand paths and uncover a thousand unexpected solutions.

The last, finally, that It seemed Itself to be promising me this aid by directing all things toward the same purpose that It inspired in me.

All was calm everywhere. Not the slightest hint of any movement within the kingdom that could interrupt or oppose my plans. There was peace with my neighbors, apparently for as long as I would want it myself, owing to the circumstances in which they found themselves.

Spain could not recover so quickly from her great losses. She was not merely without funds but without credit, incapable of any great financial or military effort, occupied by her war against Portugal that I easily complicated for her and that most of the

great nobles of the kingdom were suspected of wanting to prolong. Their King was old, in doubtful health; he had only one
son, who was very young and rather sickly. He and his minister,
Don Luis de Haro, were afraid of war; and indeed, neither the
condition of the nation nor that of the royal family made it in their
interest.[4]

I saw nothing to fear from the Emperor,[5] elected merely because
he belonged to the house of Austria, bound in a thousand ways
by a capitulation with the Estates of the Empire, disinclined to
undertake anything on his own, and whose decisions would
apparently be more in keeping with his character than with his
youth or with his rank. The electors, who had been responsible
for imposing such harsh terms upon him, could hardly doubt his
resentment and lived in continual suspicion of him. Some of the
other princes of the Empire were in my interests.

Sweden needed me for her true and lasting ones. She had just
lost a great prince,[6] and it was all she could do to hold on to her
conquests during the childhood of her new king. Denmark,
having come close to collapse in a previous war against her,
thought of nothing else but of peace and of respite.

England was barely reviving from her past troubles and sought
only to consolidate the government of a newly restored king,[7]
whose inclinations, moreover, drew him toward France.

The entire policy of the Dutch and of those who governed them
then aimed at only two things: to maintain their commerce and
to humble the house of Orange.[8] The most minor war was

4. Philip IV (1605–1665), King of Spain since 1621. His son Charles (1661–1700)
became Charles II in 1665, but his continuing bad health and lack of direct heirs
produced the problem of the Spanish succession. Don Luis de Haro (1599–1661) had
been prime minister since 1643.

5. Leopold I (1640–1705), Holy Roman Emperor since 1658.

6. Charles X of Sweden had devoted the First Northern War of 1655 to 1660 to
ravaging Poland and Denmark. Charles XI (1655–1697), his son, had become king
in 1660, at which time the Queen Mother and a Council of Regency concluded the
Treaties of Oliva with Poland and Copenhagen with Denmark. France and the
Dutch both welcomed this stabilization in the Baltic.

7. Charles II (1630–1685), restored in 1660.

8. The "States" Party, led by Jan de Witt (1625–1672), Grand Pensionary of
Holland, feared that the dynastic ambitions of the house of Orange would weaken
the dominance of Holland over the other provinces and lead to military adventures.
Louis indiscriminately refers to the Dutch as Holland, the States, United Provinces,
States of Holland, or States-General.

harmful to both, and their principal support rested in my friendship.

The Pope alone in Italy,[9] from a vestige of his old enmity for Cardinal Mazarin, harbored considerable ill will toward the French, but this amounted only to complicating for me what might depend on him, which was basically of little importance. His neighboring states would not have supported his designs, if he had devised any against me. Savoy, governed by my aunt,[10] was very favorable to me. Venice, engaged in her war against the Turks, maintained my alliance and expected more help from me than from any other Christian prince. The Grand Duke was renewing his alliance with me through the marriage of his son to a princess of my blood.[11] All the powers in Italy, finally, some of whom such as Parma, Modena, and Mantua were my friends and allies, were too weak separately to distress me, and neither fear nor hope obliged them to unite against me.

It would undoubtedly have been a waste of such perfect and such rare tranquillity not to put it to good use, although my youth and the pleasure of leading my armies would have made me wish for a few more external affairs.

Since the principal hope for these reforms rested in my own will, it was first necessary to make my will supreme through conduct that would inspire submission and respect, rendering justice meticulously to whomever I owed it, but as to graces, granting them freely and without compulsion whenever and to whomever I would please, as long as my actions made it clear that even though I gave no explanations to anyone, I was no less guided by reason, and that in my opinion gratitude for services, to reward and to promote merit, to do good in short, had to be not merely the most important occupation but also the greatest satisfaction of a prince.

Two things were necessary for me, undoubtedly: a great deal of work on my part; a careful choice of the persons who were to support me and relieve me in it.

9. Fabio Chigi (1599–1667), Pope Alexander VII since 1655.

10. Christine de France (1606–1663), daughter of Henry IV, dominant over her son, Charles Emmanuel II (1634–1675), Duke of Savoy since 1638.

11. Ferdinand II de Medici (1610–1670), Grand Duke of Tuscany since 1627. His son Cosimo (1642–1723) married Marguerite-Louise de France (1645–1721), daughter of Gaston d'Orléans.

As to work, my son, it may be that you will begin to read these *mémoires* at an age when it is far more customary to fear it than to enjoy it, delighted to have escaped from subjection to teachers and to masters, and to have no more set hours nor long and fixed concentration.

Here I shall not merely tell you that this is nonetheless how one reigns, why one reigns, and that there is ingratitude and temerity toward God as well as injustice and tyranny toward men in wanting one without the other, that these demands of royalty which may sometimes seem harsh and unpleasant to you from such a lofty post would appear delightful and pleasant to you if it were a question of attaining them!

There is something else, my son, and I hope that you will never find it out for yourself. Nothing would be more taxing for you than prolonged idleness, if you should have the misfortune of falling into it, disenchanted first with affairs, then with pleasures, then with idleness itself, and seeking everywhere in vain for what cannot be found, that is, the delight of rest and of leisure without some labor and some occupation to precede it.

I made it a rule to work regularly twice a day for two to three hours at a time with various persons, aside from the hours that I worked alone or that I might devote extraordinarily to extraordinary affairs if any arose, there being no moment when it was not permitted to discuss with me anything that was pressing, except for foreign envoys, who sometimes use the familiarity that they are permitted in order to obtain something or to pry, and who must not be heard without preparation.

I cannot tell you what fruits I immediately gathered from this decision. I could almost feel my spirits and my courage rising. I was a different person. I discovered something new about myself and joyfully wondered how I could have ignored it for so long. That first shyness, which always comes with good sense and which was especially disturbing when I had to speak at some length in public, vanished in less than no time. I knew then that I was king, and born for it. I experienced, finally, an indescribable delight that you will simply have to discover for yourself.

For you must not imagine, my son, that affairs of state are like those thorny and obscure recesses of the sciences that may perhaps have exasperated you, where the mind struggles painfully to rise beyond itself, most often for nothing, and whose apparent use-lessness discourages us as much as their difficulty. The function of kings consists primarily of using good sense, which always comes naturally and easily. Our work is sometimes less difficult than our amusements. Utility always follows a king. However experienced or able his ministers may be, he cannot take any task in hand without there being evidence of it. Success, which gratifies even in the smallest things of this world, charms in this the greatest of all, and no satisfaction can equal that of following each day the progress of glorious and lofty undertakings and of the happiness of the people, when one has planned it all himself. Everything that is most necessary to this effort is at the same time pleasant. For it consists, in short, my son, of keeping an eye on the whole earth, of constantly learning the news of all the provinces and of all the nations, the secret of all the courts, the dispositions and the weaknesses of all the foreign princes and of all their ministers; of being informed of an infinite number of things that we are presumed to ignore, of seeing around us what is hidden from us with the greatest care, of discovering the most remote ideas and the most hidden interests of our courtiers coming to us through conflicting interests, and I don't know, finally, what other pleas-ures we would not abandon for this one, for the sake of curiosity alone.

I have dwelt on this important point longer than I had intended, and for you much more than for me, for I do not ignore that at the same time that I show you these solutions and these delights to the greatest cares of royalty, I diminish, to that extent, virtually my only hope for any merit in the world. But your honor, my son, is dearer to me in this than mine, and if God should call upon you to rule before you will have acquired that spirit of dedication and of affairs that I am describing to you, the least deference that you could pay to the advice of a father, to whom I venture to say that you owe a great deal, is to do initially and for some time, even with compulsion, even with disgust, for my sake who implore you, what you will do your entire life for your own sake once you have begun.

I commanded the four secretaries of state not to sign anything at all any longer without discussing it with me, the superintendant likewise, and for nothing to be transacted at the finances without being registered in a little book that was to remain with me, where I could always see at a glance, briefly summarized, the current balance and the expenditures made or pending.

The Chancellor received a similar order, that is, not to seal anything without my command, except for letters of justice, so called because they were a mere formality that it would have been an injustice to refuse, and I also left in this category transfers of offices and granting of exemptions in clearly deserving cases, although I have subsequently changed my mind on this subject, as I shall tell you in its place.

I announced that all requests for graces of any type had to be made directly to me, and I granted to all my subjects without distinction the privilege of appealing to me at any time, in person or by petitions. The petitions were initially very numerous, which did not discourage me, however. The disorder into which my affairs had fallen produced many of them, the idle or unjustified hopes which were raised by this novelty hardly stimulated a lesser number. I was given a great many about lawsuits, which I saw no reason for withdrawing arbitrarily from the ordinary jurisdictions for trial before me. But even in these apparently useless things I discovered much that was useful. I learned thereby many details about the condition of my people. They saw that I was concerned about them, and nothing did so much to win me their hearts. From the way in which the oppression of the ordinary jurisdictions might be portrayed to me, I might find it advisable to obtain further information about it and intervene extraordinarily if necessary. One or two examples of this type prevented a thousand similar evils, and even if the complaints were unjustified or false, they restrained my officials from giving occasion for more justified and truer ones.

As to the persons who were to support me in my work, I resolved above all not to have a prime minister, and if you and all your successors take my advice, my son, the name will forever be abolished in France, there being nothing more shameful than to see on the one hand all the functions and on the other the mere title of king.

For this purpose, it was absolutely necessary to divide my confidence and the execution of my orders without entirely entrusting it to anyone, assigning these various persons to various functions in keeping with their various talents, which is perhaps the first and foremost talent of princes.

In order to concentrate the entire authority of a master more fully in myself—even though there are all sorts of details into which our occupations and our very dignity do not usually permit us to go, I resolved to enter into these with each of the ministers whom I would choose, and when he would least expect it, so that he would realize that I might do the same on other subjects and at any time, aside from the fact that by casually acquiring a knowledge of these little details as a diversion rather than systematically, we learn gradually and effortlessly about a thousand things that are by no means useless for general decisions, and which we should know and do ourselves if it were possible for a single man to know everything and to do everything.

It is not so easy for me to tell you, my son, how to go about the choice of the various ministers. Fortune always plays, in spite of us, at least as much of a part in it as wisdom; and in the part that wisdom plays, intelligence can do far more than counsel. Neither of us, my son, is going to seek for these sorts of positions those whom distance and obscurity remove from our view, whatever qualifications they may have. It is necessary to decide from a small number which chance presents to us, that is, those already in office or whom birth and inclination have attached to our personal service.

And as for this art of knowing men, which will be so important to you not merely on this but also on every other occasion of your life, I shall tell you, my son, that it can be learned but that it can not be taught.

Indeed, it is only reasonable to attribute a great deal to a general and established reputation, because the public is impartial and is difficult to deceive over a long period. It is wise to listen to everyone, and not to believe entirely those around us, except for the good that they are compelled to admit in their enemies and for the bad that they try to excuse in their friends; still wiser is it to test for oneself in little things those whom one wants to employ in greater ones. But the summary of these precepts for properly identifying the talents, the inclinations, and the potential of each one is to work at it and to take pleasure in it. For, in general, from the smallest things to the greatest, you will never master a single one unless you derive pleasure and enjoyment from them.

In my distribution of positions, the persons whom I employed most often for matters of conscience were my confessor, Father Annat,[12] whom I esteemed particularly for his integrity and disinterestedness, and for not meddling in any intrigue; the Archbishop of Toulouse, Marca,[13] whom I later made Archbishop of Paris, a man of vast learning and of great intelligence; the Bishop of Rennes,[14] because the Queen my mother had wished it; and the Bishop of Rodez,[15] later Archbishop of Paris, who had been my tutor.

As for judicial affairs, I communicated them primarily to the Chancellor,[16] an official of long standing, generally recognized by experts as very able in these matters. I also summoned him to all the public councils that I held personally, and particularly two days a week with the four secretaries of state for ordinary correspondence within the kingdom and for replies to petitions.

I even wanted sometimes to attend the council of the parties, which the Chancellor usually holds for me, and where it is only a question of suits between private individuals over jurisdictions. And if more important occupations should leave you the time for it, you would not be ill-advised to do the same sometimes in order to inspire and animate its members in their duty through your presence and in order to get to know personally the masters of requests who report and who present opinions, from whom individuals are usually drawn for the intendancies of provinces and of armies, for the embassies, and for other higher positions.

But for the most important interests of the state and for secret affairs, where a small number of heads is as much to be desired as anything, and which alone required more time and more concentration than all the others, not wanting to entrust these to a single minister, the three whom I believed could be most useful for them were Le Tellier, Fouquet, and Lionne.

12. François Annat (1590–1670), S.J.
13. Pierre de Marca (1594–1662).
14. Henri de La Mothe-Houdancourt (1602–1684) became Archbishop of Auch in 1662. Louis did not like him.
15. Hardouin de Beaumont de Péréfixe (1605–1670).
16. Pierre Séguier (1588–1672), Chancellor since 1635.

The office of secretary of state, held for twenty years by Le Tellier with great perseverance and diligence, gave him a vast knowledge of affairs.[17] He had always been employed in those of the highest trust. Cardinal Mazarin had often told me that he had recognized his competence and his loyalty on the most delicate occasions, and I had noted this myself. His conduct was wise and cautious, and I esteemed his modesty.

Lionne[18] was also endorsed by Cardinal Mazarin, who had trained him. I knew of no other subject who had so often and so successfully been employed in foreign negotiations. He was acquainted with the various courts of Europe, spoke and wrote fluently in several languages, suitable for this sort of dealing with foreigners.

As for Fouquet,[19] it might seem strange that I would have been willing to employ him once it is realized that I already knew of his thefts at that time, but I knew that he was intelligent and very knowledgeable in internal affairs, which made me imagine that if he confessed his past faults and promised me to reform, he could render me some great services. However, I took the precaution of assigning Colbert[20] to him in the finances as controller, with the title of Intendant, a man in whom I had the highest confidence, because I knew that he was very dedicated, intelligent, and honest; and I entrusted him then with keeping the register of funds that I have described to you.

I have learned since that my choice of these three ministers had been interpreted variously in the world, in keeping with the various interests into which the world is divided. But to see if I could have done any better, one has only to consider the alternatives.

The Chancellor was truly most able, but more in judicial affairs, as I have said, than in those of state. I knew him to be very devoted to my service, but he was reputed to be lacking in firmness; his age and the occupations of such a taxing function might render him less diligent and less suitable to follow me wherever the needs

17. Michel Le Tellier (1603–1685), became Chancellor in 1677.
18. Hugues de Lionne (1611–1671).
19. Nicolas Fouquet (1615–1680), Marquis de Belle Isle, Superintendant of Finances.
20. Jean-Baptiste Colbert (1619–1683).

of the kingdom and foreign wars might take me. His post, more-over, was so lofty in itself—with its capacity of first officer of the kingdom and chief of all the councils—that combined with a close participation in secret affairs, it seemed to make, at least at that time, one of my ministers too great and to raise him too far above the others, which I did not want.

The Count de Brienne,[21] secretary of state, who had the department of foreign affairs, was old, conceited, and did not usually see things either as I did nor according to reason. His son, who was to inherit the office, seemed to want to succeed, but he was so young that, far from procuring his advice on my other interests, I could not even entrust him with the functions of his own position, most of which were performed by Lionne.

La Vrillière and Du Plessis were good people whose insights appeared merely proportionate to the holding of their offices, in which nothing happened of much importance.[22]

I could undoubtedly have cast my eyes on persons of higher standing, but on none with greater qualifications than these three ministers, and this small number, as I have already told you, seemed better to me than a larger one.

But to be perfectly honest with you, it was not in my interest to select individuals of greater eminence. It was above all necessary to establish my own reputation and to make the public realize, by the very rank of those whom I selected, that it was not my intention to share my authority with them. It was important for they themselves not to conceive any greater hopes than I would please to give them, which is difficult for persons of high birth: and even with all these precautions, it took the world a rather long time to get to know me.

Many were convinced that before long some one around me would gain control over my mind and over my affairs. Most re-garded my diligence as enthusiasm that must soon slacken, and those who wanted to judge it more favorably waited to decide later.

Time has shown what should have been made of it, and here it

---

21. Henri-Auguste de Loménie (1595–1666), Count de Brienne, and his son Henri-Louis (1635–1698) were entirely supplanted by Lionne in 1663.

22. Louis Phélypeaux (1598–1681), Marquis de La Vrillière, secretary of state since 1629. Henri du Plessis-Guénégaud (1609–1676), secretary of state since 1643.

is the tenth year that I have been marching, it seems to me, rather constantly along the same route, relenting on none of my dedication, informed of everything, listening to the lowliest of my subjects, always knowing the number and the character of my troops and the condition of my strongholds, constantly issuing orders for all their needs, dealing directly with foreign envoys, receiving and reading dispatches, drafting some of the replies personally and giving the substance of the others to my secretaries, regulating the collections and the expenditures of my state, having those whom I place in important positions report directly to me, maintaining greater secrecy in my affairs than any of my predecessors, distributing graces as I choose, and keeping my servants, unless I am mistaken—although showered with graces for themselves and for their families—in modesty far removed from the loftiness and from the power of prime ministers.

The gradual observation of all these things undoubtedly began to create some opinion about me in the world, and this opinion has in no small measure contributed to my subsequent successes, nothing producing so much effect in so short a time as the reputation of a prince.

But don't be misled, my son, like so many others, into thinking that there will always be time to establish it. It cannot be put into service with the armies. Opening all one's treasures could not acquire it. It must be thought about beforehand, and not even a rather long possession assures us of it.

I already had, apparently, sufficient cause to be satisfied with my conduct, but the acclaim that this novelty drew upon me still caused me continual concern, owing to the fear, from which I am still not entirely exempt, of not sufficiently deserving it. You will be told of how suspicious I have been on this score with my courtiers and of how many times I have tested their character by encouraging them to praise me even for things that I believed I had done badly, only to reproach them for it immediately and to accustom them not to flatter me.

But however obscure their intentions may be, I shall teach you, my son, an easy way to profit from whatever they might say in your favor. It is to examine yourself secretly and to listen to your own heart more than to their praises, always interpreting these, depending on the character of the speaker, either as a malicious reproach for an opposite fault or as a secret exhortation to strive harder, convinced, even if you should feel confident of deserving them, that you have still not done enough, that a reputation cannot be preserved without adding to it every day, that glory, finally, is not a mistress who can be neglected, nor is one ever worthy of her first favors if he is not always wishing for new ones.

SECOND BOOK

First Section

T HE general arrangements that I have described to you occupied me during the entire month of March, for Cardinal Mazarin had only died on the ninth, and although during his long illness and for some time previously I had been observing the situation more carefully than ever, I did not believe I should interfere with details until I had received separate and private reports on them from each of his collaborators, carefully asking them what their principal ideas had been as well as what they might suggest for the future, and convinced that even if my insights had been much greater, they could have been immensely aided and immensely augmented by theirs.

I have believed it necessary to indicate this to you, my son, lest from excessively good intentions in your early youth and from the very ardor that these *mémoires* will perhaps inspire in you, you might confuse two entirely different things; I mean ruling personally and not listening to any counsel, which would be an extreme as dangerous as that of being governed.

The most able private individuals procure the advice of other able persons about their petty interests. What then of kings who hold the public interest in their hands and whose decisions make for the misery or well-being of the whole earth? None should ever be reached of such importance without having summoned, if it were possible, all the enlightenment, wisdom, and good sense of our subjects.

Necessity limits us to a small number of persons chosen from among the rest, and these, at least, must not be ignored. You will discover furthermore, my son, as I soon did, that in discussing our affairs we not merely learn a great deal from others but also from ourselves. The mind fulfills its own thoughts by expressing them, whereas they were previously confused, imperfect, and sketchy. Conversation, which inspires and excites it, carries it gradually from object to object, farther than would have been done by solitary and silent meditation, and the very difficulties that are raised open to it a thousand new solutions.

Moreover, my son, our loftiness somehow separates us from our people, to whom our ministers are closer; capable of seeing, consequently, a thousand details that we ignore, on which it is necessary nevertheless to decide and to make our plans. Add to this their much greater age, experience, practice, and freedom to procure information and insights from their subordinates, who themselves procure those of others, and so on down to the lowliest.

But when, on important occasions, they have reported to us on all the sides and on all the conflicting arguments, on all that is done elsewhere in such and such a case, it is for us, my son, to decide what must actually be done. And as to this decision, I shall venture to tell you that if we lack neither sense nor courage, another never makes it as well as we. For decision requires the spirit of a master, and it is infinitely easier to be oneself than to imitate someone else. For if one almost always notes a difference between the letters that we go to the trouble of writing personally and those that our most able secretaries write for us, detecting in the latter a certain lack of naturalness and the concern of a pen in perpetual fear of including too much or too little, have no doubt, my son, that in affairs of greater importance there is an even wider distance between the decisions that we make ourselves and those that we allow our ministers to make independently, where the more able they are, the more afraid they are to take events upon themselves, and hesitate sometimes over difficulties that would not stop us for a moment.

Wisdom demands that in certain instances much be left to chance. Reason itself then suggests compliance with certain blind movements or instincts beyond reason, seemingly inspired by

Heaven, known to all men, and more worthy of consideration in those whom It has Itself placed in the first ranks. To tell when to suspect them or to surrender to them, no one can. Neither books, nor rules, nor experience, can teach it. A certain judiciousness and a certain boldness of spirit always lead there, infinitely more free in one who does not have to account for his actions to anyone.

In any case, and to abandon this subject, as soon as I had begun to follow this policy with my ministers, I recognized quite plainly, not merely from what they said but also from a certain air of truth that is as distinguishable from indulgence and from flattery as a living person from the most beautiful statue—and it came back to me later through several reliable channels—that they were not merely pleased but somehow surprised to see me, in the most delicate affairs, without adhering precisely to their advice and without affecting to avoid it either, easily take my stand and one that almost always proved to have been the best. And although they saw quite clearly then that they would always be for me what ministers should be, they were all the more satisfied with a position in which they found, with a thousand other advantages, complete security in doing their duty; nothing being more dangerous for those who fill such posts than a king who usually sleeps, but who awakes with a start from time to time after having lost the thread of affairs and, in that disturbed and confused condition, blames everyone for the failures, the accidents, and the errors of which he should accuse himself.

After having thus fully informed myself through private conferences with them, I entered more boldly into matters. Nothing seemed more pressing to me than to relieve my people, to which my compassion for the poverty of the provinces was constantly urging me. The state of my finances, as I have described it to you, seemed to prevent this and suggested, in any case, a postponement. But one must always make haste in doing good. Although the reforms that I was undertaking would be useful to the public, they would prove unpleasant to a great many private individuals. It was desirable to begin with something that would please everyone, and there was no way, finally, to sustain even the pretense of peace much longer unless it were accompanied by some relief of this type that could provide greater hopes for the future. I disregarded, therefore, every other consideration and began by cutting three millions from the *taille* of the following year, which was already set and about to be levied.

I renewed at the same time, but with the intention of implementing them better, which I did, the prohibitions against gold and silver on clothing and against a thousand other foreign frills that constituted a kind of fee and tax, voluntary in appearance, obligatory in practice, that my highest-ranking subjects and my courtiers paid to neighboring countries, or putting it more properly, to luxury and to vanity.

It was necessary for a thousand reasons, including the urgently needed reform of justice, to diminish the excessive authority of the principal courts, which, under the pretext that their judgments were without appeal, or as they say, sovereign and of the last instance, had gradually assumed the name of sovereign courts and considered themselves as so many separate and independent sovereignties. I announced that I would not tolerate their schemes any longer, and to set an example, the Court of Excises of Paris having been the first to depart slightly from its duty, I exiled some of its officials, believing that a strong dose of this remedy initially would dispense me from having to use it often later, which has succeeded for me.

Soon thereafter, I made my intentions even clearer to them through a formal decision of my supreme council. For it is a fact that these courts have no authority over each other in their various jurisdictions regulated by laws and by edicts; and this sufficed formerly to make them get along; or if there arose some differences between them, especially in the cases of private individuals, these were so rare and so unencumbered by procedures that the kings themselves would settle them with a single word, most often while strolling, upon the report of the masters of requests, then also very few in number; until cases having increased in the kingdom, and chicanery even more than cases, this care has been entrusted primarily to the Chancellor of France and to the council of the parties, which I have already described to you, and which must be strongly supported in regulating the jurisdictions of these courts, as well as in other cases that we sometimes deem it appropriate for reasons of public utility and of our service to assign extraordinarily to it for judgment, depriving these courts of what they themselves hold only from us. However, from their spirit of sovereignty during the disorders of the times, they deferred to it only when they saw fit and proceeded every day in all sorts of cases in spite of its prohibitions, even claiming quite often that they recognized the king's will only in the ordinances and edicts that had been verified.

I prohibited them all in general, by this decision, from ever rendering any contrary to those of my council under any pretext whatsoever, whether of their jurisdiction or of the right of private individuals, and I ordered them, whenever they might believe that either one of them had been disturbed, to complain about it to me and to have recourse to my authority, that which I had entrusted to them being only for rendering justice to my subjects and not for procuring it for themselves, which is a part of sovereignty so essentially royal and so proper to the king alone that it can not be transmitted to anyone else.

A little later during the same year, for I shall not observe the precise chronological order, in a certain financial affair affecting all the registries in general, which no one had ever dared to execute against those of the *Parlement* of Paris because they were owned by officials of that body and sometimes by entire chambers, I made it a point, on the contrary, of showing that these officials were subject to the common law, from which nothing prevented my dispensing them either, when I would please to give this reward to their services.

About the same time, I did something that appeared even too bold, so overbearing was the judiciary and so impressed was everyone with the influence that it had acquired during the recent troubles by abusing its authority. I reduced from three quarters to two all the new salary increases deriving from alienations of my revenue, transacted at a mere pittance during the war and consuming the best part of my farmed taxes, most of which had been acquired by the officials of these courts, so that it seemed like a major undertaking to begin by shocking them so rudely in their most sensitive interests. But basically this affair was just, for two quarters was still a great deal for what they had paid; the reform was necessary; my affairs were not in such a state that I had anything to fear from their vexation. It was, rather, desirable to demonstrate to them that they inspired no fear at all and that times had changed. And those who might have had an interest in seeing these courts enraged learned from their submission, on the contrary, that which they themselves owed to me.

In all these things, my son, and in some others that you will see subsequently which have undoubtedly humiliated my judicial officials, I don't want you to attribute to me, as those who know me less well may have done, motives of fear, hatred, and vengeance for what had transpired during the Fronde, when it cannot be denied that these courts often forgot themselves to the point of amazing excesses.

But in the first place, this resentment which appears initially so just might not perhaps fare so well on closer scrutiny. They have returned by themselves and without constraint to their duty. The good servants have recalled the bad. Why impute to the entire body the faults of a few, rather than the services which have prevailed in the end? One might at least consider the account as settled and remember merely that, in reviewing history, there is hardly an order in the kingdom, nobility, clergy, or third estate that has not fallen at some time or other into terrible lapses from which it has recoiled.

Moreover, my son, even though when it comes to offenses, at least as much as in anything else, kings are men, I don't hesitate to tell you that they are this a little less so when they are truly kings because their governing and dominant passion is for their interest, for their greatness, and for their glory. The delight of vengeance is hardly made for us. It flatters only those whose power is uncertain, which is so true that even private individuals who have some honor hesitate to persecute an enemy who is entirely defeated. As for us, my son, we are only very rarely in a position to take pleasure in vengeance, for we can do everything easily, unless we find ourselves in certain delicate and difficult circumstances that do not call upon us to test our power.

Finally, just as we belong to our people, our people belong to us, and I have yet to see a wise man taking revenge to his prejudice by ruining those who belong to him under the pretext that he had been served badly, instead of providing that he would be served a little better in the future.

Thus, my son, the resentment and anger of true kings against their subjects consist of nothing but of justice and of prudence. The rise of the *parlements* in general had been dangerous to the entire kingdom during my minority. They had to be humbled, less for the harm that they had done than for what they might do in the future. As long as their authority seemed opposed to mine, whatever their good intentions, it produced some very bad effects for the state and obstructed all my greatest and most useful under- takings. It was just for this utility to prevail, and to reduce all things to their natural and legitimate order, even if it had been necessary—although I have avoided it—to deprive these bodies of part of what they had been given, just as the painter has no hesitation about softening what is most striking and most beautiful in his own work whenever he finds that it is bigger than it should be and clearly out of proportion with the rest of it.

But I know, my son, and can sincerely assure you that I feel neither aversion nor bitterness toward my judicial officials. On the contrary, if age is venerable in men, it appears all the more so to me in these ancient bodies. I am convinced that nowhere else in the state is the work perhaps greater or the rewards smaller. I hold them in the highest affection and regard, and you, my son, who from all appearances will find them even farther removed from their former wild claims, you must be all the more careful to practice what I do myself every day, namely, to display your esteem for them on occasion, to get to know the leading and the most capable individuals among them, to show that you know them—for it is wonderful for a prince to demonstrate that he is informed of everything and that services rendered in his absence are not wasted—to consider them and their families in the distri- bution of positions and of benefices if they should want to attach themselves to your personal service, to accustom them, finally, through good treatment and kind words to visit you sometimes; whereas in the last century it was part of their integrity not to approach the Louvre, and this not from any malicious intent, but from the false notion that they were defending a supposed interest of the people opposed to that of the prince, without considering that these two interests are but one, that the tranquillity of sub- jects lies only in obedience, that there is always greater evil in popular control than in enduring even the bad rule of kings, of whom God alone is the judge, that what they seem to do sometimes against the common law is based on reason of state, which is the first of all laws by common consent, yet the most unknown and the most obscure to all those who do not rule.

The smallest moves were important in these beginnings, which showed to France what would be the spirit of my reign and of my conduct from then on. I was disturbed by the customary manner of dealing with the prince, or rather with the minister, almost always putting conditions on what should have been awaited either from my justice or from my kindness. The Assembly of the Clergy, which had been lasting for a long time in Paris, was as usual postponing its separation, which I had desired of it, until the issuance of certain edicts for which it had been pressing. I made it clear to it that nothing would be gained by such means. It separated, and it was only then that the edicts were issued.

About the same time, the death of the Duke d'Epernon[23] vacated the office of Colonel-General of French Infantry. His father, the first Duke d'Epernon, had been raised by the favor of Henry III and had expanded this office to suit his ambitions. Its power was immense and the appointment of subordinate officers which had been attached to it gave him the means of placing his followers everywhere and gave him more control than the king himself over the principal forces of the state. I found it advisable to abolish it, although I had already reduced this great power in various ways, insofar as propriety and time had permitted me.

As to the governors of strongholds who so often abused of theirs, I first deprived them of the tax funds that had been given over to them during.the war under the pretext of providing for the security and for the maintenance of their strongholds, but which, amounting to immense sums for individuals, made them too powerful and too absolute. In the second place, I slowly but surely changed almost all the garrisons, replacing the troops dependent on them with others who recognized only me, and what would have seemed inconceivable a few months previously was executed without the slightest commotion, everyone awaiting and indeed receiving more legitimate rewards from me by doing his duty.

I saw, in the meanwhile, to continuing the fortifications of the Château Trompette in Bordeaux and to the construction of

23. Bernard de Nogaret de La Valette (1592–1661), Duke d'Epernon.

the citadel in Marseilles, not so much from any fear of these two cities then as for security in the future and to serve as an example to all the others. There was no movement within the kingdom, but anything that ever so slightly approached disobedience—as on occasion at Montauban, at Dieppe, in Provence, and at La Rochelle—was suppressed immediately and punished without dissembling, for which the peace and the good number of troops that I had resolved to maintain gave me ample means.

I believed, finally, my son, that under the circumstances, a little severity was the greatest kindness that I could bestow my people, the opposite attitude necessarily producing an infinite number of misfortunes for them by itself and by its consequences. For as soon as a young king relents on his commands, authority flees and tranquillity accompanies it. Those who are closest to the prince, being the first to know his weakness, are also the first to abuse it; then come those of the second rank, and so on down the line for those in any position of power. Everything falls upon the lowest classes, oppressed thereby by thousands of tyrants in the place of a legitimate king, whose indulgence alone creates all this disorder.

The marriage of my cousin of Orléans to the Prince of Tuscany took place at that time. I paid for her dowry and had her escorted at my expense into the domains of her father-in-law.

That of my brother to the sister of the King of England[24] had just taken place in the month of March, to my great pleasure, even for reasons of state, for my alliance with this nation under Cromwell had virtually struck the last blow in the war against Spain by reducing the enemy to not being able to defend the Low Countries any longer and consequently to grant me, if I had wanted, better terms than they did by the Treaty of the Pyrenees. The situation had subsequently changed in England. Cromwell was dead and the King restored. The Spanish, taking stock for the future of Flanders in case of a break with me and hoping for nothing then from Holland, wanted above all to place this prince in their interests. The marriage of my brother was intended to keep him in mine. But the one that I resolved to propose between this King himself and the Princess of Portugal[25] seemed capable of detaching

24. Philippe de France (1640–1701), Duke d'Orléans, married Henrietta of England (1644–1670).
25. Catherine de Braganza (1638–1705).

him entirely from Spain and of producing two effects of greater importance for me: the first, to protect the Portuguese from the danger of imminent collapse; the second, to give me greater means of assisting them myself if I deemed it necessary, notwithstanding the Treaty of the Pyrenees which prohibited it.

I shall touch here, my son, on what is perhaps one of the most delicate points in the conduct of princes. I am far from wanting to teach you dishonesty, and I believe I have recently shown to all Europe at the Peace of Aix-la-Chapelle what store I set on keeping my word, preferring this even to my greatest interests, but there is a distinction to be made in these matters. The state of the two crowns of France and of Spain is such today and has been such for a long time in the world that it is impossible to raise one without humbling the other, which has almost nothing else to fear. This makes for a jealousy between them that, I might venture to say, is essential and a kind of permanent enmity that treaties can cover but that they could never extinguish, because its basis persists, and that each one of them in working against the other is less conscious of harming another than of sustaining and preserving itself, which is such a natural duty that it prevails easily over all others.

And to tell the honest truth, they always enter into every treaty with this spirit. Whatever specious clauses may be included of union, of friendship, of procuring each other all sorts of advantages, the true sense that each side understands perfectly well from long experience is that they will refrain from all sorts of hostilities and from all public manifestations of ill will; and as for the secret infractions that will go unnoticed, one always expects them of the other, from the natural principle that I have mentioned, and promises the contrary only in the sense that it is promised to him. Thus it might be said that by dispensing each other mutually from observing treaties, strictly speaking they are not violated, because the words of the treaty have not been taken literally, although there is no alternative but to employ them, as is the case with compliments in society, absolutely necessary for getting along, and meaning far less than they sound.

The Spanish have set the first example for us, for however profoundly we have been at peace with them, have they ever failed to foment our domestic discords and our civil wars? And the capacity of Catholics *par excellence*, has it ever at any time prevented them from furnishing money underhandedly to rebellious Huguenots? They are always careful to welcome, at some expense, all the malcontents who leave this country, even persons of no worth and of no importance, not from any ignorance of who they are but to show thereby to those of greater worth what might be done in their favor. I could not doubt that they had been the first to violate the Treaty of the Pyrenees in a thousand ways, and I would have felt lacking in my responsibility to my domains if, by observing it more scrupulously than they, I had left them free to ruin Portugal so as to return upon me subsequently with all their forces and to disturb the peace of Europe by reclaiming from me all that they had ceded to me by this same treaty. The more extraordinary, reiterated, and ringed with precautions were the clauses that prohibited me from assisting this still shaky crown, the more this indicated that I was not expected to comply; and all that I believed I should concede to them was to aid it only when necessary, with moderation and restraint, which could best be accomplished through the medium and in the name of the King of England, once he was the brother-in-law of the King of Portugal.

I neglected nothing, therefore, that could dispose him toward this marriage; and because this is a court where money usually accomplishes a great deal, and that the ministers in this nation have quite often been suspected of being in the pay of Spain, and that Chancellor Hyde,[26] a man very able in internal affairs, then appeared to have a great deal of influence over the King, I engaged him privately in a very secret negotiation, unknown even to my ambassador in England, and sent a capable man to him who, under the pretext of purchasing lead for my buildings, possessed letters of credit for five hundred thousand *livres*, which he offered to this minister on my behalf, asking only for his friendship. He refused my offers with all the more merit, since he confided at the same time to this envoy that he himself favored the Portuguese marriage in the interest of the King his master, with whom he later let him speak secretly.

The Spanish, for their part, were proposing the Princess of Parma to him, offering to pay her dowry as if she were an infanta;

26. Edward Hyde (1609–1674), Earl of Clarendon.

then, when I had this proposal rejected, the daughter of the Prince of Orange, on the same terms, without remembering then their great zeal for the faith, since to give that state a Protestant queen meant depriving the Catholics of all the consolation and of all the support that they could hope from this source. But I arranged things so that the second proposal was rejected as well and even served to further my own wishes for Portugal and for its infanta.

Of all the foreign affairs of that year, this was the most important. I shall not fail to touch here on some others of lesser importance, which will still make you realize that while consolidating my authority at home more and more every day, I lost no opportunity to maintain the dignity and the interests of the crown abroad.

The ambassadors of Genoa, by an often repeated artifice which they wanted to turn into a kind of title of possession, had for some years been usurping the royal honors at my court. They had acceded, for this purpose, to taking their audiences only with some royal ambassador, so that by entering the Louvre directly behind him and to the sound of the drum, it was impossible to tell whether this honor was for them or not; vanity all the more ridiculous since, to go back a little further, this entire state long possessed by our ancestors has only the sovereignty that it has assumed for itself by its revolt of 1528 and belongs to us on many grounds, such as the voluntary and solemn treaties by which all the people had submitted to us, often renewed with full and entire consent and repeatedly confirmed by right of arms.[27] I made it clear to these ambassadors how far I was from tolerating their foolish claim, which they had even presumed to justify, and neither they nor their superiors have dared to speak of it since, trembling with fear at the slightest movement of my troops toward Italy, from their knowledge of what I could easily and justly demand.

The Emperor had found it in his interest to inform me of his election, as his predecessors did mine, but he had fancied that it was beneath his dignity to write to me first and had addressed his letter to the Spanish ambassador, with orders not to deliver it

27. For the long and turbulent relationship between France and Genoa, see François de Mézeray, *Histoire de France* (Paris, 1643–1651), I, II.

without having obtained some letter of compliment from me which made it appear that I had anticipated him. I refused not merely to write one, but in order to teach this prince to know me better, I obliged him soon thereafter to delete the titles of Count of Ferrette and Landgrave of Alsace from the powers of his ministers, these domains having been ceded to me by the Treaty of Münster. I also made him suppress the title of Chief of Christendom that he assumed in a proposed league against the Turks, as if he had actually possessed the same empire and the same rights as Charlemagne after having defended religion against the Saxons, the Huns, and the Saracens!

And on this subject, my son, lest they should try to impress you sometimes with the wonderful names of Roman Empire, of Caesar, of Imperial Majesty, of successor to the great emperors from whom we derive our origin, I feel obliged to indicate to you how far the emperors of today are removed from the greatness of the titles that they affect.

When these titles were introduced into our house, it reigned all at once over France, the Low Countries, Germany, Italy, and most of Spain, which it had distributed among various individual lords, while preserving sovereignty over it. The bloody defeats of many peoples issuing from the north and from the south for the ruin of Christendom had made the French name the terror of the whole earth. Charlemagne, finally, seeing no king in all Europe, nor, to tell the truth, anywhere else in the world, whose fortunes could compare with his, this title seemed henceforth unsuitable either for them or for him. He had risen to this high point of glory not by the choice of some prince, but by courage and by victories, which are the choice and the votes of Heaven Itself when It has resolved to subordinate the other powers to a single one. And there had not been any dominion as extensive as his except for the four famous monarchies to which the empire of the entire world is attributed, although they had never conquered nor possessed any more than a small part of it, yet important and well known in the world. That of the Romans was the last, entirely extinct in the West and with only some feeble remnants in the East, miserable and languishing.

However, as if the Roman Empire had recovered its strength and begun to revive in our climes, which was not the case at all, this the greatest title then in the memory of man alone seemed capable of defining and designating the extraordinary loftiness of Charlemagne, and even though this loftiness itself, which he derived only from God and from his sword, gave him every right to assume whatever title he would have wanted, the Pope, who along with the entire Church was extremely indebted to him, was most pleased to contribute whatever he could to his glory and to render this capacity of emperor more authentic in him through a solemn coronation, which, like the consecration, even though it does not give us royalty, proclaims it to the people and renders it more august, more inviolable, and more sacred in us. But this greatness of Charlemagne, which was so fit to establish the title of emperor or even more magnificent ones if there had been any, did not long survive him; diminished first by the partitions that were made then among the sons of France, then by the weakness and by the lack of dedication of his descendants, particularly of the branch that had established itself on this side of the Rhine; for empires, my son, are preserved only as they are acquired, that is, by vigor, by vigilance, and by work.

The Germans, excluding the princes of our blood, soon thereafter appropriated this dignity, or rather, substituted another in its place that had nothing in common either with the old Roman Empire nor with the new empire of our ancestors, by which they tried, as in all great changes, to arrange that everyone would find his advantage and thus not oppose it. The people and the individual states entered into it owing to the great privileges that were given to them in the name of liberty, the princes of Germany because this dignity was made elective instead of hereditary and they thereby acquired the right to appoint to it, to claim it, or both; the popes, finally, because one always professes to derive it from their authority and, basically, a great and true Roman emperor could assume more rights than they would have liked over Rome itself; so that those who have most carefully investigated antiquity [28] hold that Leo III, in crowning Charlemagne, did not invest him with the title of Roman Emperor, which the voice of the people gave him later, but merely with that of Emperor and that of Advocate of the Holy See, for the term advocate then meant

28. Compare with *ibid.*, I, 186–188.

protector. In this sense, the kings of Spain still titled themselves, only a few years ago, advocates of some of the cities that I have conquered in Flanders, that country being almost entirely divided into different advocacies or protectorates of this type.

But to return to the emperors of today, you can easily, my son, understand from this entire discussion that they are in no way comparable to the old Roman emperors, nor to Charlemagne and his first successors. For, to give them their due, they can be considered merely as heads, or captains-general, of a German republic, rather new by comparison with many other states, and which is neither so great nor so powerful that it should claim any superiority over neighboring nations. Their most important decisions are subject to the deliberations of the Estates of the Empire. One imposes whatever conditions one wants upon them at their election. Most of the members of the republic, that is, the princes and the free cities of Germany, defer to their orders only when they please. In their capacity as emperors they have very little revenue, and if they did not possess other hereditary domains of their own, they would be reduced to residing, out of all the Empire, in the sole city of Bamberg, which the bishop who is its sovereign lord would be obliged to cede to them. Thus many princes who might have attained to this dignity by election have rejected it, believing it to be more of a burden than of an honor. And the Elector of Bavaria [29] could have been emperor in my time if he had not refused to appoint himself, as the law permits, by combining his vote with those that I had secured for him in the electoral college.

I fail to see, therefore, my son, for what reason the kings of France, hereditary kings who can boast that there isn't either a better house, nor greater power, nor more absolute authority than theirs anywhere else in the world today, should rank below these elective princes. It cannot be denied, nevertheless, that the popes, as a consequence of what they had done, have gradually given precedence at the court of Rome to the ambassadors of the Emperor over all the others and that most of the courts in Christendom have imitated this example without our predecessors having made any effort to prevent it, but in every other respect they have

29. Ferdinand Maria von Wittelsbach (1636–1679), Elector since 1651.

defended their rights. There are public treaties from the tenth century in which they are named first before the emperors with whom they deal, and our ambassadors at the Porte of the Grand Seigneur, and most recently the Marquis de Brèves under Henry the Great, my grandfather, have not merely disputed but also won the precedence over those of the emperors.[30] In short, my son, while I have not believed I should ask for anything new in Christendom on this matter, I have believed even less that, in my position, I should in any way tolerate anything new by which these princes might affect to assume the least superiority over me; and I counsel you to do the same, noting, however, how much virtue is to be esteemed, since, after such a long time, that of the Romans, that of the first Caesars, and that of Charlemagne still secure, without adequate reason, more honor than is due to the empty name and to the empty shadow of their empire.

These minor disputes with the Emperor led me to devote myself even more to diminishing his influence in Germany, or that which the house of Austria has acquired there in the last two centuries; and having even more carefully investigated the state of opinions, I detached, through a negotiation of several months, the Elector of Trier from that conspiracy. He entered into the Alliance of the Rhine,[31] that is, into a powerful and important league that I had formed within the Empire, under the pretext of maintaining the Treaty of Münster and the peace of Germany.

Ten imperial cities that this same treaty had placed under my protection then lent me the oath of fidelity that they had been refusing me.

In order to consolidate my conquests in that area and in Flanders by a closer union with my old domains, having no grounds to imitate the practice of the Greeks and of the Romans, who sent colonies of their native subjects into newly conquered areas, I tried at least to establish French customs there. I converted the sovereign courts into presidial ones. I put these under the

---

30. François de Savary (1560–1628), Marquis de Brèves, got this right confirmed by a celebrated treaty in 1604.

31. Charles Gaspard van Leyen (1618–1676), Archbishop-Elector of Trier since 1654. He joined the Electors of Mainz and of Cologne, the Bishop of Münster, the Duke of Neuburg, the King of Sweden, the three dukes of Brunswick-Lüneburg, the Landgrave of Hesse, the Count of Waldeck, and some other princes. Louis shows great concern in the *Mémoires* for maintaining this league.

appellate jurisdiction of my *parlements*. I placed Frenchmen, and insofar as I possibly could, people of merit, in the principal offices. I wrote for the generals of orders to unite the convents of these areas to the old provinces of France. I prevented the churches of Artois and of Hainault from continuing to receive rescripts from Rome by way of the internuncio of Flanders and insisted on appointing the abbots in the three bishoprics of Metz, Toul, and Verdun, merely agreeing to choose them from three individuals who would be presented to me at each vacancy.

I had granted my protection to the Prince d'Epinoi during the war. I put him in possession of the property of the Count de Bucquoi until the Spanish had fulfilled their promise to restore his own.[32] I delivered the area of Lalleu, then in dispute between us, from various reprisals with which they threatened it, for under the pretext of some arrears on a sum of twelve thousand *écus* that they customarily levied there, they had imprisoned twelve of the principal inhabitants and had already extorted from them, for their expense, two thousand florins that I regained for them with their liberty, refusing even to consider the hard and ruinous proposal of Spain to double the tax of this area during the dispute so that France and herself would each obtain its right.

I put a stop in Artois to some levies that the magistrates made there under the pretext of tolls granted by the King of Spain. I wanted, in order to relieve the people, for the officers of the garrisons themselves to pay, like the inhabitants, all the other duties that were levied on commodities, and I gave three years of grace to the poor families of the frontier, pursued mercilessly by their creditors since the peace. I arranged for a good part of the boundary to be marked out during that year in execution of the Treaty of the Pyrenees; the fortifications of Nancy demolished; all my strongholds repaired, put in readiness, and provisioned with all the necessities of war, fearing nothing so much as the reproach that has for so long been levied at the French, but which I hope to efface completely by my conduct, that they can conquer but cannot preserve.

It is usual for mature minds, which have received their first disposition for piety at an early age, to turn directly toward God

32. Alexandre-Guillaume de Melun (d. 1679), Prince d'Epinoi. Charles-Albert de Longueval (d. 1663), Count de Bucquoi.

in the midst of good fortune, although, as a major consequence of our weakness, a long sequence of successes, which we then regard as being naturally and properly due us, will customarily make us forget Him. I confess that in these beginnings, seeing my reputation growing each day, everything succeeding for me and becoming easy for me, I was as deeply struck as I have ever been by the desire to serve Him and to please Him.

I empowered Cardinal Antonio Barberini and D'Aubeville,[33] my representative in Rome, to form a league against the Turk, in which I offered to contribute much more in money and in troops than any other Christian prince. I gave one hundred thousand *écus* to the Venetians for the war in Crete, re-engaging myself to furnish them with large forces whenever they might want to make an effort to drive the Infidels from that island. I offered the Emperor an army of twenty thousand men against this common enemy, composed entirely of my troops or of those of my allies.

I revived, by a new ordinance, the rigor of the old edicts against swearing and blasphemy and wanted some examples to be made immediately; and I can say in this regard that my cares and the aversion that I have displayed toward this scandalous disorder have not been useless, my court being, God be thanked, more exempt from it than it long has been under the kings my predecessors.

I took additional precautions against duels, and in order to show that neither rank nor birth dispensed anyone, I banished the Count de Soissons from my court for having extended a challenge to the Duke de Navailles and put his messenger in the Bastille,[34] although nothing came of the matter.

I dedicated myself to destroying Jansenism and to breaking up the communities where this spirit of novelty was developing, well-intentioned perhaps, but which seemed to want to ignore the dangerous consequences that it could have. I made various appeals to the Dutch on behalf of the Catholics of Guelderland.

33. Cardinal Antonio Barberini (1608–1673), Co-protector of French Affairs at Rome. Jean de Sève (1610–1687), Sieur d'Aubeville. Louis secretly instructed them not to enter the league.

34. Eugène-Maurice de Savoie (1635–1673), Count de Soissons and husband of Cardinal Mazarin's niece, Olympia Mancini. Philippe de Montault-Benac (1619–1684), Duke de Navailles.

I ordered alms to be distributed liberally among the poor of Dunkirk, lest their poverty tempt them to follow the religion of the English, to whom the war against Spain had obliged me to give this stronghold during the ministry of Cardinal Mazarin.

And as to my great number of subjects of the supposedly reformed religion, which was an evil that I had always regarded, and still regard, with sorrow, I devised at that time the plan of my entire policy toward them, which I have no grounds for regretting, since God has blessed it and still blesses it every day with a great number of conversions.

It seemed to me, my son, that those who wanted to employ violent remedies did not know the nature of this disease, caused in part by the excitement of tempers, which must be allowed to pass and to die gradually instead of rekindling it with equally strong contradictions, always useless, moreover, when the corruption is not limited to a clearly defined number, but spread throughout the state.

As far as I have been able to understand, the ignorance of the clergy in previous centuries, their luxury, their debaucheries, the bad examples that they set, those that they were obliged to tolerate for that very reason, the excesses, finally, that they condoned in the conduct of individuals contrary to the public rules and sentiments of the Church gave rise, more than anything else, to those grave wounds that it has received from schism and from heresy. The new reformers obviously spoke the truth on many matters of fact and of this nature, which they decried with both justice and bitterness. They presumed in regard to belief, and people cannot possibly distinguish a well-disguised error when it lies hidden, moreover, among many evident truths. It all began with some minor differences which I have learned that the Protestants of Germany and the Huguenots of France hardly consider any more today. These produced greater ones, primarily because too much pressure was put upon a violent and bold man [35] who, seeing no other honorable retreat for himself, pushed ahead into the fray and, abandoning himself to his own reasoning, took the liberty of examining everything that he had accepted, promised the world

---

35. Martin Luther. Compare with Mézeray, *op. cit.*, II, 400. It will be recalled (see note 3) that Louis prepared this text while in a conciliatory mood toward the Jansenists.

an easy and shortened path to salvation, a means very suitable for flattering human reasoning and for drawing the populace. Love of novelty seduced many of them. The interests of various princes mingled in this quarrel. The wars in Germany, then in France, intensified the animosity of the wrong side. The lower classes had even fewer doubts that a religion for which they had exposed themselves to so many perils was not good. The fathers, filled with this preoccupation, bequeathed it to their children with as much of its violence as they possibly could, yet basically similar in nature to all the other passions, which time always moderates, and often all the more successfully if one makes less of an effort to combat them.

From this general knowledge, I believed, my son, that the best means to reduce gradually the number of Huguenots in my kingdom was, in the first place, not to press them at all by any new rigor against them, to implement what they had obtained from my predecessors but to grant them nothing further, and even to restrict its execution within the narrowest limits that justice and propriety would permit. I appointed for this purpose, that very year, commissioners to execute the Edict of Nantes. I carefully put a stop everywhere to the schemes of these religionists, as in the Faubourg Saint-Germain, where I learned that they were beginning to conduct secret meetings and schools of their sect; at Jametz, in Lorraine, where they had taken refuge in great numbers during the disorders of the war and were carrying on their services without the right of assembly; at La Rochelle, where the old inhabitants who were permitted to reside there with their families had slowly but surely attracted a number of others whom I obliged to leave.

But as to the graces that depended solely on me, I resolved, and I have rather scrupulously observed it since, not to grant them any, and this out of kindness rather than out of bitterness, so as to oblige them thereby to consider from time to time, by themselves and without constraint, if they had some good reason for depriving themselves voluntarily of the advantages that they could share with all my other subjects.

However, to profit from their greater willingness to be disabused of their errors, I also resolved to attract, even to reward, those who might be receptive, to do all I could to inspire the bishops to work at their instruction and to eliminate the scandals that sometimes separated them from us; to place, finally, in these highest posts and in all those to which I appoint for any reason whatsoever, only persons of piety, of dedication, of learning, capable of repairing, by an entirely different conduct, the disorders that their predecessors had primarily produced in the Church.

But I am still a long way, my son, from having exhausted everything that I have in mind for recalling peacefully those whom birth, education, and most often a zeal without knowledge hold in good faith to these pernicious errors. Thus I shall have, as I hope, other occasions to discuss this with you, without explaining plans to you in advance to which time and circumstances can bring a thousand changes.

I assumed all these cares out of true gratitude for the blessings that I was receiving every day, but I also noticed at the same time that they were very useful to me in preserving the affection of the people, very pleased to see that I was not too occupied to continue my pious devotions with the same regularity in which the Queen my mother had raised me, and particularly edified that year when I performed the stations of a jubilee on foot with my entire household, something that I did not even think worthy of note.

And to tell you the truth, my son, we are lacking not merely in justice but also in prudence when we are lacking in veneration for Him whose lieutenants we are. Our submission to Him is the rule and the example for that which is due to us. Armies, councils, all human industry would be feeble means for maintaining us on the throne if everyone believed he had as much right to it as we and did not revere a superior power, of which ours is a part. The public respects that we pay to this invisible power could indeed justly be considered the first and most important part of our entire policy if they did not require a more noble and more disinterested motive.

Watch out, my son, I implore you, not to approach religion with only this idea of self-interest, very bad when it stands alone, but which, moreover, would not succeed for you because artifice always comes out and does not long produce the same effects as truth. All the advantages that our post gives us over other men are undoubtedly so many new titles of servitude to Him who has given them to us. But in His sight, the external without the internal is nothing at all and serves more to offend Him than to please Him. Judge for yourself, my son, if you should ever find yourself, as it can hardly fail to happen in the course of your life, in the position that is so usual for kings, and in which I have seen myself so often. Even when my rebellious subjects have had the temerity to take up arms against me, they have made me less angry, perhaps, than those who were in the meanwhile remaining at my side being more dutiful and more attentive to me than all the others, while I was well aware that they were betraying me and had neither true respect nor true affection for me in their hearts.

In order to preserve this internal disposition that I desire above all and most of all for you, it is useful, my son, to review from time to time the truths in which we believe, but which our occupations, our pleasures, and our very greatness are constantly making us forget.

It is not for me to play the theologian with you. I have been extremely careful to choose for your education those whom I have believed best suited to instill piety in you by instruction and by example, and I can assure you that this is the first quality that I have sought and considered in them. They will not fail, and I shall watch out for it, to confirm you in the good maxims, and more so every day as you will grow more capable of reasoning with them.

If, nonetheless, from a rather natural curiosity, you would like to know what has struck me most in what I have ever seen or heard about such matters, I shall relate it to you quite simply, following what good sense might suggest to me without affecting a depth of knowledge that I do not possess.

I have attributed a great deal, in the first place, to the general consensus of all nations and of all ages, and particularly of almost all the most famous men of whom I have ever heard—whether for literature, or for arms, or for statesmanship—who have esteemed piety in general although in different ways, whereas over all this time the impious and the atheists have comprised only a very small number of mediocre minds who have wanted to appear greater than they were, or at least than the public has found them, since they have not been able to create, like the others, an influential party in the world, a long sequence of supporters and admirers. This universal consensus has always carried great weight with me. For, after all, it is not surprising for reason to mislead a small number of individuals since the senses themselves, which are so reliable, also mislead some individuals, and since there are some who see things as entirely different from what they actually are. But if, in the most important and the most carefully studied thing in the world, human reason taken generally has always been regularly mistaken at all times, in all natures, and in the same way, so as to make us embrace a nonexistent phantom and fantasy as the greatest and the most important of all our duties, it would no longer be reason but an untenable folly, which is the greatest absurdity and the greatest contradiction that a rational mind could maintain because it maintained this only through its own reasoning.

I have considered subsequently that if the intellect balks initially against everything that we have not seen and consequently against everything that we have been taught about divinity, judgment submits to it easily upon longer reflection and closer scrutiny, for we can judge things that are unknown to us only by comparing them to those that we know and by drawing inferences from one to the other. However, we see nothing in the world, out of all that has some relation and some resemblance to the world itself, such as machines for building and a thousand other similar things, which is not the plan and the work of some rational mind. This being so, why should we not believe, even if natural instinct and the voice of the people had not taught it to us, that the world itself, which so far surpasses all these things in order, in greatness, and in beauty, is also the work of some rational mind, infinitely greater and higher than ours; and if we are subsequently told a thousand marvels about it, we need merely determine who is telling them to us and what assurances he has of them, without astonishment at not being able to understand them, since in the world itself, which is but the handiwork, there are so many other incomprehensible although undeniable miracles constantly before our eyes. Thus, if what were incredible in itself is supported, moreover, by some good authority, it becomes not merely credible but very likely when it is a question of that superior and higher reason, that is, of something very obscure for us who know only very imperfectly what our own reason is.

These first bases laid, it has always seemed to me, my son, that all the rest followed easily. The infinite variety of religions may be distressing, but they all have basically so much relation to each other, so many principles and so many bases in common that their very diversity obviously establishes a single religion, of which all the others are imperfect or false copies that still preserve the most notable traits of the original.

And if it is only a question of disentangling this original from among these copies, what other religion can prevail over ours, to which all the able and enlightened people in the world have submitted when it has appeared; which is embraced and followed today, not by barbarous, ignorant, and crude nations like the others, but by all those where intellect and learning are most cultivated; which, moreover, if one considers antiquity, is the same as the Jewish, the oldest of all, of which it is only the perfection and the culmination, long predicted, promised, and announced by extraordinary men at the same time that they were making a thousand other predictions that events were confirming each day; which since that time has claimed boldly that upon reaching the point of perfection that it awaited it would entirely destroy the pagan, by which it was then despised and oppressed; nor has it failed to do so, all the gods who used to be worshipped having given way to its own without retaining a single worshipper in the world.

The truths that it reveals are surprising, but we have established that nothing that is so far beyond us need surprise us nor appear too great. The world has learned them from eyewitnesses whom good sense prevents us from suspecting even today either of folly, since their ethics, by admission of the impious themselves, far surpasses that of the wisest philosophers; or of imposture, since it is agreed that they have lived without self-interest, without property, without ambition, without pleasures, most often satisfying their limited needs by the work of their hands, traversing the whole earth with both labor and peril in order to convert it, scorned, persecuted, and almost all concluding their life in martyrdom, yet neither they nor their successors ever relenting or denying themselves. This religion that preached mysteries so contrary to human reason and maxims so hard and so unpleasant to the worldly without ever arming subject against prince or citizen against citizen, without ever doing anything but suffering and praying, has disarmed its oppressors and all the powers that opposed it, has established itself throughout the world, and has become dominant in less than three centuries, which can only make good sense by the miracles that fill Christian history, which we no longer see today, but which this great and astonishing progress of Christianity verifies for us, aside from a thousand other proofs of great authenticity.

There you have, my son, the considerations which have struck me the most. I have no doubt that these very ones, or some others, will produce a similar effect on you and that you will try to answer sincerely to our title of *très-chrétien*;[36] if you cannot do it in all your actions, which would be desirable, never lose sight, at least, of what makes for all the merit of the good ones and all the remedy of the bad and the weak ones.

Some of my ancestors have waited until the end of their life to make similar exhortations to their children. I have believed, on the contrary, that these would have a greater impact on you while the vigor of my age, the clarity of my mind, and the flourishing state of my affairs would prevent your suspecting any deception in them or your attributing them to the idea of peril. Spare me the disappointment, my son, that they will only have served one day to compound your guilt, which they would undoubtedly do, if you should ever forget them.

Second Section

It was then that I believed I should give serious attention to the re-establishment of the finances, and the first thing I deemed necessary was to remove the principal officials responsible for the disorder from their positions. For ever since I had assumed the care of my affairs, I had every day discovered new evidence of their squandering, and particularly by the superintendant. The sight of the vast establishments of this man and of his insolent acquisitions could not but convince me of his wild ambition, and the general distress of my entire people constantly urged my justice against him.

36. The kings of France possessed the title of "Most Christian" kings, the kings of Spain that of "Catholic" kings.

But what compounded his guilt toward me was that, far from profiting from the kindness I had shown him by retaining him in my councils, it gave him renewed hope of deceiving me, and that far from being the wiser for it, he merely tried to be more skillful at it. But whatever artifice he might employ, I was not long in recognizing his bad faith, for he could not refrain from continuing his extravagant expenses, fortifying strongholds, decorating palaces, forming conspiracies, and purchasing important offices for his friends at my expense, in the hope of soon becoming the sovereign arbiter of the state.

Although this behavior was assuredly most criminal, I had initially intended only to exclude him from affairs, but having subsequently considered that with his restless disposition he would not endure this change of fortune without trying something new, I thought it best to arrest him. I postponed, nevertheless, the execution of this plan, and this plan distressed me greatly, for not merely did I see that he was in the meanwhile employing new subterfuges to steal from me, but what disturbed me more was that in order to appear more influential, he made a point of asking me for private audiences, and that in order not to arouse his suspicions, I was compelled to grant them and to submit to his useless discussions, while I knew all about his disloyalty.

You can imagine that I was at an age when it required a great deal of self-control for me to act with such restraint. But, on the one hand, I saw that the removal of the superintendant was necessarily connected with transferring the farmed taxes, and on the other hand, I knew that it being summer, this was the worst season of the year for making such innovations, aside from wanting above all to have a fund of four millions on hand for whatever needs might arise. Thus I resolved to wait for autumn to execute this plan.

But having gone to Nantes toward the end of the month of August for the meeting of the Estates of Brittany and getting a closer look from there at the ambitious enterprises of this minister, I could not refrain from having him arrested in that very place on September 5. All France, as convinced as I was of the misconduct of the superintendant, acclaimed this action and praised particularly the secrecy with which I had kept a decision of this nature for three or four months, primarily in regard to a man who had such private access to me, who was in contact with all those who were around me, who was receiving information from within and from outside the state, and whose own conscience should have given him ample warning that he had everything to fear.

But what I believed I had done on this occasion that was most worthy of being observed and most advantageous to my people was to abolish the office of superintendant, or rather to assume it myself.

Perhaps in considering the difficulty of this undertaking, you will one day be astonished, as all France has been, that I have undertaken this labor at an age when it is usual to love only pleasure. But I shall tell you frankly that although this work was unpleasant, I felt less repugnance for it than another might have, because I have always considered the satisfaction of doing one's duty as the sweetest pleasure in the world. I have even often wondered how it could be that love for work being a quality so necessary to sovereigns should yet be one that is so rarely found in them.

Most princes, because they have a great many servants and subjects, do not feel obliged to go to any trouble and do not consider that, if they have an infinite number of people working under their orders, there are infinitely more who rely on their conduct and that it takes a great deal of watching and a great deal of work merely to insure that those who act do only what they should and that those who rely tolerate only what they must. All these different conditions that compose the world are united to each other only by an exchange of reciprocal obligations. The deferences and the respects that we receive from our subjects are not a free gift from them but payment for the justice and the protection that they expect to receive from us. Just as they must honor us, we must protect and defend them, and our debts toward them are even more binding than theirs to us, for indeed, if one of them lacks the skill or the willingness to execute our orders, a thousand others come in a crowd to fill his post, whereas the position of a sovereign can be properly filled only by the sovereign himself.

But to be more specific, it must be added to this that of all the functions of sovereignty, the one that a prince must guard most jealously is the handling of the finances. It is the most delicate of all because it is the one that is most capable of seducing the one who performs it, and which makes it easiest for him to spread corruption. The prince alone should have sovereign direction over it because he alone has no fortune to establish but that of the state, no acquisition to make except for the monarchy, no authority to strengthen other than that of the laws, no debts to pay besides the public ones, no friends to enrich save his people.

And indeed, what would be more ruinous for the provinces or more shameful for their king than to raise a man who has his own private objectives and affairs, who claims the right to dispose of everything without rendering any account and to fill his coffers and those of his creatures constantly with the most liquid public funds? Can a prince be more foolish than to favor private individuals who use his authority in order to become rich at his own expense and whose squandering, although it gains him nothing, ruins both his affairs and his reputation? And putting it more piously, can he fail to consider that these great sums which compose the exorbitant and monstrous wealth of a small number of financiers always come from the sweat, the tears, and the blood of the wretched, whose defense is committed to his care?

The maxims that I am teaching you today, my son, have not been taught to me by anyone, because they had never occurred to my predecessors. But know that your advantage in being instructed in them at such an early age will come back to haunt you if you don't profit from it.

Aside from the councils of finances and the boards that had always been held, I decided, in order to acquit myself more responsibly of the superintendancy, to establish a new council, which I named Royal Council. I composed it of Marshal de Villeroi, of two Councillors of State, D'Aligre and De Sève,[37] and of an Intendant of Finances, who was Colbert, and it is in this council that I have been working ever since to disentangle the terrible confusion that had been introduced into my affairs.

This was assuredly no minor undertaking, and those who have seen the point at which things were and who see the precision to which I have now reduced them are astonished, with reason, that

37. Nicolas de Neufville (1598–1685), Duke de Villeroi and Marshal of France, who had been Louis' governor. Etienne d'Aligre (1592–1677) and Alexandre de Sève (1604–1672).

I was able to penetrate in so short a time into an obscurity that so many able superintendants had never yet clarified. But what must put a stop to this surprise is the natural difference between the interest of the prince and that of the superintendant. For these private individuals, approaching their position with no greater care than to preserve their own liberty to dispose of everything as they see fit, often put much more of their skill into obscuring this matter than into clarifying it, whereas a king, who is its legitimate lord, puts as much order and precision as he can into everything, aside from the fact that I was personally often relieved in this work by Colbert, whom I entrusted with examining things that required too much discussion and into which I would not have had the time to go.

The manner in which the collections and the expenditures had been made was something incredible. My revenues were no longer handled by my treasurers but by the clerks of the superintendant who combined them haphazardly with his private expenses. Money was disbursed when, how, and as they pleased, and one looked afterwards at leisure for false expenses, orders for cash, and canceled notes to consume these sums. The continual exhaustion of the public treasury and the perpetual avidity for more money made for the easy awarding of exorbitant commissions to those who offered to advance it. The wild disposition of Fouquet had always made him prefer useless expenses to necessary ones, so that the most liquid funds having been consumed in gratuities distributed to his friends, in buildings constructed for his pleasure, or in other things of a similar nature, it was necessary, at the slightest need of the state, to have recourse to alienations that could only be negotiated at a pittance because of the extreme necessity. By these means the state had become so impoverished that notwithstanding the immense *tailles* that were levied, the treasury netted no more than twenty-one millions per year, which had itself been spent for two years in advance, aside from my having been made liable for seventy millions in notes issued for the profit of various individuals.

The thing that I was most eager to correct about this general abuse was the use of orders for cash, because these had assuredly contributed more than anything else to the squandering of my money; for in this way one gave freely to whomever one wanted, without shame and without any fear of discovery. To avoid this confusion in the future, I resolved to draw up and to record personally all the orders I would sign, so that no expenditure has since been possible without my knowing the reason.

I also wanted to recontract my farmed taxes, which had not been brought to their just value, and in order to avoid the frauds that were so common on these occasions—whether through the corruption of the judges who awarded them or through the secret compacts between the bidders—I was present at the bidding personally; and this first effort of mine increased my revenues by three millions, aside from making the value of the contracts payable monthly, which then gave me enough to provide for the most pressing expenses and enabled me to save the state a loss of fifteen millions a year in interest on loans.

As for the contracts for the direct taxes, I reduced the commission from five *sols* to only fifteen *deniers* per *livre*, a diminution that amounted to such a large sum for the entire kingdom that it permitted me, in my great exhaustion, to lower the *taille* by four millions.

I was astonished myself that in such a short time and by such entirely just means I should have been able to procure so much profit for the public. But what might cause still greater astonishment is that those who dealt with me on these terms made almost as great and much more solid a gain than those who had dealt previously, because the respect of my subjects for me then and my care in protecting my servants in all their just requests made them find as much facility in their collections then as there had previously been chicanery and obstruction.

I resolved, a short time later, to reduce from three quarters to two the payments on the salary increases that the officials had acquired at a pittance and that had greatly diminished the value of my farmed taxes. But I have already explained the justice and the facility of this reduction to you in discussing the sovereign courts, and I shall only indicate it to you now in passing as one of the good effects of the economy that was so necessary to my state.

But my last decision of that year concerning the finances was the establishment of the Chamber of Justice, in which I had two principal motives: the first, that it was not possible, in the state to which things were reduced, to diminish the ordinary taxes sufficiently and to relieve the poverty of the people promptly enough without making those who had grown wealthy at the expense of the state contribute heavily to its expenses; and the second, that for this chamber to examine the contracts that had been made was the only means to facilitate the settling of my debts. For they had been raised to such prodigious sums that I could not have paid them all without ruining most of my subjects, nor cancel them arbitrarily without running the risk of committing an injustice, aside from not wanting to return to the abuse that had been practiced in the redemption of treasury notes, by which means influential people were paid sooner or later for sums that were not due them while the real creditors would have drawn only a small portion of their due. This is why I believed that I should liquidate exactly what I owed and what was owed to me in order to pay the one and to be paid the other, but because these discussions were delicate and because most of those concerned had a great deal of influence and a good many relatives in the ordinary courts of justice, I was obliged to form a special one out of the most disinterested men in all the others.

I have no doubt that from reading all these details you will get the impression that the effort required for all these sorts of things was not very pleasant in itself, and that this great number of ordinances, contracts, declarations, registers, and accounts that it was necessary not merely to see and to sign but to conceive and to resolve, was not too satisfying a matter to a mind capable of other things, and I will grant you this. But if you consider the great advantages that I have drawn from it later, the relief that I have granted to my subjects each year, of how many debts I have disengaged the state, how many alienated taxes I have repurchased, with what punctuality I have paid all legitimate burdens, and the number of poor workers I have supported by employing them on my buildings, how many gratuities I have given to people of merit, how I have furthered public works, what aid in men and in money I have furnished my allies, how greatly I have increased the number of my ships, what strongholds I have purchased, with what vigor I have taken possession of my rights when they were challenged, without ever having been reduced to the unfortunate necessity of burdening my subjects with any extraordinary tax, you would certainly find then that the labors by which I have reached this position must have appeared very pleasant to me, since they have borne so much fruit for my subjects.

For indeed, my son, we must consider the good of our subjects far more than our own. They are almost a part of ourselves, since we are the head of a body and they are its members. It is only for their own advantage that we must give them laws, and our power over them must only be used by us in order to work more effectively for their happiness. It is wonderful to deserve from them the name of father along with that of master, and if the one belongs to us by right of birth, the other must be the sweetest object of our ambition. I am well aware that such a wonderful title is not obtained without a great deal of effort, but in praiseworthy undertakings one must not be stopped by the idea of difficulty. Work only dismays weak souls, and when a plan is advantageous and just, it is weakness not to execute it. Laziness in those of our rank is just as opposed to the greatness of courage as timidity, and there is no doubt that a monarch responsible for watching over the public interest deserves more blame in fleeing from a useful burden than in stopping in the face of imminent danger; for indeed, the fear of danger can almost always be tinged by a feeling of prudence, whereas the fear of work can never be considered as anything but an inexcusable weakness.

I was in the midst of these occupations when news reached me from London that on October 10, at the entry of a Swedish ambassador, the Spanish ambassador, Baron de Vatteville,[38] had presumed to claim a competition of rank between my ministers and those of the King his master, and that under this delusion, having underhandedly and by means of money instigated a popular disturbance, he had dared to have the coach of the Count d'Estrades,[39] my ambassador, stopped by a band of armed rabble, killed the horses with musket fire, and had prevented it, finally, from parading in its rightful place. You may judge my indignation by your very own, for I have no doubt, my son, that you shall still be stirred by reading this and shall be just as sensitive as I have always been about the honor of a crown that is destined for you.

38. Charles (d. 1670), Baron de Vatteville.
39. Godefroi (1607–1686), Count d'Estrades.

What disturbed me even more was that I could not view this offense as the outcome of a sudden and unpremeditated quarrel. It was, on the contrary, a decision made long before by this minister in order to flatter his own vanity and that of his nation. He had been very mortified at not having been able to prevent the Portuguese marriage, although he had formed a great conspiracy in London for this with the most important persons at court, to the point of iring the King himself by this behavior. The money that he had requested from Spain in order to parry this blow had arrived, but too late. And not being able, apparently, to divest himself of his supporters, to whom he had promised it, he sought at least to use the expense for something striking that could redound to the honor of the King his master.

With this intention, sometime previously, on the very similar occasion of the entry of a Venetian ambassador extraordinary, he had sent word to D'Estrades that in order to preserve the friendship between the kings their masters and in order to imitate Cardinal Mazarin and Don Luis de Haro, who, according to him, had divided everything—earth, water, and sun—at Conference Island,[40] he was of the opinion that neither one of them should send his coach to meet this ambassador; whereupon having met with a most formal refusal and D'Estrades having assured him that, on the contrary, he intended to send one and to preserve his rank there, he indicated that he would do the same thing for his part by sending his coach, unless, he added, the ambassador had made the same decision as other ambassadors extraordinary not to notify anyone of his arrival and of his entry, in which case no one was obliged to be there. Thereupon, having brought in the Venetian resident, who was his friend and with whom he was already in agreement, this resident confirmed that the ambassador wanted to imitate the Prince de Ligne, who, having been ambassador extraordinary sometime previously, had sought to emphasize the distinction between himself and the ordinary ambassadors by not notifying anyone at all of his arrival. The King of England, whose only interest in this dispute was to prevent any sort of commotion and turmoil in his capital city and who was being

40. The Isle of Pheasants on the French Spanish border, where they had concluded the Treaty of the Pyrenees.

urged by Vatteville, did not hesitate to intervene subsequently and to request my ambassador and all the others not to send off to the entry of the Venetian one, who did not desire it either, since he was not informing them of it: in short, this is how they did it that time.

I was very ired by the first rather vague rumors that reached me about it. It seemed to me that the King of England, who was then displaying a good deal of friendship for me, had been wrong to meddle in this dispute, that D'Estrades should have defended himself not merely against his requests, but also against his explicit orders, if he had sent any, and replied that an ambassador took orders only from his master, should have withdrawn, finally, before consenting to this shameful solution. But I had no retort when I learned from his letter what had transpired and that the King had added only his simple request to the decision of the Venetian ambassador, which would commonly prevent all the others from sending off to meet him; and I had less cause for complaint than anyone, because I had practically invented this solution at my own court a short time previously in order to avoid the competition of some ambassadors, admittedly better founded than the one that was contrived between France and Spain.

But I could see where the subterfuge of the Spanish was aiming and how, by similar negotiations with ambassadors who would enter in the future, they would try, under the ever plausible pretext of avoiding disorder, to suppress the memory of a precedence that is so legitimately mine. I was in possession of it throughout all Europe, and especially in Rome, where the papal guards themselves have sometimes been employed to preserve it for my predecessors, and it had been a long time since the Spanish ambassadors either there or in Venice had been present at the public ceremonies that mine attended. At no time, not even in the most flourishing state of their monarchy, has it succeeded in establishing the equality to which it aspired. And when my predecessors, occupied by their domestic troubles, have relented the most on this subject, all that its ministers have been able to achieve was to usurp, as at the Council of Trent, some bizarre rank that, being neither the first nor equal to the first, could pass in their imagination as not being the second, although it actually was.

Thus I could not stomach seeing my right circumvented by the artifice of Vatteville, and this artifice often repeated could ultimately constitute not merely a claim but almost the possession of a conflicting right. At the point to which I had already brought the dignity of the French name, I did not think I should leave it to my successors any lesser than I had received it. And remembering that in matters of state it is sometimes necessary to cut what cannot be untied, I instructed D'Estrades precisely that at the first entry of an ambassador, whether ordinary or extraordinary, whether or not he had been notified, he should not fail to send his coach to him and to have it assume and preserve the first rank.

He was in a position to obey me at this entry of the Swedish ambassador, who in truth had notified him initially of his arrival and of the date of his entry, but who subsequently, at the urging of the Spanish and perhaps of the King of England himself, had requested him not to send off to meet him, as if he had changed his mind and wanted to do the same as the last ambassadors extraordinary. To this, D'Estrades, instructed by my letters, replied that the close alliance and friendship between France and Sweden did not permit him to neglect this duty without incurring my displeasure. But even though he had gathered all the French who were in London, that he had brought in from Gravelines, where he was governor, some officers from his regiment and some cavalrymen from his son's company, that all this together might have amounted to four or five hundred men, that those who were accompanying his coach, or those who were to support them, and the Marquis d'Estrades, his son, who was at their head, did all that brave men could in a similar tumult, it was not possible for them to prevail over a huge mob of people already naturally ill-disposed toward the French and even more aroused then by the emissaries of Vatteville, who, if I have heard correctly, had armed more than two thousand men and spent almost five hundred thousand *livres* in this fine undertaking. The King of England, who had secretly promised D'Estrades to preserve my rank for me, had some days before issued prohibitions to all subjects against taking either side and stationed his guards throughout the city in order to prevent what happened. But he could not control it, and all he could do was to pacify the tumult after many persons had been killed or wounded on both sides, and almost as many on the Spanish side as on the French.

However, they believed they had already defeated my armies by this miserable advantage, which was to cost them still more later, but they changed their minds when they saw how I reacted to this outrage and how capable I was of redressing it. I had no sooner received news of it than I commanded the Count de Fuelsandaña,[41] their ambassador, to leave the kingdom immediately without seeing either me or the queens, charging him, furthermore, with informing the Marquis de Fuentes,[42] who was coming from Germany to take his place, that he was not to enter my domains. I revoked the passport I had issued to the Marquis de Caracena, governor of Flanders, for passing through France on his way back to Spain. I ordered the governor of Peronne to inform him of this on my behalf. I instructed the commissioners whom I had appointed for the execution of the peace to suspend and to break all contact with those of the Catholic King. I hastily dispatched a gentleman ordinary of my household to Madrid with orders for the Archbishop of Embrun,[43] my ambassador, to demand the personal and exemplary punishment of Vatteville and a reparation not merely proportionate to the offense but which would also assure me that the ministers of Spain would not attempt any more similar undertakings against mine in the future. I commanded him, finally, to declare emphatically that I could easily procure justice for myself if it were refused to me. I also had D'Estrades appeal to the King of England for the punishment of those responsible and subsequently ordered him to withdraw from that court as a place where it was neither safe nor dignified nor proper for him to remain any longer.

It was not difficult for these manifestations to convince everyone of how I actually felt. For it is a fact that I would have carried my just resentment to the last extremes, and even in that unfortunate eventuality, I would have found cause for satisfaction in a legitimate war where I could acquire honor at the head of my armies.

41. Alonzo de Perez de Vivero (d. 1661), Count de Fuelsandaña.

42. Gaspar de Teves de Guzman (c. 1608–1673), Marquis de La Fuente (or de Fuentes).

43. Georges d'Aubusson de La Feuillade (1609–1697).

The court of Spain did not share these sentiments, but it trusted to the art of negotiation, in which this nation considers itself unsurpassed. Don Luis de Haro, who was nearing the end of his life, feeling the weakness of the state as well as his own, feared nothing so much as this break. He sought merely to gain more time in this affair by long and repeated conferences with my ambassador, imagining that everything would become easier once the initial excitement had been allowed to pass. He was very much surprised to see that things had changed between France and Spain, for at the Treaty of the Pyrenees it was Cardinal Mazarin who tried to convince him by reasoning, to which he always replied briefly that he neither could nor dared exceed the precise orders of his King and of the Council of Spain; here, on the contrary, it was he who did the reasoning and my ambassador who held firmly to my precise orders, continually obliging him to make very unpleasant concessions. He died about then. I played on the circumstance. I acted with new ministers who were still uncertain as to their conduct as if all the conditions that had merely been proposed to him had already been decided so as to have the means of demanding still others of them. Each of my couriers carried stricter and more pressing orders, and the Council of Spain, seeing that every moment of delay made its situation worse, hastened by itself to settle on my conditions.

In order to begin to satisfy me, Vatteville had already been re-called and had been relegated to Burgos without being permitted to go to court, punished, perhaps, for a fault that he had not committed without authorization but for which he was primarily responsible owing to the ease with which the ministers of a prince in a foreign country can always make their distant master agree to proposals for glorious and easy undertakings.

Aside from this, a public reparation was settled upon in writing, which was punctually executed subsequently as I had been promised, and whose record has been published, signed by my four secretaries of state. I believe it necessary to relate its sub-stance to you, for even though I am writing here about the events of 1661 and that this satisfaction was not offered to me until May 4, 1662,[44] I have told you elsewhere that I don't intend to

44. Actually, on March 24, 1662.

follow the precise chronological order when it is a question of gathering everything that belongs to the same matter.

The Count de Fuelsandaña,[45] ambassador extraordinary of the Catholic King, came to my great chamber at the Louvre, where the papal nuncio and all the ambassadors, residents, and envoys at my court and the most important persons in my state were waiting. There, having first presented me with the letter that declared him ambassador, he immediately handed me a second one, authorizing what he would tell me regarding this matter on behalf of the King his master. Subsequently, he declared to me that His Catholic Majesty had been no less displeased nor less surprised than I by what had transpired in London and that he had no sooner heard of it than he ordered Baron de Vatteville, his ambassador, to leave England and to return to Spain, dismissing him from his position in order to offer me satisfaction and to demonstrate to him the resentment that his excesses merited; that he had also commanded him to assure me that he had already sent orders to all his ambassadors and ministers, both in England and in all other courts where similar difficulties might arise in the future, to abstain from any competition with my ambassadors and ministers in all public ceremonies that my ambassadors and ministers might attend.

I replied that I was very pleased to hear his declaration on behalf of the King his master, because it would obligate me to continue to live on good terms with him. After which, this ambassador having withdrawn, I addressed the residents or envoys who were present and told them that they had heard the declaration of the Spanish ambassador and that I requested them to communicate it to their masters so that they might know that the Catholic King had issued orders for his ambassadors to cede the precedence to mine on every occasion.

I shall not be displeased, my son, as this affair is important, for you to make some useful reflections upon it.

In the first place, this notable example will confirm for you what I have already established by reason at the beginning of these *mémoires:* I mean that after having procured counsel, it is for us to make our decisions, there being no one sometimes who could

45. Actually, the Marquis de La Fuente.

venture to inspire us with better or more royal ones than we can find in ourselves. This success can undoubtedly be considered fortunate, since I have obtained more than my predecessors had even hoped, obliging the Spanish not merely to stop claiming the competition, but even to declare formally and by an authentic act that they would not claim it any longer. And I don't know whether anything has transpired since the beginning of the monarchy that is more glorious for it, for the kings and the sovereigns that our ancestors have sometimes seen at their feet to render them homage were not there as sovereigns and as kings but as lords of some minor principality that they held in fief and that they could renounce. Here the kind of homage is truly of another sort, of king to king, of crown to crown, which could not even leave our enemies in any more doubt that ours is the first in all Christendom. This success, however, would not have been the same, I can say it in all truth, if from the beginning to the end I had not followed my own impulses much more than those of others, which has been a source of great and lasting joy to me.

It must not be assumed that interest leads everyone to deceive us. This would be unjustified distrust, as irksome and as cruel to ourselves as to others. But there are few people in the world who are not misled by their interest into giving more frequent and more serious consideration to the reasons that flatter them than to the contrary reasons. The King of England was not satisfied with Vatteville and undoubtedly preferred my friendship then to that of the Spanish, but he could not prefer it to his sole interest, which was to avoid all sorts of commotion and disorder in London at the beginning of a still shaky reign and consequently to lend his support to all the solutions proposed by Vatteville and by Spain in order to suspend a decision. D'Estrades was undoubtedly not badly intentioned. I can say, on the contrary, that he has rendered me some very useful services, and I had, indeed, good cause to esteem his zeal and his conduct. But it was not in his interest, as distinct from mine, to take upon himself in the course of his embassy such an important, difficult, and uncertain affair, instead of getting out of it by a compromise that did not seem to prejudice him, no ambassador being obliged to have his coach and his servants at an entry of which he has not been informed. So, when I sent him my precise orders for that one, he replied to me, in truth, that he would be there in greater strength, the Scottish colonels who had served in France having promised him a good number of their soldiers; but at the same time he added that the conspiracy for Spain being large and powerful in London, all the Irish colonels in the interests of that nation, the people naturally enemies and envious of the French, and Vatteville receiving and distributing infinite sums of money for these sorts of things, he left me to consider if the advantage that would have been gained once could always be preserved in other sallies and if, consequently, it might not be better to presume it as still entirely acquired for France without ever risking it. He was undoubtedly doing well, as ambassador, to foresee and to propose these difficulties, but I was doing well as king not to fear them. I make it sufficiently clear to all France whether I consider my ministers loyal and enlightened, but it should not be astonishing if their state, their condition, their age, their inclination, and their purposes would have made them a little more afraid of war at that time than I was, and particularly fear being responsible toward me and toward the public for all its consequences.

In any case, it is very certain, my son, that if I had attributed too much to their counsels, I would have accepted a much lesser satisfaction and would be leaving you with this inestimable advantage greatly impaired. But, as for me, I reflected on the circumstances, on the condition of France and of Spain both at home and abroad, which permitted me to hope for everything. I listened to my own heart, which could not consent to anything that left my right and yours in any sort of doubt. I acted, finally, on a general principle that I ask you to note carefully: It is, my son, that in such unpleasant instances, which can hardly fail to happen in the life of kings, it is not enough to redress the evil if one does not add some good in the bargain. When a wound is healed and closed, it still leaves its mark. Few people will refuse you some words when they have offended you with deeds. But if what they have undertaken does not cost them anything, what assures you that they will not undertake it again? One is not too discouraged from striking a second blow when he has merely missed with the first. It was necessary, so as not to recoil before the eyes of all Europe, for me to step forward as I did, drawing a new utility from this disaster. This tumult in London was a misfortune. It would be the misfortune now if it had not happened.

The second reflection for you to make here is that in these incidents that strike us so sharply and so deeply, one must maintain a balance between timid wisdom and wild resentment, trying, so to speak, to imagine for ourselves what we would counsel to another in a similar case. For whatever effort we may make in order to attain this degree of tranquillity, our own passion works against us and is always strong enough to prevent us from reasoning calmly and fairly. I have noted on this occasion, as on a thousand others, that the rules of justice and of honor almost always lead to utility itself. When war is necessary, it is in justice not merely permitted but commanded of kings. It is an injustice, on the contrary, when one can dispense with it and obtain the same thing by milder means. I regarded it in this manner and that is what enabled me to succeed. If I had not been sincerely disposed to wage it, if necessary, for the honor of my crown, the negotiation would assuredly not have produced the same effect for me. If I had closed the door to all negotiation, initially carrying things to the last extremes, I don't know what battles and what victories would have acquired a similar advantage for me, without considering the enormous bloodshed, the ever uncertain outcome of battle, and the interruption of all my plans for the interior of the kingdom.

And from this reflection, my son, I pass to a more general one, which still appears very necessary to me for both of us. I am trying, and shall always try, in these *mémoires* to arouse but not to inflate your courage. If pride is legitimate in our rank, modesty and humility are no less praiseworthy. Don't think, my son, that these virtues are not made for us. On the contrary, they are more proper to us than to the rest of mankind. For after all, however low an opinion those who have neither the fortune nor the merit to be eminent may have of themselves, they can never be modest or humble, for these qualities necessarily presume that their possessor has both some loftiness and some greatness which could inspire his vanity. We, my son, who are particularly susceptible to this natural human failing, we cannot be too careful in guarding against it. But if you can see what I mean, it seems to me that we must be at the same time humble for ourselves and proud for the post we occupy.

I hope that I shall leave you with still more power and more greatness than I possess, and I want to believe that you will make still better use of it than I. But when everything that will surround you will conspire to fill you with nothing but yourself, don't compare yourself, my son, to lesser princes than you or to those who have borne or who may still unworthily bear the title of king. It is no great advantage to be a little better; think rather about all those who have furnished the greatest cause for esteem in past times, who from a private station or with very limited power have managed by the sole force of their merit to found great empires, have passed like comets from one part of the world to another, charmed the whole earth by their great qualities, and left, after so many centuries, a long and lasting memory of themselves that seems, instead of fading, to intensify and to gain strength with every passing day. If this does not suffice, be still more fair to yourself and consider for how many things you will be praised that you will perhaps owe entirely to fortune or to those whom it has itself placed in your service. Get down to some serious consideration of your own weaknesses, for even though you may imagine that all men, and even the greatest, have similar ones, nevertheless, since you would find this harder to imagine and to believe of them than of yourself, it would undoubtedly diminish your conceit, which is the usual pitfall of brilliance and of fame.

Thereby, my son, and in this respect you will be humble. But when it will be a question, as on the occasion that I have just described to you, of your rank in the world, of the rights of your crown, of the king, finally, and not of the private individual, boldly assume as much loftiness of heart and of spirit as you can, and do not betray the glory of your predecessors nor the interests of your successors, whose trustee you are. For then your humility would become baseness, and this is what I could have replied myself to the supporters of Spain, who were secretly murmuring in their concern for her, as if I had taken a little too much advantage of her.

I can add as a consequence of this affair that I then discovered and opposed another artifice of the Spanish. With the same intention of attaining this supposed equality they had won over those who drew up the powers of the Venetian ambassadors, who, whenever these referred to France and to Spain, combined them with the words, *delle due corone*.[46] I complained about it and put a stop to this novelty.

I also obliged the Catholic King to render me justice on another point; that is, to remove from his titles the quality of Count of Roussillon, which he still assumed although this area was mine by right of arms and had been ceded by the Treaty of the Pyrenees, aside from the old right of France to retrieve it from the hands of the Spanish, who have never executed the conditions under which it had been given to them.

Around that time, the Poles and the Muscovites chose me as mediator of their differences. The Dukes of Savoy and of Modena submitted theirs to my judgment.

You were born, my son, the first of the month of November. I drew from the fact that all these glorious things for the state and for my own person had just been accomplished or appeared well advanced a secret augury that Heaven had not destined you to humble your fatherland. The very great joy of my subjects at your birth showed me, on the one hand, their natural affection for their princes and, on the other, all that they expected from you one day, and they would, my son, reproach you forever if you were not to fulfill their expectation.

I subsequently issued various orders for the interior of the kingdom, at which I shall not stop, having already partly touched upon them in describing to you the reforms that I had undertaken.

I dismissed the old soldiers, who constituted only a useless expense. I began to regulate, by an edict, the age and the conduct of the judicial officials, to which I have added a great deal since, as you will see in its place. I continued to introduce troops into my strongholds, in order to moderate the excessive authority of the governors. I put the finishing touches on this useful ordinance on duels, which has had such great and such prompt effect that it has virtually eliminated an evil against which my predecessors, with the best of intentions, had uselessly employed all sorts of remedies.

I finished this year and began the following one with the promotion of eight prelates and sixty-three knights of the Order of

46. Louis felt that "of the two crowns" implied equality.

the Holy Spirit, no posts having been filled since the year 1633; that is what made for the great number, but I would have wished to be able to raise still more people to this honor, finding no purer joy for a prince than to obligate deeply many persons of quality with whom he is pleased without burdening the least one of his subjects. No reward costs our people less and none strikes noble hearts more than these distinctions of rank, which are virtually the first motive of all human actions, but especially of the most noble and of the greatest. It is, moreover, one of the clearest manifestations of our power to give infinite value when we please to what in itself is nothing. You have learned, my son, what use the Romans, and particularly Augustus, the wisest of their emperors, could make of these purely honorific distinctions, which were much more common in their time than in ours. Some excellent men have criticized recent times for not having enough of them.[47] It is desirable not merely to make whatever use we can of those that our fathers have introduced, but even to invent new ones sometimes, as long as this is done judiciously, selectively, and with dignity, as you will see by the example that I have tried to show you elsewhere.

47. Compare with Jean Bodin, *Les Six Livres de la République,* Book IV, Ch. I.

1662

THIRD BOOK

First Section

I BEGAN the year 1662 with the firm intention, not merely of continuing what I had undertaken for the good of my people, but also of adding to it each day whatever I might find to be advantageous and useful. In working at the reorganization of the finances, I had already acceded, as I have told you, to signing personally all orders issued for the slightest expenses of the state. I found that this was not enough, and I was willing to go to the trouble of marking in my own hand, in a little book that I could always see, on one side, the funds that I was to receive each month, on the other, all the sums paid by my orders during that month, always taking one of the first days of the following month for this work, so as to have it more clearly in mind.

It may be, my son, that among the great number of courtiers who will surround you, some, attached to their pleasures and glorying in their ignorance of their own affairs, will someday portray this care to you as far beneath royalty. They will tell you, perhaps, that the kings our predecessors have never done such a thing and that even their prime ministers would have believed they were lowering themselves if they had not relied for these details on the superintendant and he, in turn, on the treasurer or on some lowly and obscure clerk. But those who speak this way have never considered that in the world, the greatest affairs are hardly ever concluded without the smallest, and that what would be baseness if a prince were acting through mere love of money becomes loftiness and superiority if its ultimate object is the welfare of his subjects, the execution of an infinite number of great plans, his own splendor, and his own magnificence, of which this attention to details is the most secure basis; that if they will be honest with you and admit how many times they take the wrong measures, or are compelled to abandon the ones that they had taken because it so pleases their intendant, who is the sole master of what they can or cannot do, what setbacks and what vexation this causes them, you will easily see that they would have infinitely less trouble in knowing their affairs than in not knowing them.

Imagine, my son, what an entirely different thing it is for a king, whose plans must be more varied, more extensive, and more hidden than those of any private individual, of such a nature indeed that there is sometimes hardly a single person in the world to whom he can entrust them all in their entirety. There are, however, none of these plans in which the finances do not enter somewhere. This is not saying enough. There are none of these plans that do not entirely and essentially depend on them, for what is great and wonderful when the state of our finances allows it becomes fantastic and ridiculous when it does not. Think then, I beg of you, how a king could govern and not be governed if his ignorance of these financial details subjects his best and most noble thoughts to the caprice of the prime minister, or of the superintendant, or of the treasurer, or of that obscure and unknown clerk, whom he would be obliged to consult like so many oracles, so that he could not undertake anything without obtaining their advice and their consent.

But there are, you will be told, loyal and wise people who, without penetrating into your plans, will not mislead you about these financial details. I wish, my son, that these qualities were as common as they are rare. This is still saying nothing. Were their heart merely of a different mold than ours, and it always is, were their ideas and their inclinations different from ours, which never fails to happen, they would mislead us out of affection. They would then secretly oppose our wishes for the good of the state as they see it, and their good intentions would render us just as incapable of doing anything as their disloyalty.

Moreover, my son, make no mistake about it. We are not dealing with angels but with men, in whom excessive power almost always ultimately produces a temptation to use it. In the affairs of the world, the discussion of details and true merit are absolutely inseparable. No one shares in your work without participating in your power. Leave only as much of it to others as you must, for however careful you are, you will always lose much more of it than you should.

There arose soon thereafter an occasion, unpleasant in itself, yet useful in its outcome, that gave my people a clear indication of how capable I was of this same attention to details in regard to their own interests and their own advantages. The great dearth of 1661 did not actually make itself felt until the beginning of the year 1662, when most of the wheat of the previous ones had been consumed, but then it afflicted the entire kingdom in the midst of these first successes, as if God, who is careful to temper His blessings, had wanted to balance the great and joyful hopes for the future with a present misfortune. Those who in such a case are accustomed to profit from public calamity did not fail to close their stores, expecting higher prices and greater profits.

One may imagine, however, my son, what effect markets empty of all sorts of grains, peasants compelled to abandon the cultivation of the soil in order to go elsewhere in desperate search for their sustenance produced in the kingdom, even causing apprehension that the misfortune of that year would continue into the following ones; artisans who raised the prices of their products in proportion to the cost of living, the poor making their complaints and their murmurs heard everywhere, middling families who held back their usual charities from fear of an impending need, the most wealthy burdened with their servants and unable to do everything—all the orders in the state, finally, threatened with the grave diseases that accompany a poor diet, and which, beginning with the people, subsequently spread to persons of the highest quality: all this caused indescribable dismay throughout France.

It would have been infinitely greater, my son, if I had merely agonized uselessly over it or if I had relied on the remedies at hand, on the ordinary magistrates, who are all too often weak and incompetent, lacking in zeal, or even corrupt. I became intimately acquainted with the needs of the people and with conditions. I obliged the more affluent provinces to aid the others, private individuals to open their stores and to put up their commodities at a fair price. I hastily sent orders everywhere to bring in as much wheat as I possibly could by sea from Danzig and from other foreign countries. I had my treasury purchase it. I distributed most of it free to the lower classes of the biggest cities, such as Paris, Rouen, Tours, and others. I had the rest sold at a very

modest price to those who could afford it, and any profit from
this was immediately employed for the relief of the poor, who
derived, by this means, voluntary, natural, and imperceptible aid
from the more wealthy. In the countryside, where distributions of
wheat could not be effected so promptly, I dispatched money
with which each one subsequently tried to relieve his need. I
appeared, finally, to all my subjects, as a true father of a family,
who provides for his household and equitably distributes nourishment to his children and to his servants.

I have never found any expense more useful than this one. For
our subjects, my son, are our true riches and the only ones that
we conserve purely for themselves, all the others being good for
nothing unless we know the art of using them, that is, of spending
them wisely. And if God gives me the grace to execute everything
that I have in mind, I shall try to bring the prosperity of my reign
to such a point, not in truth that there should be no more rich or
poor, for fortune, industry, and intelligence will always retain this
distinction among men, but at least that there should be no more
indigence or begging throughout the kingdom; I mean no one,
however impoverished he may be, who is not assured of his sustenance either through his work or through normal and regulated
aid.

But without looking forward, I was abundantly and immediately rewarded for my cares by the upsurge of affection that they
produced for me in the hearts of the people. And this is how, my
son, we may sometimes fortunately turn into blessings the greatest
troubles of the state. For if anything can tighten the sacred knot
that attaches subjects to their sovereign and awaken in their hearts
their natural sentiments of respect, of gratitude, and of love for
him, it is undoubtedly the aid that they receive from him in time
of some unexpected public misfortune. We hardly note the admirable order of the world and the regular and useful course of
the sun until some disturbance in the seasons or some apparent
disorder in the machine makes us give it a little more reflection.
As long as everything in a state is prosperous, it is easy to forget
the infinite blessings that royalty provides and merely envy those
that it possesses. Man, naturally ambitious and proud, can never
understand why another should command him until he feels the
need for it. But habit makes him insensitive to this very need, as

soon as it is constantly and regularly satisfied. It is extraordinary incidents that make him consider what he ordinarily gains from this; and that, without authority, he would himself fall prey to the strongest, finding in the world neither justice, nor reason, nor security for his possessions, nor recourse against his losses; and this is how he comes to love obedience as much as he loves his own life and his own tranquillity.

I also had, about the same time, various other opportunities to display my affection to my people.

The Chamber of Justice, having discovered that a million in bonds for which I had not received any payment had been alienated from the *taille*, ordered their invalidation to my profit, but I immediately commanded this amount to be subtracted from the warrant for the *taille*, deriving no advantage from this than that of my subjects.

The same reason prevented me from putting, in something else of this nature, the interest of the investors before that of all France. Common law permits any private individual to repurchase bond issues by repaying their original price and crediting to the principal any arrears beyond the legitimate interest. The Chamber of Justice judged that I was to be no less favored for the bonds issued in my name by the *Hôtel de Ville*[1] of Paris. The private individuals who had acquired them at a pittance and had long enjoyed them did not find this crediting, which made their repayment very small, to their advantage, but I did not believe I should lose such a perfect opportunity to avoid the necessity of levying four millions in annual interest upon my people.

The overwhelming taxes during the war and my minority had reduced almost all the communities and all the cities of my kingdom to borrowing large sums, first by mortgaging the toll rights, their sales taxes, and other public revenues, then on the credit of the principal inhabitants, who assumed full obligation for the others. The interest that was constantly accumulating rendered them virtually incapable of ever servicing it with their own funds. The richest, actively pursued for these common debts, were becoming more impoverished than the others, forced to abandon their patrimonies, the cultivation of the soil, and trade in the most

1. City Hall.

vital necessities by the continual seizures to which they were sub-jected and by fear of imprisonment. The worst part of it was that the consuls and other administrators used these debts as a pretext for squandering public money. I delivered the communities from their poverty by appointing commissioners to liquidate and to regulate the payment of their debts as conditions permitted and ordering that this be done by my own receivers.

I could also easily see that my people responded to my affection in the farthest provinces as in the nearest.

The *taille*, which had taken at least two or three years to levy, was then levied in fourteen or fifteen months, partly, in truth, because the lighter burdens were easier to bear, but primarily through the good will of those who bore them, who, seeing them-selves relieved, did all they could do happily and good-naturedly.

The *pays d'états*,[2] which had formerly considered themselves as independent in matters of taxation, began to use their liberty only for making their submission more pleasing to me. In the previous year 1661, the Estates of Brittany had already granted to my commissioners, without deliberation and on the very spot, all that had been asked of them on my behalf, ready to go further at my slightest wish. But I was at Nantes, and it might be believed that my presence alone had produced this effect. The Estates of Languedoc, which were held two hundred leagues away from me at the beginning of this year 1662, followed this propitious trend by granting me the sum requested, without any of their previous difficulties and without any reductions.

It had been the custom not merely to ask them for large sums in order to obtain meager ones, but also to tolerate their putting conditions on everything, to promise them everything, to circum-vent everything they had been promised soon thereafter under various pretexts, even to issue a great number of edicts with no other intention than to grant, or rather to sell, their revocation soon thereafter. I found this method undignified for the sovereign and unsatisfactory for the subject. I chose an entirely different one that I have always followed since, which was to ask them for

2. Provinces with Estates, where local assemblies would meet periodically to grant taxes to the king, as opposed to *pays d'élection,* where the king taxed without consent.

precisely what I intended to obtain, to promise little, to keep my promises faithfully, hardly ever to accept conditions, but to surpass their expectations when they appealed to my justice and to my kindness.

I made two separate treaties that year for two very important acquisitions, Lorraine and Dunkirk. I combine them here for your instruction, my son, as two examples of a similar nature, although the treaties were concluded and signed some months apart.

The location of Lorraine could leave me in no doubt that it would be very advantageous and desirable for me to control it. It was a passage to my troops for Germany, for Alsace, and for some other area that already belonged to me, an open door to foreigners for invading our domains. It was the seat of a neighboring power, incapable, in truth, of disturbing a king of France by itself, but always participating in all the quarrels of the kingdom, always ready to ally itself with the malcontents and to ally them with other more distant princes; and if honor need be added to utility, it was the former patrimony of our fathers, which it was wonderful to reunite to the body of the monarchy from which it had so long been separated.

I could easily have acquired this area by arms; and the restless and vacillating conduct of the Duke, always unmindful of treaties and of promises, gave me every justification for doing so. But basically, this meant breaking the peace of Europe, which I did not want to do then without absolute necessity. The Treaty of the Pyrenees gave the other powers grounds for interfering in this quarrel, and if my behavior had been in the least questionable, the prejudice against the stronger would have subjected me to accusations of injustice and of violence.

On the other hand, it hardly seemed possible to accomplish this by negotiation and by treaty. As difficult as it is to convince a prince who is free and master of his actions of such a thing, even his consent would seem to be insufficient without that of the others concerned, that is, all those who have a right to the succession. Finally, unless the treaty is most formal and most authentic, unless it is basically very equitable, one might still wonder if the unborn successors of the successors would not have the right to protest someday against the prejudice that has been done to them.

I had, therefore, all of these difficulties to consider, which made some of my ministers believe that there was no hope for this plan. But there is a great difference, my son, between general insights on things and particular knowledge of times, circumstances, persons, and interests.

I knew the Duke of Lorraine[3] as a naturally restless prince, to whom all novelties were pleasing, strongly attached to money, without any legitimate children, and eager to amass treasures which he carefully hid throughout Europe, whether from his own confidence in such fortunes or in order to enrich his beloved natural children someday. He was master in name rather than in fact of an area devastated by war, where he did not hold any stronghold of importance and was thereby all the more disposed to cede what he would always have a great deal of difficulty in defending.

As to those of his blood and of his house, I knew of their passion to be regarded as our relatives on the side of Charlemagne, that everything might be obtained by giving them some prerogative that could flatter this claim; that basically, their house was sufficiently illustrious to be considered, after ours, superior to all the others in the state, especially if the state could then derive some great and signal advantage from this, as, for their part, they received a very great and very glorious one from such a distinction.

There was lacking a perfectly natural occasion to propose what I had in mind, and a better one than I could have hoped for arose. Prince Charles,[4] nephew of the Duke, and, as his heir presumptive, the most concerned in this affair, dissatisfied with him and suspicious of the affection that he displayed toward his natural children, was then trying to contract a marriage with Mademoiselle de Nemours, now Duchess of Savoy, primarily in the hope that I would protect him after the death of his uncle and maintain him against one and all in the domains he was to inherit. The Duke,

---

3. Charles IV (1604–1675), Duke of Lorraine, had been dispossessed during the wars.

4. Charles of Lorraine (1643–1690), wished to marry Marie-Jeanne de Savoie (1644–1724), Duchess de Nemours. He was to enter the service of the Emperor and distinguish himself as a general. He succeeded his uncle in 1675, but never obtained possession of the Duchy.

ired and jealous that this young Prince was trying to make a connection with me, let some words slip in his anger that were reported to me and that could have been interpreted as favorable to my plan. I worked immediately to profit from this lest he change his mind once his vexation had passed, which was not unusual for him. Lionne, whom I charged with the negotiation, reported to me from time to time on what was going on. I pressed the affair so actively that it was entirely resolved soon thereafter.

The Duke, by a treaty that we signed on February 6,[5] ceded all his domains to me, except for their proceeds during his life, for which I paid him seven hundred thousand *livres* of revenue, without any increase in taxes. I gave him, furthermore, one hundred thousand *écus* in income, which he could bequeath to the Count de Vaudemont,[6] his natural son, or to any other person he pleased: namely one hundred thousand *livres* on one of my farmed taxes and two hundred thousand in lands, of which there was one carrying the title of duchy and peerdom. I assumed all the debts of the Duke and of his predecessors, to which these three hundred thousand *livres* of income could have been mortgaged, in return for his transferring the ownership of the *Hôtel de Lorraine* to me.[7] Finally, I gave to the house of Lorraine the privileges of princes after the last princes of my blood, with all the other rights that this rank might give them in the future, more remote, undoubtedly, but also infinitely greater than what they and their families abandoned by this treaty. But the Duke and I had agreed that none of them could take advantage of it until all had signed it, and that this condition would be added, as it was, at the registration in *Parlement*, where I brought it myself on the 27th of the same month of February.

But to tell the truth, I had nothing to lose and everything to gain from this affair. The Duke, at least, was bound personally by this treaty, obliged by it to be more dependent upon me, which was always a great deal. If all of his house consented, they established

5. The Treaty of Montmartre, by which Charles IV retained possession of his Duchy, but agreed to allow the French to garrison Marsal. The Duke immediately proceeded to ignore the treaty, and in 1663, Louis came up with his army in order to force the surrender of the city.

6. Claude-Henri de Lorraine (1649–1723), Count de Vaudemont.

7. A bond issuing institution, like the *Hôtel de Ville* of Paris.

my right for the future beyond any legal question, for they merely abandoned uncertain rights for other rights infinitely greater and so illustrious that they should have considered themselves eternally honored by them. Some who, for being closer to the succession, regarded it as imminent, could well refuse to sign, but in that case I had no commitment toward the others, whom I thereby even placed in my interests. There remained only a personal treaty between me and the Duke that worked in my favor and gave me the opportunity of gradually winning over all the parties concerned through other general advantages in the course of time.

This treaty was made public and registered in *Parlement*, with the stipulation that I have mentioned, and with the consent of all the house of Lorraine except for Prince Charles, who withdrew from my court as soon as he saw the matter settled, giving me grounds to suspend all the others from enjoying the privileges of prince of the blood. It is still uncertain, as I write these *mémoires*, what advantages I will one day derive from this treaty, but you have seen, at least, that it could not be harmful to me.

The acquisition of Dunkirk was not so extensive, but it was no less important and clearly more useful. Few persons have known exactly how such an important stronghold had fallen into the hands of the English during the ministry of Cardinal Mazarin. It is necessary for this to go back to my minority and to the factions that twice obliged this minister to leave the kingdom.

Cromwell, in whom intelligence, opportunity, and the misfortune of his country had inspired ideas far above his birth, beginning as a mere officer in the rebel troops of Parliament, then general, then Protector of the Republic, and secretly desiring the title of king while publicly refusing it, inflated by the success of most of his undertakings, saw nothing so great, either within or outside his island, that he thought it beyond his reach; and even though he had no lack of problems at home, he regarded the troubles of my state as a means of establishing a strong foothold in France, which would be equally advantageous for him if the royal power were confirmed in his person and in his family or if the caprice of the people and the same fortune that had raised him to such heights were to undertake his overthrow.

He knew how almost all the governors of strongholds and of

provinces then dealt with Cardinal Mazarin and that there was hardly any loyalty among my subjects not bought with money or with whatever honors anyone might wish. He dispatches the Colonel of his Guards to the Count d'Estrades, Governor of Dunkirk. He exhorts him to consider his private advantages in the situation, offers him two millions payable in Amsterdam or in Venice for surrendering the stronghold and to make no peace with France without obtaining for him any dignities and establishments that he might want. He adds that the affairs of the Cardinal, his benefactor, who had placed him in this post, are desperate, there being no evidence that this minister, who had a price on his head, could by his own strength re-enter either the ministry or the country, that he could not support him with Dunkirk alone, but would perish with him. If, nonetheless, he wants to carry his affection and his gratitude for him to the end, he should take this opportunity to be useful to him in the only way, perhaps, that fortune left open, that he can offer the Cardinal, with the same condition of turning Dunkirk over to the English, not merely the two millions but also whatever aid in troops that he would need for returning to France; that if this minister is restored, he would have so much merit with him that he could hope for everything.

D'Estrades, acting very laudably, after having obliged this envoy to make these proposals to him in a council of war and subsequently to sign them, sends him back with his reply. He complains at having been believed capable of disloyalty or of surrendering this stronghold without my orders, that all he can do is to propose the two millions to me, along with a close alliance by which the Protector would engage to break with the Spanish on land and on sea, to furnish me with ten thousand foot soldiers and two thousand horse for fighting them in Flanders, and to maintain fifty warships on the coasts during the six months of summer and a squadron of fifteen on patrol during the winter, cooperating according to plan.

Cromwell accepted these proposals, which were immediately sent to me in Poitiers by D'Estrades, and which arrived only two days after the return of Cardinal Mazarin. This minister found them very advantageous, his maxim being to provide for the present at any cost and to let the future take care of itself. But the

Keeper of the Seals, Châteauneuf,[8] whom it had been necessary to recall during these troubles, prevailed over him in the council and with the Queen my mother and had them entirely rejected. The same day that Cromwell received this reply, he signed a treaty with the Spanish to furnish them with ten thousand men and twenty-five ships for the sieges of Gravelines and of Dunkirk, which were taken from me by this means, one at the end of May and the other on September 22, with the Spanish as the only ones to profit.

However, my authority having been consolidated in the king-dom, and the factions they fomented there having been entirely dissolved, they were reduced sometime thereafter to hardly being able to withstand the efforts of my arms in Flanders. Cromwell, who had allied himself with them only for that particular under-taking and who had continued to increase in power and in import-ance throughout Europe, saw himself equally courted by both sides. They regarded him as the sole recourse for their affairs in Flanders and I as the sole obstacle to their progress at a time when I could see the entire conquest of these provinces as virtually certain if peace were not made on my terms. He, not having for-gotten his original intention of acquiring an important post for himself on this side of the water and not wanting to settle without this condition, was proposing at the same time to the Spanish to join with them in this war, to besiege Calais, which he would retain, and which they were about to accept joyfully, and to me to besiege Dunkirk and to turn it over to him.

Cardinal Mazarin, to whom this overture was not new, and who had formerly approved of it even when Dunkirk was in the hands of the French, was less opposed to it than ever; and although I was very reluctant about it, I finally submitted to it, not merely from my esteem for his counsels, but also from its indis-pensable advantages for the war in Flanders and from the necessity of choosing the lesser of two evils, seeing no comparison, if it was necessary to see the English in France, between seeing them there as my enemies or as my friends, or between risking the loss of Calais or promising them Dunkirk.

It was therefore through this arrangement that, after having

8. Charles de l'Aubespine (1580–1653), Marquis de Châteauneuf.

retaken Dunkirk, I turned it over to them, and there can be no doubt that it was our alliance that virtually struck the last blow against Spanish resistance and produced such a glorious and advantageous peace for me.

I confess, however, that this stronghold in the hands of the English disturbed me greatly. It seemed to me that the Catholic religion was concerned. I remembered that they were the old and irreconcilable enemies of France, from whom she had formerly been saved only by a miracle,[9] that their first establishment in Normandy had cost us one hundred years of war and the second in Guyenne three hundred years, during which the war was always waged in the midst of the kingdom at our expense, so that we considered ourselves fortunate just to make peace and send the English back home with huge sums of money for their trouble, which they regarded as ordinary revenue or tribute. I did not ignore the fact that times had changed greatly; but because they could still change again, I was disturbed by the thought that my most remote successors might reproach me someday for having caused such great troubles to recur; and without going to such extremes, without going so far into the past or into the future, I knew what immense sums the city of Calais alone, their last remaining one, had cost the French through the usual ravages of the garrison and through the raids that it had facilitated—any of their posts in my kingdom, moreover, being at the same time an open sanctuary to rebels and furnishing that nation with contacts throughout the kingdom, especially among those naturally bound to it by a common religion. Perhaps in giving up Dunkirk I had not paid too much for the advantages that the Peace of the Pyrenees had brought me, but it is certain that I could not have paid too much afterwards to repurchase Dunkirk, which I had definitely resolved to do but which in truth seemed hopeless.

However, since the first step in order to accomplish anything is to believe that it is possible, when I sent D'Estrades back to England in the year 1661, I charged him most explicitly with making this matter his principal concern.

The newly restored King of England was in desperate financial need. I knew that the state of his revenues and of his expenditures

9. Joan of Arc. See François de Mézeray, *Histoire de France* (Paris, 1643–1651), II, 11–19.

always left him with a deficit of two or three millions a year, and it is the essential fault of this monarchy that the prince may not levy any extraordinary taxes without the Parliament nor keep the Parliament in session without gradually losing his authority, which is sometimes left shattered, as the example of the previous King had sufficiently demonstrated.

Chancellor Hyde had always been rather favorable to France. He felt then that his influence over the King was diminishing, although this was not yet noticeable, and saw himself opposed by a powerful conspiracy in the state, which made it all the more necessary for him to acquire friends and protectors abroad: all these reasons disposed him to please me whenever my interests should coincide with those of the King his master.

D'Estrades, executing my orders and skillfully using his long-standing free and familiar access to this Prince, had no difficulty in bringing casual conversations around to Dunkirk. The King, who was then talking about making it his armed stronghold, willingly discussed this plan with a man who, having long been its governor, could give him some useful insights. As for him, he agreed with everything, merely indicating some disadvantages in its location and especially that the great expense necessary for its maintenance and its protection was such that Cardinal Mazarin, who was acquainted with it from past experience, had often wondered about its advantages for France even if she had been able to keep it. The King replied that he could easily deliver himself of this expense at any time, the Spanish even then offering him large sums for Dunkirk. D'Estrades always counseled him to accept their offers until the King, pressed more than we thought, came out on his own to say that if he was to deal on it, he preferred to deal with me.

Thus began a negotiation that brought me great joy, and even though he wanted five millions, undoubtedly a very large sum that moreover had to be paid very promptly, I did not find it advisable to let him reconsider, the improved state of my finances permitting even greater efforts for something as important as this. The treaty was concluded, nonetheless, at four millions payable in three years, both for the stronghold and for all the munitions of war, cannons, rocks, bricks, and wood. I even saved five hundred thousand *livres* in the bargain without the English noticing it. For, never imaginging from the state of my affairs a short time previously that I would have had the means of furnishing them with this large sum as promptly as they desired it, they joyfully accepted the offer of a banker to pay it in cash in return for five hundred thousand *livres* of commission, but this banker was a man introduced by me, who made the payment with my own money and did not profit from the commission.

The importance of this acquisition caused me continual concern until everything was finished, and not without reason, for the secret of the affair having gradually leaked out, the city of London was informed of it and delegated its principal magistrates, the mayor and the aldermen, to offer the King any amount in return for not alienating Dunkirk. Of the two couriers that D'Estrades had dispatched to me by two different routes with two copies of the treaty for ratification, one was stopped on the road to Calais by the orders of the King of England, the other having already reached France through Dieppe; and whatever indulgence this King—to whom D'Estrades portrayed at the same time that if he did not keep his word to me, it would no longer be a question of Dunkirk but of breaking with me forever—was obliged to have for them, he finally made them accept the inevitable.

These two affairs, which initially appeared entirely out of the question, and which, nevertheless, proved so easy for me, must teach you, my son, not to be easily discouraged in your plans when you believe, moreover, that they are advantageous to the state. Don't be astonished if I so often exhort you to work, to see everything, to listen to everything, to know everything. I have already told you: there is a vast difference between general insights that are usually useful only for discussions and particular ones that must almost always be followed in practice. Maxims are most often misleading to vulgar minds. Things are rarely as they should be. Laziness stops at common notions in order to avoid thinking and acting. The effort lies in evoking particular circumstances in order to profit from them, and one never accomplishes anything extraordinary, great, and wonderful without thinking about it more and more often than others.

You can derive still another lesson from these two examples, my son. Have no doubt that I would always, and especially in these beginnings and in my earlier youth, have preferred conquering states to acquiring them. But it is not enough to practice only one virtue, for no true one is inconsistent with all the others, since they all consist of acting rationally, that is, as time and circumstances require, even if this does violence to our own inclinations. If it is not wonderful to adopt a favorite, however able he may be, and listen to no one else, it is hardly better to develop a passion, however noble it may be, and accept no counsel but its own; unless by this you mean one for good in general, which comes in as many forms as there are just, honest, and useful things. Variety is necessary in glory as in everything else, and to princes more than to private individuals, for whoever says "great king" means almost all the talents of his best subjects.

Valor is among the principal of these qualities, but it is not the only one. It leaves a great deal to justice, to prudence and to good conduct, and to ability in negotiations. The more perfect the valor, the more it aims not to appear inopportunely and not to show itself until the last, in order to succeed where all the others have failed. If the other qualities are less brilliant, they still acquire for the prince honor all the more solid in that their good effects seem to be owing to him rather than to fortune. Always be in a position, my son, to inspire fear by your arms, but employ them only if necessary, and remember that even at its height our power is most formidable when it is rarely tested; someone who might not think he could defend himself against us finding among his friends, among his neighbors, among the envious, and sometimes even in his own despair the means to resist us.

Second Section

I shall now cover in a few words, my son, a number of things that would fill volumes if I wanted to expand on them, and which tended in general to make me feared, loved, or respected throughout Europe.

With these ideas in mind, the acquisition of Dunkirk did not prevent me from paying the Archduke of Innsbruck [10] a good part of the three millions granted to him by the Treaty of Münster in

10. Ferdinand-Charles (1618–1662), Archduke of Innsbrück.

compensation for Alsace, an important debt to discharge in order not to leave the house of Austria any claim to that area.

The Bishop of Speyer[11] having sent me his chancellor in order to settle some differences between us concerning Philippsburg, I found a means of satisfying him equitably without losing any of my rights.

The Duke of Neuburg,[12] a very important prince in Germany, who had great aspirations to the crown of Poland whenever there was a new election and who was my friend and ally, had recourse to me in order to recover from the Dutch the sovereign county of Ravenstein, which he had inherited in the partition of the house of Cleves. I obtained from the States a promise to compensate him with other lands, thereby confirming their hold on that important possession. I also interceded to conclude another important dispute between him and the house of Brunswick. I gave him, finally, much stronger proof of my friendship, for upon his complaint that the Elector of Brandenburg[13] had excluded him from the Treaty of Oliva, I refused to sign an agreement concluded between this Elector and myself, although it was extremely important for me to detach him gradually from the interests of the house of Austria, of which he was one of the most important supporters in the Empire. But I believed, and it is very true, my son, that when we act both reasonably and vigorously for those who are in our interests against those who are not, this powerfully confirms the ones in our friendship and no less attracts the others to it whenever they have a favorable opportunity.

The Alliance of the Rhine, which was so useful to me in Germany, and which I have already described to you elsewhere, was unfortunately about to split between the Protestants and the Catholics, owing to a quarrel between the Landgrave of Hesse, on the one hand, and the Count of Waldeck, supported and protected by the Elector of Cologne, on the other. I pacified this

11. Lothar Frederick von Metternich (1617–1675), Bishop of Speyer since 1652. He complained that the French garrison of Philippsburg was harassing his subjects in the surrounding countryside.

12. Philip William von Simmern (1615–1690), Duke of Neuburg.

13. Frederick William von Hohenzollern (1620–1688), Elector of Brandenburg since 1640, the "Great" Elector. He had sided first with the Swedes and then with the Poles in the First Northern War and was a signatory to the Treaty of Oliva. Louis also refers to him as the Marquis of Brandenburg.

quarrel so that both sides were grateful to me for it, and we all remained better friends than ever.[14]

There remained some difficulties between my commissioners and the deputies of the United Provinces over the renewal of our alliance, and the affair had been dragging for eighteen months. I dedicated myself to it personally and concluded it in a few days to the equal satisfaction of both sides.[15]

I rendered useless by this, and by a thousand other means that I shall not explain to you here, the proposals of a league for the defense of the Low Countries that the Spanish were constantly making to the United Provinces. I likewise circumvented their intrigues to have the Swiss urge the neutralization of the two Burgundies.[16]

I obstructed and foiled the proposals of the Emperor to the Electors of Bavaria, of Saxony, and of Brandenburg for a league to oppose the Alliance of the Rhine.

Add to this, my son, the marriage of the King of England to the Infanta of Portugal, which I have described to you because it was negotiated in 1661 although it was concluded only in this year 1662, a marriage that resulted in the settlement between England and Holland, the settlement between Holland and Portugal, and the closer alliance of all these powers with me, which was virtually the bond of their own union.

All these things, some already executed, others obviously about to be, contributed in no small measure to something else that I have already explained to you in advance in order to describe it to you all at once: I mean the satisfaction that I received around this same time on the affair of London. I shall not repeat myself to you. I have merely wanted to indicate to you here in passing and in their proper place the circumstances that alone forced Spain, against its maxims and its inclination, to give me full satisfaction, and which rendered my measures certain, although they may not have appeared that way to everyone.

14. William IV (1629–1663), Landgrave of Hesse. George Frederick (1620–1692), Count of Waldeck. Maximilian Henry von Wittelsbach (1621–1688), Archbishop-Elector of Cologne since 1650.

15. The Franco-Dutch Treaty of April 27, 1662, on the basis of which Louis went to the aid of the Dutch in 1666.

16. The Duchy of Burgundy, belonging to France, and Franche-Comté, the Free County of Burgundy, still held by Spain.

I cannot even refrain, my son, from reflecting on this with you, for considering how true it is that the entire art of politics consists of playing on circumstances, I sometimes begin to wonder if its discussion and these very *mémoires* must not be classed as useless things, since the summary of all its precepts lies in good sense and in dedication, which we do not receive from others, and which we find rather in ourselves. But this disenchantment with our own reasoning is not reasonable, for dedication comes to us primarily through habit, and good sense is developed only through long experience or through repeated and continual meditation on things of a similar nature, so that we owe to rules and to examples themselves the advantage of being able to dispense with examples and with rules.

Another equally dangerous error is spread among men, for since the greater and more perfect this art of profiting from all things, whether or not people are ignorant of them, the more its glory lies hidden and remote from view, they will often try to obscure the merit of good actions by imagining that the world is governed by certain fortuitous and natural changes that were impossible to predict or avoid, a notion that ordinary minds easily accept because it appeals to their limited insights and to their laziness and permits them to call their errors misfortune and the industry of others good fortune.

As much, my son, as you must acknowledge your submission to a Superior Power capable of upsetting your best-laid plans whenever It pleases, always rest assured, on the other hand, that having Itself established the natural order of things, It will not easily or constantly violate it, either in your favor or to your prejudice. It can assure us in time of peril, strengthen us in our labors, enlighten us in our doubts, but It hardly does our work without us, and when It wants to make a king fortunate, powerful, supported, and respected, Its most normal course is to make him wise, clear-sighted, fair, vigilant, and industrious. But I resume the narrative.

As I had only done my duty in maintaining the dignity of my crown, this dispute with a nation whose interests will always be opposed to ours did not prevent the King of Spain from subsequently giving me tokens of his esteem and of his friendship in every instance.

He displayed his esteem for me in a manner that I confess flattered me pleasantly when, after the death of Don Luis de Haro, he stated publicly in front of all the foreign ambassadors that he wanted to follow my example in not having a prime minister any longer; for it seemed to me both very generous of him and very glorious for me that, after so much experience in affairs, he acknowledged that I had been his guide in the path of royalty; and without being too presumptious, I have reason to believe that many other princes have also imitated my conduct in this, which must truly exhort both of us, my son, to weigh all our actions when we consider how much good we do in doing good and how much harm, consequently, in doing harm, since bad examples find many more imitators than good ones.

He displayed his friendship for me in something that he could justly have refused me. By the Treaty of the Pyrenees, the Spanish possessed the right to inspect all French ships encountered within fifty miles of the Portuguese coast, and this was an important right for them to preserve. He was, nevertheless, willing to abandon it upon my pressing appeals, thus favoring the maritime commerce of my subjects, which was suffering great prejudice from it.

I had taken umbrage because of a French monk who resided secretly at his court, but even though he was not obliged to do so, he volunteered, in order to show that he wished to live on good terms with me, to give me his word as king that this monk had not discussed any affair regarding France, and indeed, I learned that he had made only some proposals concerning Portugal.

I responded to these manifestations of esteem and of friendship with my own whenever the opportunity arose, and this is why I then gave to the Marquis de Fuentes, his ambassador, free and familiar entries to me, which the other ambassadors have never even presumed to have, accepting him as one of my own servants in my household and in my amusements. This would not have been without danger in other times, when all those who were around the king or the minister participated in their secrets and virtually in their decisions, or could at least penetrate them through a hundred outward signs. I think I have provided against this, and unless I am mistaken, however carefully one keeps an eye on my plans, those who never budge from the Louvre know hardly any more about them than those who never go near it.

I would not dwell with you, my son, upon a carrousel that took place at the beginning of the summer if it were not the first amusement of any brilliance that I encounter in the course of these *mémoires* and if, your life having necessarily to include these sorts of things as well as greater ones, it were not desirable to indicate to you what legitimate use may be made of them.

I shall not merely tell you, as one might tell a mere private individual, that honest pleasures have not been given to us by nature without reason, that they are a relaxation from work, furnishing new strength for dedicating oneself to it, are good for the health, soothe the troubles of the soul and the restlessness of the passions, inspire with humanity, refine the mind, soften manners, and deprive virtue of a certain rigidity that sometimes renders it less social and, consequently, less useful.

A prince and a king of France can still consider something else about these public amusements, which belong not so much to us as they do to our court and to all our people. There are some nations where the majesty of kings consists mostly of not letting themselves be seen, and this may have its reasons among spirits accustomed to servitude who can only be governed by fear and by terror; but this is not the character of our French, and as far back as we can go in our history, if there is any unique characteristic about this monarchy, it is the free and easy access of the subjects to the prince. It is a community of justice between them that holds them, so to speak, in a mild and courteous association, notwithstanding their almost infinite difference in birth, rank, and power. That this system is good and useful for us, experience has already shown, since there is no memory in all past times of any empire having lasted as long as this one, and yet it does not seem about to end.

And it is a notable thing, my son, that the most unscrupulous political thinkers, the least affected by principles of equity, of goodness, and of honor[17] seem to have predicted immortality for this state, insofar as it is humanly possible, for they maintain that these other empires where terror rules and where the caprice of

17. See Machiavelli's *Prince*, Ch. IV.

the prince is the only law are perhaps more difficult to pierce, but that their first wound is mortal, there being hardly any subject who does not wish for a change and who does not favor it as soon as there is any hope for it; whereas in France, they say, if it is easy to depart from natural conditions, it is even easier to return to them, there being no other empire where private individuals, and especially the principal ones, once they have had a taste of it, find so many things to their interest and advantage as in this one.

It may seem to you, perhaps, my son, that I am carrying this reflection a little too far, but it does not fail to come right to the point. I confess, my son—and everything that I have already told you makes it sufficiently clear to you—that this liberty, this mildness, and, so to speak, this laxity of the monarchy had gotten out of hand during my minority and the troubles of my state, and that it had turned into license, confusion, and disorder. But the more necessary it was to find some acceptable remedies to this excess, the more I was obliged to preserve and cultivate carefully whatever, without diminishing my authority and the respect that was due me, bound my people, and especially persons of quality, to me by affection, so as to show them thereby that it was neither aversion for them, nor affected severity, nor rudeness of manners, but simply reason and duty that rendered me more reserved and more strict toward them in other things. This community of pleasures that produces a courteous familiarity between our courtiers and ourselves strikes them and charms them beyond words. The people, on the other hand, enjoy a spectacle which, basically, is always aimed at pleasing them, and all our subjects, in general, are delighted to see that we share their tastes for what they do best. We sometimes hold their minds and their hearts more effectively by this, perhaps, than by rewards and by favors; and in regard to foreigners, when they see that a state is otherwise flourishing and orderly, what might be considered as superfluous expenses make a very favorable impression of magnificence, power, wealth, and greatness upon them, aside from the fact that physical dexterity, which can only be maintained and confirmed by this, is always becoming in a prince and produces a favorable estimate of his hidden qualities.

All these considerations, my son, even if it had not been for my age and for my inclination, obliged me to favor amusements of this nature and must oblige you to do likewise, without going, however, to undesirable extremes in your attachment; for then, my son, whatever gravity you might otherwise affect in your other actions, make no mistake about it, you would not deceive the public. Even if you always wore your crown and your royal mantle, it would soon be recognized that you make pleasure your business and disregard business when you should disregard pleasures. For this reason, it is sometimes dangerous for young princes to excel in certain skills and especially in those of this type, for our natural pride is so inexhaustible that it always makes us cultivate, esteem, and love immoderately everything in which we think we excel. To hear the dancing master, the fencing master, and all the others, each one will tell you, and it is true, that his art requires the whole man and that there is always more to learn about it, but it is enough for us to know this truth without having to experience it or to seek the ultimate limits of their skill, which they never find themselves. Even if we could reach this perfection, it would indicate a degree of attention and care unworthy of us, which can only be given by neglecting much more important things. You know the words of that ancient King to his son, "Aren't you ashamed of playing the lyre so well?"[18] Allow some of your subjects to surpass you in these sorts of things, but let none be your equal, if possible, in the art of governing, which you cannot know too well, and which must be your principal concern.

The carrousel, which has furnished me the subject for these reflections, had initially been planned only as a light amusement, but the excitement gradually mounted, and it developed into a rather great and magnificent spectacle, owing to the number of the drills, to the originality of the costumes, and to the variety of the emblems.

It was then that I adopted the one that I have retained ever since and that you see everywhere. I believed that, rather than dwelling on something private and minor, it should in some way portray the duties of a prince and always inspire me to fulfill them. Chosen as the symbol was the sun, which, according to the rules of this art, is the noblest of all, and which, by virtue of its uniqueness, by the brilliance that surrounds it, by the light that it imparts

18. Philip of Macedon to Alexander. See Plutarch's *Lives*, "Pericles."

to the other heavenly bodies that seem to pay it court, by its equal and just distribution of this same light to all the various parts of the world, by the good that it does everywhere, constantly producing life, joy, and activity everywhere, by its perpetual yet always imperceptible movement, by never departing or deviating from its steady and invariable course, assuredly makes a most vivid and a most beautiful image for a great monarch.

Those who saw me managing the cares of royalty with such ease and with such confidence induced me to add the sphere of the earth, and as its motto, NEC PLURIBUS IMPAR,[19] by which they meant to flatter the ambition of a young king, in that with all my capacities, I would be just as capable of ruling still other empires as would the sun of illuminating still other worlds with its rays. I know that some obscurity has been found in these words, and I have no doubt that the same symbol might have suggested some happier ones. Others have been presented to me since, but this one having already been used in my buildings and in an infinite number of other things, I have not deemed it appropriate to change it.

It was this same year that, continuing with my plan to diminish the authority of governors of strongholds and provinces, I resolved to give out vacant governorships for only three years, merely reserving the right to extend this term by new commissions whenever I might find it advisable.

The governorship of Paris becoming vacant by the death of Marshal de l'Hôpital, I gave it, with this same condition of three years, to Marshal d'Aumont, a person of importance, one of the four captains of my bodyguard, long attached to my personal service, so that after this example no one else could feel slighted when the same regulation was applied to him.[20] I have always observed it since, and I have found that it has produced two good effects: one that the subordinates of the governors no longer make connections and arrangements with them; the other that since the governors themselves depend for their position on my continuing good will, they are much more submissive.

I also gave Paris an archbishop after having given it a governor.

19. "Not unequal to many."
20. François de l'Hôpital (1583–1660). Antoine d'Aumont (1601–1669).

Everyone knows what little cause I had then to be satisfied with Cardinal de Retz and how important it was for me that this dignity be filled by another. As long as he had hoped to be reinstated through intrigues or through changes at the court during the life of Cardinal Mazarin, he had obstinately refused to resign on any terms. He no sooner saw me acting for myself and all conspiracies rendered useless by the consolidation of authority in my hands that he thought it best to submit unconditionally to my will.

I had initially appointed the Archbishop of Toulouse, Marca, a man of extraordinary learning and merit, to this important post, but he died soon thereafter, and I chose the Bishop of Rodez, who had been my tutor, to succeed him.

I was not displeased, undoubtedly, my son, to acknowledge his care for my childhood by this token of my affection, and there is no one to whom we owe more than to those who have had both the honor and the burden of forming our mind and our manners. But I would never have made this choice if he did not seem to be better qualified than anyone else for such an important post. I have very often resisted my inclinations, I can say it in all truth, in order not to bestow this type of favor on persons to whom I would gladly have bestowed favors of any other sort, noting in them neither the qualifications nor the dedication of a true clergyman.

Who would believe, my son, that there could be something more important than our service and the tranquillity of our subjects? However, the distribution of benefices, by its consequences and effects, is infinitely more, and by as much as heaven rises above the earth. It appears to be a rich and abundant harvest that we reap in all seasons of the year in order to shower our servants and our favorites with graces. But perhaps there is nothing more thorny in all royalty if it is true, as it cannot be doubted, that our conscience becomes involved at our least attributing of too much either to our own inclination or to the memory of services rendered, or even to some present utility of the state in favor of persons who are otherwise incapable or much less capable than others on whom we might cast our eyes.

I don't want, nonetheless, my son, to instill rigorous opinions in you, which are hardly ever practical and are most often also

untrue. One of our ancestors,[21] from fear of not adequately ful-
filling such a delicate obligation, voluntarily relinquished the
nomination to benefices. But who is to say if others would perform
this better than we and if we would not be doing our duty badly
for wanting to do it too well? God most assuredly does not mean
for us to do the impossible, my son, and make our choice as well
as He could make it Himself. It is enough for us to make it as men,
and as well-intentioned men, who neglect nothing in order to
avoid mistakes. Then, I venture to say, we can be sure that it is
He Himself who makes it for us. Nor is it true that our servants
and our courtiers should have no advantage over the others in this.
They have the one of making their worth better known to us,
undoubtedly a great one with an enlightened prince who believes
much more in what he sees than in what is reported to him by
others, which is always mingled with good or bad offices.

I have always believed that three things had to enter into this
examination: learning, piety, and conduct.

In regard to learning, it is perhaps more difficult for us to
judge than all the rest, for it rarely happens that kings are experts
in these sorts of things or that, if they were, they would find the
time to study the talents and potential of each one in them. I have
countered this difficulty, insofar as I could, by giving out important benefices only to Sorbonne doctors—not that there isn't considerable variation in the knowledge and the insights of those who
bear this title, but, basically, it cannot be attained without a
reasonable degree of competence, far removed from that former
ignorance of prelates that has caused so much harm to the Church.
Thus this proof combined with all the others at our disposal undoubtedly suffices to reassure us on this subject.

As to piety and to morals, what is good and what is bad cannot
long be hidden from the world. Listen calmly to the various
reports that you will receive, even while doing other things. Look
carefully around you. You will soon know as much about it as is
humanly possible, and you are not obliged to penetrate the rest.

The same is true of what I call conduct, which is a third point
of great importance. For if the apostles themselves, in their
original simplicity, would not choose a bishop without examining

21. Charles VII, who accepted the Pragmatic Sanction of Bourges in 1438.

what prudence he had shown in his household and in his own affairs, what about today, when the state is so constituted that these sorts of dignities participate actively in the civil government?

Thus, my son, I would not recommend as common practice what can sometimes be done with dignity and with brilliance in order to pay homage to exceptional piety: I mean to seek out individuals from their solitude for these posts on the basis of an often rather misleading reputation. They might perhaps have perfect attributes for the state in which God has placed them and would not have those that they need for the state to which we call them. On the contrary, I have often thought that in order to get to know the qualifications of our clergymen better, it would be desirable to implement in this sacred militia what I carefully observe today with most of my troops, where one advances step by step through the ranks, which I understand is also entirely in conformity with the original spirit of the Church in instituting the five sacred orders. But since times and customs have changed, it would suffice today, it seems to me, to admit to bishoprics and to other important dignities only those who would actually have served the Church for a certain time, either in diligent and continual preaching in the great parishes of Paris or in the provincial missions, or in particular dedication to converting heretics, or most importantly, in performing the functions of curate or vicar, which include all these things and many others; for which young people of the highest birth should no more be pitied than they are when they carry a musket in my guards in order to attain someday to the command of my armies. But both of us, my son, must improve gradually on our times, without expecting to reform them all at once; and even so, I would not want to resort in these matters to public edicts, which commit us either to weaken the authority of our own laws by not always observing them or to continue with the same policies, although they may not always be appropriate. It suffices to show the path to graces by word and by example, and you will soon see that there will be a rush to take it.

Third Section

It was around this same time, my son, that I formed and put into service your company of light horse, not merely in order to give you a token of my affection, but also owing to a particular situation that I should explain to you.

The peace permitted me to dismiss most of my troops; the intention of relieving my people committed me to it. Out of eighteen hundred infantry companies, I retained only eight hundred, and out of a thousand troops of cavalry, only a mere four hundred and nine; but war could easily return, and it would be difficult to find such seasoned troops again, especially if it had been necessary to lose through retirement the great number of officers who comprised their main strength. Some depended on their position for their living and struck me with pity. Many, not able to reconcile themselves to idleness, thought of taking service abroad. I believed it advisable to retain as many as I could at my side. I placed a number of them in my bodyguard and in my musketeers, and it was in order to occupy the others that I founded your company of light horse, giving them, aside from their regular pay in their new units, pensions proportionate to their previous positions. I thus supported a great many fine people, and I retained the means of putting other troops not much different from the first ones into service in less than no time, since it is the officer who usually inspires the soldier, not merely with discipline, but also with courage; and moreover, I had often noted with pleasure the almost infinite difference between the other troops and those of my household, whose pride at being in my personal service, stricter discipline, greater assurance of rewards, long traditions, and high morale rendered absolutely incapable of an unworthy action. Thus it seemed both fitting and proper for me to increase rather than diminish their number.

That year I also dedicated myself to a regulation for the forests of my kingdom, whose extreme disorder displeased me all the more since I had long before devised great plans for the navy. The principal causes of this disorder can serve for your instruction, my son.

It is undoubtedly foolish to entrust our financial interests to the same persons to whom we do, on the other hand, considerable injury in our levies and who can repair it by cheating us. It belongs only to kings, in truth, to procure justice for themselves, ever since private individuals have renounced this right by submitting to the civil law for their personal and for the public welfare. But if they could freely and secretly regain possession of this natural right, their loyalty would hardly meet the test unless it were an almost heroic virtue beyond the capacity of ordinary men.

The war and the financial schemes of the contractors had produced an infinite number of officials of waters and forests as of every other sort. The war and these same schemes deprived them of all or part of their wages, of which they had received only a token at the establishment of their offices. They took their revenge and their payment for it usuriously at the expense of the forests that were committed to them, and this all the more easily since few persons are knowledgeable in these matters except for those who participated in the crime and in the profit. There was no artifice that had not occurred to these officials, even to burning part of the standing wood on purpose, in order to be able to take the rest as burned by accident.

I had learned about and deplored this devastation of my forests since the previous year, but a thousand more pressing things preventing me from seeing to it entirely, I had merely prevented the evil from spreading by prohibiting all sales until further orders. That year I applied, through the regulation that I have already described to you, two principal remedies to it: one was to reduce the number of officials to a few who could easily be paid from their earnings, and on whom it was easy to keep an eye; the other was to investigate past irregularities, which served not merely as an example for the future, but the substantial restitutions that they were condemned to make partly contributed to reimbursing the abolished officials and rendered this reduction both just and easy.

That year, moreover, I increased my ordinary revenues by four millions under a single title, on the one hand, by combining the entry tolls of Paris with the farm of the excises, which saved the tax farmers a great deal of expense and gave them the means of bidding higher for it; on the other, by acceding to awarding both of them only during the best season, that of the October quarter, and under mutually advantageous conditions; but primarily by returning and reuniting to that of the excises a number of duties that had been detached from it during the war and alienated to the most powerful persons, each one having acquired whatever was to his fancy, wherever, moreover, he had the most revenue and influence, and this usually at a mere pittance, or even without cash, in exchange for very poor merchandise. I committed no injustice, equitably reimbursing everyone for what was due him. But even this justice required an authority as established as mine then was in order to be received with submission and without murmuring. After the reunion of these alienated duties, the two farmed taxes combined were brought from eight millions to twelve, without my having done anything, nevertheless, but to restore all things to their natural condition, where they should always have been.

My aim in this was not merely the present interest, as important as it was, but an infinitely greater and more general good for the future, which was to arrange, if possible, that never again would things be reduced to those miserable alienations that had devastated my finances and my state. I knew the greatest amount that had been spent on the war in a year. I did not think it impossible to bring my revenue to this through the very same economies whose great effects I was seeing each day, and I found great happiness in establishing that of my people to such a point that the return of war itself would hardly be capable of disturbing it; that they would no longer, at least, be exposed to the many vexations of extraordinary measures, nor be obliged to groan at home for successes abroad, where they found only empty honor acquired through real misery.

But I went still further, my son, for in assuming, as it has actually happened since, that I would soon bring my revenues to the sum that I had set as sufficient for sustaining the greatest war without loans and without extraordinary aid, I resolved privately not to add to this revenue, but to subtract each year from the ordinary taxes in favor of my subjects, whatever I might have added to my income by peace and by economy, by repurchasing my old domains, or by other just and legitimate means, so that there never would have been, if possible, a prince more wealthy or a people less burdened.

With these thoughts in mind, two things appeared very necessary to me for their relief.

One was to diminish the number of those exempt from the *taille* in the provinces, who by this means shifted the entire burden

upon the poorest. I accomplished this by abolishing and reimbursing every day a number of new and very useless petty offices,
to which this exemption had been attached during the war in
order to dispose of them.

The other was to take a closer look at the exemptions claimed
by certain particular areas of my kingdom, and which they possessed less through any title or through any important service
than through the laxity of the kings our predecessors or through
the weakness of their ministers.

The Boulonnais was among these. The people there have been
warlike since the war against the English and even have a kind
of militia dispersed throughout the governorship, which is rather
well trained and can be easily assembled when needed. Under this
pretext, they had long regarded themselves as exempt from contributing in any way to the *taille*. I wanted to levy a very small sum
there merely to make them realize that I had the power and the
right to do it. This initially produced a bad effect, but the use that
I painfully and sorrowfully made of it rendered it good for the
future.

The lower classes, either frightened by something that appeared
new to them or secretly aroused by the nobility, stirred seditiously
against my orders. The protestations and the mildness of those
whom I had entrusted with their execution, being taken as timidity
and as weakness, increased the tumult rather than pacified it. The
rebels gathered in various places to the number of six thousand
men: their fury could not be tolerated any longer. I sent troops
there to punish it. Most of them [sic] dispersed. I readily pardoned
all those whose repentance was demonstrated by their retreat.
Some, more obstinate in their errors, were taken under arms and
turned over to justice. Their crime merited death. I arranged that
most were merely condemned to the galleys, and I would even
have exempted them from this punishment if I did not believe
that on this occasion I had to follow my reason rather than my
inclination.

We should be too happy, my son, if we had only to oblige and
to give out graces. But God Himself, whose goodness has no
limits, cannot always reward and is sometimes compelled to
punish. However much it pains us to do harm, we must be con-
soled about it when we feel in ourselves that, like Him, we are

doing it solely with the just and legitimate idea of a good a thousand times greater. It is not spilling the blood of our subjects to exterminate murderers and evildoers. It is, rather, sparing it and preserving it. It is letting ourselves be struck by compassion for an infinite number of the innocent rather than for a small number of the guilty. Indulgence for these individual wretches would constitute universal and public cruelty.

I would not speak to you thus, my son, if I had noted in you the least tendency toward excessive severity, not to mention toward a bloodthirsty and wild disposition, unworthy of a man, far from being worthy of a king. On the contrary, I shall try to make you realize the charm of clemency, the most royal of all the virtues since it can only belong to kings; the only one by which we can be owed more than we can ever be repaid: I mean life and honor; the greatest thing, finally, for which we can be revered, since it is virtually one step above our power and our justice. But insofar as I can judge from carefully observing the actions of your childhood as I do, you will be—and I praise God for it with all my heart—sympathetic, easily pacified, and will have to guard much less against anger, hatred, and vengeance than against the opposite faults. Only don't let them take advantage of your own love for glory by passing these faults off to you as virtues. Acclaim follows them initially, but scorn will be quick to follow when it is recognized that if they are not the source, they are at least the most dangerous of all vices in a prince. To deprive the laws of their rigor is depriving the world of order, of peace, and of tranquillity: it is depriving ourselves of royalty.

Whoever pardons too often, almost punishes uselessly the rest of the time, for the hope of impunity has hardly less effect on the terror that restrains men from evil than impunity itself. You will not finish the reading of these *mémoires*, my son, without finding places where I have conquered myself and pardoned offenses that I could never justly forget. But on this occasion, when it was a question of the state, of the most pernicious examples and of the most contagious disease in the world for the rest of my subjects, of an armed revolt that attacked a no less important part of my authority than its very basis, I believed I should conquer myself in a different way by allowing the punishment of these wretches instead of pardoning them. My sorrow has been well rewarded by the satisfaction of seeing that their punishment has prevented me from ever having to use such a remedy again.

It was then all the more important to suppress such movements, since my success was beginning to cause envy and since it is the custom of our neighbors to await their recourse from revolutions in France, building up vain and fantastic hopes at the least appearance of novelty.

I was then carefully observing the actions of Prince Charles of Lorraine, who was dissatisfied at my treaty with his uncle, and I was trying to anticipate whatever he could stir up against me, since he was in no way dangerous on his own.

In regard to the electors and to the other princes of the Empire, without waiting for him to engage them to speak to me on his behalf in the hope that the very answers I would be obliged to give them would embroil me with them, I myself asked them first not to ask me anything in his favor. I obtained this, and it proved easier for me to forestall their appeals than it would have been to repulse them.

The Emperor was extremely occupied by the war against the Turks, and he had displayed some desire to get along with me, having resolved to write to me first, as I have already told you elsewhere,[22] contrary to his former pretension. But this good disposition could change. He could make peace without the participation of any other European powers and employ the aid that he had been given against the common enemy against me. I arranged, through various negotiations, that this aid be given to him not in money, as he wished, but in troops so that he could not misuse them, and I was everywhere heeded all the more willingly since my particular interest in this accorded with the public welfare.[23]

As to the King of Spain, I wished to secure his approval of the treaty with Lorraine and to commit him in such a way that Prince Charles could not expect anything from him either. But in view

22. The complicated exchange of letters had taken place in June, 1662. This development seems to have been omitted inadvertently from the second section of this text.

23. Louis and his allies of the League of the Rhine did go to the aid of the Emperor in 1664, and the French contingent, under Gaspard de Coligny, was instrumental in repulsing the Turks at the Battle of Saint-Gothard on August 1, 1664.

of the character of the Spanish, a formal negotiation would have rendered my success more difficult by making them realize my desire and interest in obtaining it. I took a more subtle and more simple approach. I wrote a letter to the Catholic King on this subject, conceived in such a way that it was impossible to answer it without praising or condemning my behavior. It was in my own hand, so that courtesy obliged him all the more to reply to it. He did so, and being in no position or disposition to contradict me, he also gave me in his own hand a more formal and a more explicit approval of this treaty than I could have ventured to hope.

1665

EDITOR'S NOTE

THE *Mémoires* for 1665 are lost, which is unfortunate not merely because of the importance of this year in the King's life, but also because of the particular contribution of these *Mémoires* to the work as a whole. It is possible, however, to obtain some idea of what they contained from allusions found throughout the other documents and by the exercise of a little imagination.

The *Mémoires* for this year may well have begun with Louis congratulating himself, and perhaps Colbert, on the excellent state to which they had brought the royal finances. We know that the King intended to mention two developments of early 1665 relating to this topic: the repurchase of the *Impôt* and *Billot* of Brittany and of other alienated excises, and the action of the Chamber of Justice in adjudicating the Duchy of Penthièvre to him.[1] Louis, moreover, was thinking of terminating this inquisitorial court,[2] particularly if he could extract one last sum of money from the financiers in the process, and was emphasizing a more positive approach to the economic welfare of his kingdom. Indeed, he probably describes the establishment of a council of commerce, possibly commenting on his new manufacturing establishments and commercial companies,[3] and it is not excludable that he takes the occasion to present some personal reflections on political economy, especially with an Anglo-Dutch commercial war having broken out on February 22.

The King also had time now for some more decorative reforms, and the *Mémoires* for 1665 relate his efforts to re-establish the Order of St. Michel.[4] This order had been founded by Louis XI in 1469, but its aristocratic character had subsequently been diluted through the

---

1. Both Colbert's two-part document, published in *Lettres, instructions, et mémoires de Colbert,* ed. Pierre Clément (Paris, 1861–1882), II, CCXII–CCXVII, and Périgny's copy of its second part (Bibliothèque Nationale, *Manuscrit Français* 6732, ff. 110–117, published in *Mémoires de Louis XIV,* ed. C. Dreyss (Paris, 1860), I, XXI–XXIII) mark these two items for insertion into the *Mémoires* for 1665.

2. See Colbert's *Mémoire sur la resolution à prendre pour la conclusion de la Chambre de Justice,* published in *Lettres, instructions, et mémoires de Colbert, op cit.,* II, CCIV–CCX.

3. See the *Mémoires* for 1666, p. 143, where Louis casually says, "The morning was *still* devoted to the regular councils of justice, of commerce, etc.," as well as p. 122, where the King claims that in the first part of the *Mémoires* his son has found "advantageous establishments."

4. See the *Mémoires* for 1661, p. 80.

admission of undistinguished persons. Louis XIV, by a decree of July 14, 1661, had designated commissioners, before whom all those who claimed membership were to produce their titles. This investigation having been concluded, the King proceeded, by an ordinance of January 12, 1665,[5] to announce the limitation of the order to a hundred persons, including those whom he would retain from the previous membership. On April 19, the reconstituted order held its first assembly at the Cordeliers in Paris,[6] marking a small but symbolic step in the purification of the monarchy.

Louis may even have stopped to express his grief at the illness of Anne of Austria,[7] which became extremely serious that year and which, in spite of some occasional moments of slight improvement, was obviously drawing toward its fatal conclusion.

As to foreign affairs, the King did not neglect to describe his efforts to prolong the war between Spain and Portugal.[8] He was not only giving the Portuguese indirect aid but he also desired to arrange a marriage between their erratic King, Alphonso VI, and a French princess. Louis had initially approached his cousin, Mlle. de Montpensier, who would not even hear of the match. He found the eligible Mlle. de Nemours more amenable, but when the Duke of Savoy expressed his interest in her, she chose sanity over rank. The King finally proposed her sister, Marie-Françoise, another Mlle. de Nemours, but the death of Philip IV of Spain on September 17, 1665, seemed to increase the prospects of peace and made the Portuguese more hesitant about strengthening their connection with France just at a time when Louis needed them for his purposes.

The central topic of the *Mémoires* for 1665, however, seems to have been the reform of justice. In May, the King had confided his rather ambitious ideas on these reforms to his closest ministers, and there is no doubt that he expressed similar views in the *Mémoires*.[9] Louis envisaged

5. *Recueil général des anciennes lois Françaises,* ed. François André Isambert (Paris, 1821–1833), XVIII, 44–48.

6. *Journal d'Olivier Lefèvre d'Ormesson,* ed. Pierre Adolphe Chéruel (Paris, 1861), II, 345.

7. Périgny's document cited above, note 1, adds the item, "Illness of the Queen, Concern of the King, Good qualities of this Princess," for insertion into the *Mémoires* for 1665.

8. In the third text for 1666 (Bibliothèque Nationale, *Manuscrit Français* 6733, f. 214, published in Dreyss, *op. cit.,* I, 146), Louis says, "It is necessary to resume the marriage of the Queen of Portugal where I left it off last year."

9. See the *Mémoires* for 1666, p. 122, where Louis claims that in the first part of the *Mémoires,* his son has found, "regulations of justice," as well as p. 142, where the King casually says, "I *continued* to work at the general restoration and reform of justice." See also the *Mémoires* for 1667, p. 223, where he begins, "In regard to the general regulation on justice about which I have already told you something."

a comprehensive ordinance that would both simplify procedures and reduce the number of judges, even hoping eventually to make justice available free to all his subjects. Colbert enthusiastically applauded this design and suggested a twofold approach to the problem. On the one hand, he recommended that the King establish a council of justice to work on the simplification of procedures; on the other, he called for the gradual elimination of the *droit annuel,* or *paulette,* a tax through the payment of which judicial officials could dispose of their offices by sale or inheritance. He also favored reducing the current prices of the offices and strict adherence to the regulations regarding the age of admission to them.[10] In short, this entire reform could have been catastrophic to the entrenched French judiciary and epochal for the monarchy.

Louis possibly goes on to mention how, in August, 1665, he dispatched a special court, the *Grands Jours,* to investigate irregularities in the Auvergne[11] and probably describes the establishment of the council of justice on September 27.[12] However, as the council settled down to its labors on the ordinance, Colbert surprisingly moderated his stand on the elimination of the *droit annuel* and advocated a generally more cautious policy toward the judicial officials.[13] The King just as amazingly appears to have followed suit. What was his reasoning? The *Mémoires* for 1665 might at least have given us his justifications and might possibly even have permitted us to see Louis sacrificing this far-reaching reform at the altar of territorial expansion against the Spanish monarchy.

In foreign affairs, the King may also have expressed his interest in the turbulent affairs of Poland.[14] Maria-Louisa de Gonzaga, the energetic Queen of that elective monarchy, had long been planning, with his support, to have her docile husband, John Casimir, abdicate once she could get an Estates, or Diet, to designate the Prince de Condé's son, the Duke d'Enghien, as the successor. Even though the Polish nobility, led by the Grand Marshal, Jerzy Lubomirski, had rejected the idea of a premature election as a threat to its "liberties," she had gone ahead with

10. See Colbert's *Mémoire sur la reformation de la justice,* published in *Lettres, instructions, et mémoires de Colbert, op. cit.,* II, 5–12.

11. *Recueil général des anciennes lois Françaises, op. cit.,* XVIII, 60–64. See also the *Mémoires* for 1666, p. 142, where Louis casually mentions renewing the *Grands Jours.*

12. See the *Deliberation du Conseil de la Reformation de la Justice,* published in *Lettres, instructions, et mémoires de Colbert, op. cit.,* VI, 369–391. On the council of justice, see note 3.

13. See Colbert's *Mémoire* on this subject, published in *Lettres, instructions, et mémoires de Colbert, op. cit.,* VI, 15–17.

14. See the *Mémoires* for 1666, p. 135, where Louis almost imperceptibly resumes his discussion of Poland.

the marriage of the Duke to her own niece, thus augmenting its suspicions. By 1665, the Grand Marshal was in open revolt and the Queen appealed to Louis for help. The King initially seemed willing, even eager, to oblige, but in October, he sent his troops to aid the Dutch against Bernard van Galen, the Bishop of Münster, who was allied with the English. The gratitude of the Dutch was more necessary to Louis' plans than the throne of Poland.

The *Mémoires* for 1665 seem to conclude with a description of four edicts that the King issued in the month of December,[15] which accurately reflect both the thrust and the limitations of his activities for the year. The first was a decree devaluating the currency, which he promulgated on December 7 with the intention of putting more money into circulation.[16] Then came three edicts that Louis himself took to the *Parlement* of Paris for registration on December 22. The first was on the price of offices.[17] It announced the continuation of the *droit annuel* and set the price of judicial offices at a rate somewhat higher than that initially suggested by Colbert. It also regulated the ages for admission to them, categorically denying the possibility of obtaining dispensations. The second concerned the Chamber of Justice.[18] It granted amnesty to most of the financiers under prosecution in return for substantial payments to the royal treasury. This act virtually terminated the work of the Chamber. The third[19] reduced the official interest rate from $5\frac{1}{2}$ per cent to 5 per cent, again with the intention of increasing the money in circulation. The judicial officials and the financiers had a great deal to mutter about, but they had survived to fight another day.

All these topics echo throughout the *Mémoires*. It is for the reader to check the allusions and to judge our imagination.

15. The first two texts for 1666 specifically state that these edicts had been described at the end of the previous year. Périgny crossed out this entire section in the second text, but it is reproduced in *Oeuvres de Louis XIV*, ed. Ph. A. Grouvelle (Paris, 1806), II, 45–47.

16. *Recueil général des anciennes lois Françaises, op. cit.*, XVIII, 66.

17. *Ibid.*, 66–69. See the *Mémoires* for 1661, pp. 31 and 79, where Louis twice specifically alludes to his discussion of this edict.

18. *Lettres, instructions, et mémoires de Colbert, op. cit.*, II, 758–759.

19. *Recueil général des anciennes lois Françaises, op. cit.*, XVIII, 69–71.

SECOND PART

MÉMOIRES
FOR THE INSTRUCTION OF
THE DAUPHIN

1666

 N THE first part of these *mémoires*, which con-
tains nearly five years, I have described to you
in what manner I had conducted myself
during the peace, and in this second one, I
intend to show you how I have acted in war.
There I have tried to teach you by what
means a wise prince can profit from the
public tranquillity. Here I shall teach you how he must see to all
the needs produced by the tumult of arms. There you have most
often seen me as the father of a family, occupied peacefully with
the cares of domestic administration. Here you will see me as a
vigilant captain, constantly adjusting my position and my conduct

according to the posture of my enemies. Finally, there you have found only releases of troops, reductions of taxes, increases in revenue, regulations of justice, advantageous establishments, useful and peaceful acquisitions. Here you will encounter only levies of soldiers, armaments of ships, provisioning of strongholds, constant cares, bloody battles, continual alerts. But I am sure that in this variety of things you will always note in me the same constancy for work, the same firmness in my decisions, the same passion for the greatness of the state, and the same ardor for true glory.

The death of the King of Spain and the war between the English and the United Provinces occurring at almost the same time, offered me two important opportunities at once for exerting my arms: one against the Spanish, in pursuit of the rights inherited by the Queen through the death of the King her father;[1] and the other against the English in defense of the States of Holland, according to our recent treaty. The King of England, of course, did furnish me with a rather plausible pretext for disengaging myself from this last quarrel, maintaining that the Dutch were the aggressors and that I had promised to aid them only if they were attacked. But even though it may have been in my interest to accept such a fine opportunity for remaining neutral, I could not refrain from acting in good faith, knowing that the English were the aggressors.

I postponed declaring myself, however, in the hope of reconciling them. But seeing that my intercession was not succeeding and fearing that they might reach an agreement between themselves to my prejudice, I finally openly took the stand that I should. But it remained for me to decide if it was in my interest as well as that of my allies to go to war against both England and Spain, or if I should merely assume the quarrel of the Dutch and wait for a better time to settle my own, undoubtedly an important deliberation, owing to the importance and the weight of the arguments on both sides.

On the one hand, I envisaged with pleasure the prospect of these two wars as a vast field that could create great opportunities

1. Louis now claimed that certain territories in the Spanish Low Countries were subject to a law of devolution, by which a daughter of the first marriage (Maria Theresa) succeeded prior to a son by a second marriage (Charles II).

for me to distinguish myself and to fulfill the great expectations that I had for some time inspired in the public. So many fine men whom I saw enthusiastic for my service seemed to be constantly urging me to furnish some scope for their valor, and it would not have been satisfied through a maritime war in which the most valiant hardly ever have the opportunity to distinguish themselves. But thinking of my own interest, I considered that the good of the kingdom not permitting me to expose myself to the caprices of the sea, I would be obliged to commit everything to my lieutenants without ever being able to act in person; that, moreover, my various ideas always obliging me to maintain a great number of troops, it would be more convenient for me to thrust them upon the domains of the King of Spain than to feed them constantly at the expense of my subjects; that besides, the entire house of Austria, convinced of my intentions, would not fail to harm me indirectly with all its power; that if there was to be a war, it was better to fight it for some apparent profit than to direct all my efforts against islanders, from whom I could hardly conquer anything without it being burdensome to me; that if I undertook the two wars at once, the States would serve me better against Spain in order to have my support against England, whereas if they were entirely out of danger they would perhaps fear the increase of my power instead of recalling my favors; that, finally, many of my predecessors had been confronted with equally great affairs and that if I refused to expose myself to similar difficulties, I was in danger of not meriting similar praises.

But in support of the contrary opinion, I knew that the glory of a prince actually consists of magnanimously overcoming the difficulties that he cannot honestly avoid, but that he is always in danger of being accused of recklessness when he rushes voluntarily into complications from which a little skill might have saved him; that the greatness of our courage must not make us neglect the aid of our reason, and that the more dearly one loves glory, the more cautiously one must try to acquire it; that to attack these two powerful enemies at once would create a connection between them of incalculable prejudice to me; that the English by themselves were not to be feared, but that their aid would carry great weight in the defense of the Spanish lands; that I could hardly make much progress in Flanders once they had filled it with their troops; that the Catholic King would be obliged to surrender some ports to these islanders, from which they would not easily be expelled; that once these two nations had united for war, they would hesitate to make peace separately and that thus I would always be obliged to fight them together or to reach an agreement with both of them on worse terms; that such a close alliance between Spain and England would advance a settlement with Portugal; that under the pretext of the war against England, I could organize my forces and my connections so as to begin the one in Flanders more propitiously; that the aid of the Dutch, quite preoccupied now with their own defense, would not compensate for the prejudice that the English would cause me and that, in regard to the future, there was no more honest nor better way to engage them to keep their word to me than to display my entire good faith by beginning the war purely for them; and that, finally, it would be glorious for me in the sight of all the nations of the earth if, having on the one hand my rights to pursue, and on the other my allies to protect, I would have suspended my interests in order to undertake their defense.

I remained for some time undecided between these two opinions, but if the first struck my heart more, the second satisfied my reason better, and I believed that in my post I had to violate my inclinations in order to adhere to the interests of my crown. This is why I finally resolved to engage only in the war against the English, but to fight it all the harder.

From the end of the previous year, I had incorporated two hundred new companies of infantry into the old regiments so that they would gradually pattern themselves after the others and the number of my men would increase without any weakening of discipline. I had planned to organize two hundred companies of light horse, for which I issued, however, only one hundred and twenty commissions, most of the officers being drawn from my household troops, where I had retained them since the last war. A great number of others who had also been in the service claimed to have as much right to be appointed as they, but I felt that it was only fair in this instance to prefer those who had remained at my side in a continuing function to those who had withdrawn to the comfort of their homes, aside from the fact that the latter having shown that they could dispense with the position, it was undoubtedly more humane to employ the others, who might otherwise perhaps have found it difficult to make a living.

Your company of two hundred gendarmes was not included in these, nor was the regiment that I formed when I dismissed the Queen my mother's company of light horse, in order not to deprive Tury who commanded it and the cavalrymen who composed it of their livelihood. I did not feel obliged to take the same precautions in regard to Bouligneux, lieutenant of this Princess' gendarmes, because his salary remained on the books, and I thought that it sufficed, as a token of my esteem, to add a pension to it, but in order not to abandon his cavalrymen, I retained them in my service in my company of Scottish gendarmes.

I don't know if I write to your taste when I go into these details, which may perhaps appear unimportant to you, but as for me, I am convinced that by these little cares for the fortune of his servants a prince produces a very great effect on the people in this profession. Not all the reputation of great men is formed by great actions. Since the most menial ones are performed the most often, it is on them that our true inclinations are judged. In disentangling the minutest affairs, there is a certain point of honesty which, when scrupulously observed, is no less to be prized than the most brilliant virtues. The account of the actions that it directs is not as intriguing, perhaps, but their imitation is no less useful. It does not cause such a commotion in the world, but it secretly makes more of an impression upon hearts. It does not acquire such vast renown for us, but it contributes more to our happiness, for whatever love we may have for glory, it must be confessed that a good prince cannot be entirely satisfied if he does not have the love of his servants as well as their admiration.

However, because giving out so many offices left many empty posts among the troops who served at my side, I filled some with cavalrymen chosen from all the individual companies, but I picked to fill the others a good number of young noblemen whom I wanted, so to speak, to train with my own hands in the maxims of their profession, so that they would take my lessons along with them into other units as vacancies occurred.

I even wanted, in the meanwhile, to review my guards regiment more often, not wanting these new levies to weaken the old units, and for this reason I cautioned all those who were forming companies to take only new men, because to recruit old soldiers was a useless expense that did not actually increase the number of my men. But my efforts to prevent this disorder were so effective that, far from being depleted, my household troops were stronger than ever, for they alone amounted to two thousand five hundred effectives of horse and six thousand foot soldiers, although I had not yet made any increase in the companies of French guards, knowing how easy this would be once I saw the need for it.

Convinced that the French infantry had not been very good, I sought to find ways of improving it, and one of the first that occurred to me was to place the colonelcies, insofar as it was possible, into the hands of the highest-ranking young people at my court, whose desire to please me and emulation of each other could inspire with greater dedication; aside from the fact that being in a position to sustain the expense necessary for earning the respect of their units, they would be more capable of maintaining them in their proper condition.

The same reasons also made me desire that subordinate offices be filled by persons of importance, and therefore I not merely intended to choose them henceforth with the greatest possible care, but so that these posts would be in greater demand I declared publicly that I would no longer give out positions in the cavalry except to those who had served in the infantry.

And so that all these units would have the same opportunities for service and that some would not always remain in the garrisons while the others were at war, I resolved that each would always have twenty-four companies in the field, out of which two battalions would be formed, while the others would remain to guard the strongholds, each to be drawn from them in its turn. And so that the execution of this regulation would not leave my frontiers depleted, I levied sixteen Swiss companies of two hundred men each, which I put into the garrisons to replace the French.

I intended at that time to negotiate for troops with the Duke of Brunswick in case I would need them for my service. But in regard to the Duke of Lorraine, I did not believe that it was desirable for me to make him any proposal about his, for I had no doubt that once we entered into negotiations he would insist on making me buy them for more than they were worth and that he would even add the condition that they be maintained as a unit, which was absolutely unacceptable to me. I actually, of course, did plan to secure them, whether for my own service or in order to deprive my enemies of them, but I wanted the offer to come from him, and in order to bring him to this, I resolved to send word to him that I desired for him to dismiss them, according to our treaty, which did not permit him to maintain any troops except for his regular bodyguard. This proposal was particularly embarrassing to him at that time, because the Elector of Mainz, to whom he had lent his troops, had peaceably concluded his dispute with the Palatine, leaving them unemployed, so that he was faced with the alternative either of dismissing them, as I was requesting, or of breaking with me openly, unless this Duke himself found a compromise solution, which could only be to keep his men in service by placing them at my entire disposal.

But finally, before coming to grips with my enemies, I believed that it was necessary to conclude the disputes over rank and over command that so often arose among my own troops. These disputes were not new, but my predecessors, seeing them sustained everywhere with such intensity, had not yet ventured to settle them, wondering perhaps whether their judgment would be accepted by the parties or whether the advantage that it would procure for the public would not be outweighed by the personal hatreds they would incur. As for me, I was sufficiently assured of the respect of my subjects not to be deterred by such considerations, but it must be confessed, however, that it was not without some regret that I resolved to issue this regulation, because my affection for all the troops in my service prevented me from condemning any of them without sharing in their vexation. However, I realized that this was no time to give way to my feelings, for it must be agreed that of all the instances when the authority of a single person is useful to the public, none is so obvious as war, where everyone knows that decisions must be prompt, discipline strict, orders final, obedience punctual, where the least moment of indecision is fatal to success, and where the slightest errors must often be repurchased in blood.

That ancient Rome which was so averse to sovereign authority, submitted to it, nevertheless, whenever it was threatened by some formidable enemy, and realizing that the equality between its consuls was not suitable for military operations, it elected a dictator who ruled it with absolute power.

But then, what could ever be expected but tumult and confusion in a body where those who must obey cannot tell who has the right to command them and where those who aspire to authority are more interested in venting their private differences than in seeking the welfare and the security of their troops? Nothing inflames tempers as much as jealousy of rank. The claims of the commanders invariably engage their subordinates, each of the soldiers believes that his own interest is at stake, all are inspired by envy, and a single camp is turned into two hostile armies, both of which, immediately forgetting the service of their prince and the safety of their country, think of nothing else but of satisfying their wild frenzy at the cost of their own blood: misfortune that could not be effectively avoided without settling all these differences as I did, so that wherever troops might henceforth come together, there would be no more grounds for questioning the rank or the authority of their commander.

I found that the most convenient solution for this matter was to eliminate the difference of titles, which was the principal basis of the disputes, and to give all my household cavalry the rank of gendarmes, so as to be free to settle the rank of each of their companies later as I would deem it appropriate.

I desired to bring the King of Denmark[2] over to our side so that he would close the Baltic Sea to the English and prevent them from obtaining naval stores from there, and because this Prince was then disputing with the Dutch about a sum of money, I furnished a portion of it in order to bring this Prince around to my terms.

Meanwhile, having learned that in spite of the eruption of full-scale war between them and the English, the States of Holland still retained their ambassador at the court of the King of Great Britain whereas mine had left, I was afraid that they might use this channel for making some deal to my prejudice. This is why I obliged them to recall him. But to insure myself further against similar surprises, I subsequently extracted a formal promise from them not to negotiate on this matter without my express consent.

2. Frederick III (1609–1670), King of Denmark since 1648.

I then sent all governors of provinces and of maritime strongholds back to reside at their posts, and the Duke de Mazarin[3]
having recently returned from inspecting the coasts of Brittany,
I had him give me an exact report on their condition.

Meanwhile, I was making levies everywhere and was providing
my frontiers with troops and with munitions. But the partly
demolished condition of Mardick gave me some concern because
I could not decide whether it would be better for me to rebuild it
hastily or to finish its demolition; for I feared that if I were to
repair it, the enemy would profit from my work by surprising it
partly rebuilt, and if I were to finish its demolition, they would
plan to seize it and to fortify it. But while waiting to make my
final decision on this question, I commanded Marshal d'Aumont
to remain there with a small body of men. I also had some fear
for the ships in the Toulon roadstead, which was defended only
by two very distant towers and was exposed to the insults of the
English, particularly since they had some pilots in their pay who
knew the area. But I sent Vivonne to devise means of preventing
such an incident with the Duke de Beaufort.[4]

The only thing that remained for me to do before beginning
the war was to decide how I would declare it; for still intending
to conclude it as soon as possible, I wished to act as courteously
as I could with the King of England, and it appeared to me that
the best solution was to arrange for the Queen his mother,[5] who
was then in Paris, to bear the news herself, thinking that she was
bearing only a compliment, so I requested her to express merely
to this Prince that my singular esteem for him made me feel very
sorry about the decision that my commitment had forced upon
me; and this appeared so courteous to her that not merely did she
promise to inform him of it, but she even believed that he should
have felt obligated for it.

I can also say that there was nothing in this speech that was
not entirely in conformity with my thoughts, because actually

3. Charles-Armand de La Porte (1631–1713), Duke de La Meilleraye, assumed
the title of Mazarin in 1661, when he married the Cardinal's niece, Hortense Mancini.

4. Louis-Victor de Rochechouart (1636–1688), Duke de Vivonne, Captain-
General of the French Galleys. François de Vendôme (1616–1669), Duke de Beaufort,
illegitimate grandson of Henry IV, commanded the French navy.

5. Henriette de France (1609–1669), Louis' aunt, widow of Charles I. Louis refers
to her as the Queen of England.

I was convinced that in starting this war he had perhaps been carried further by his subjects than he would have liked, so that I believed that in this squabble between our states I had less reason to complain about him than to pity him, for there is no doubt that this subjection that makes it necessary for a sovereign to take orders from his people is the worst calamity that can befall a man of our rank.

What makes for the greatness and the majesty of kings is not so much the scepter that they bear as the manner in which they bear it. It is perverting the order of things to attribute decisions to the subjects and deference to the sovereign, and if I have described to you elsewhere the miserable condition of princes who commit their people and their dignity to the conduct of a prime minister, I have good cause to portray to you here the misery of those who are abandoned to the indiscretion of a popular assembly; for indeed, the prime minister is a man whom you choose as you see fit, whom you associate to your power only insofar as you please, and who has the greatest influence in your affairs only because he has the first place in your heart. In appropriating your possessions and your authority, he at least retains some gratitude and some respect for your person, and however great we may make him, he cannot avoid his ruin if we have but the strength to will it. At the most, you have only a single partner on the throne. If he despoils you of part of your glory, he unburdens you at the same time of your thorniest cares. The interest of his own greatness engages him to sustain yours. He wishes to preserve your rights as a possession that he enjoys in your name, and if he shares your diadem with you, he at least works to leave it intact to your descendants.

But this is not the case with the power of a popular assembly. The more you grant it, the more it demands; the more you caress it, the more it scorns you; and what it once has in its possession is retained by so many hands that it cannot be torn away without extreme violence. Out of so many persons who compose these great bodies, it is always the least sensible who assume the greatest license. Once you defer to them, they claim the right forever to control your plans according to their fancy, and the continual necessity of defending yourself against their assaults alone produces many more cares for you than all the other interests of your crown, so that a prince who wants to bequeath lasting tranquillity to his people and his dignity completely intact to his successors cannot be too careful to suppress this tumultuous temerity.

But I am dwelling too long on a reflection that seems useless for you, or that can at most serve you only to recognize the misery of our neighbors, since it is patent that you will reign in a state where you will find no authority that is not honored to derive its origin and its status from you, no body that dares to depart from expressions of respect, no corporation that does not see its principal greatness in the good of your service and its sole security in its humble submission.

After having informed my enemy of my decision to go to war, it was necessary to announce it to my subjects, and for this purpose I ordered it to be published in the customary manner. But my care for present affairs did not prevent me from thinking of those that I had postponed for another time.

Knowing how much trouble the war against Portugal gave to Spain and how capable the continuation of this internal disease was of eventually sapping the strength of this crown, I believed that it was desirable to protract it for as long as I could, and for this reason I arranged the marriage of Mademoiselle de Nemours to the King of Portugal. Still later, I sent Romainville[6] to that court to circumvent the proposals of the Spanish with advantageous offers of aid in men and in money and even, as a last resort, with hopes of the offensive and defensive league that the Portuguese had always ardently desired.

From Germany, Count Wilhelm von Fürstenberg[7] was working with the Elector of Cologne and the Duke of Neuburg to convince the Elector of Mainz, the Dukes of Brunswick, and their neighboring princes to ally with me in order to prevent the Emperor from sending troops into Flanders, showing them that this was the only way to maintain the peace in their country and to keep my armies away from it. I sent the abbé de Gravel on a similar mission to reside personally at the court of the Elector of

6. Melchior de Harod de Senevas (1614–1694), Marquis de Saint-Romain, also known as the abbé de Saint-Romain.
7. Wilhelm Egon (1629–1704), Count von Fürstenberg, a Councillor of the Elector of Cologne, was one of the principal French agents in Germany.

Mainz, so as to observe his actions more closely, since they were not always very sincere.[8]

Moreover, in order to engage the Elector of Brandenburg to the defense of the States of Holland, I first sent Du Moulin[9] to him with some general proposals on this subject, and I subsequently intended to transfer D'Estrades, my ambassador in Holland, there with more precise ones, but the refusal of this Prince to give him the hand prevented me from continuing the negotiation through this channel. I dispatched Colbert,[10] master of requests, to him a short time later as a mere envoy, yet with power to do everything possible to interest this Elector and his councillors in making a favorable decision, for although I had been deeply stung by his pretension in regard to my ambassador, I would not let this deprive me of the advantages of this treaty. It was still rather difficult to achieve it, however, but few things can resist one who can conquer himself. Thus, although I had to combat the arguments of the dowager and the influence of the Prince of Orange in that court,[11] this Elector finally assumed the obligation to maintain ten thousand men at his expense for the defense of the States of Holland.

This example can teach you, my son, how useful it is for a prince to control his feelings on occasions of this nature, when we can choose to dissemble or to evoke. We must not concentrate so much on the wrong that we have presumably suffered as on the circumstances in which we find ourselves. When we become unduly embittered, instead of affronting our antagonist, we usually cause prejudice to ourselves. For the empty satisfaction of exhibiting our vexation, we often lose the opportunity of garnering solid advantages. The excitement that transported us vanishes quickly, but the losses it has caused us remain forever present to our mind, along with the sorrow of having brought them upon ourselves.

8. Jacques de Gravel. John Philip von Schönborn (1605–1673), Archbishop-Elector of Mainz since 1647.

9. P. du Moulin, equerry of the Queen.

10. Charles Colbert (1629–1696), Marquis de Croissy, brother of Jean-Baptiste, was the minister for foreign affairs from 1679 to 1696.

11. Amalia von Solms (1602–1675), dowager Princess of Orange, mother-in-law of the Elector. William III (1650–1702), Prince of Orange, the future King of England.

I know better than anyone how sensitive of the least things that seem to affect their dignity are hearts jealous of their glory. And yet, it befits prudence not to evoke everything, and perhaps it sometimes even befits the greatness of our rank and the nobility of our motives to ignore what is transpiring beneath us. Exercising a divine function here below, we must try to appear incapable of the agitations that could belittle it, or if our heart not being able to belie the weakness of its nature feels the rise of these vulgar emotions in spite of itself, our reason must be extremely careful to hide them if they are harmful to the good of the state, for which alone we are born. One never reaches the end of vast undertakings without experiencing difficulties of different kinds, and if there are some where we apparently relent on our pride, the beauty of the successes that we await from them gently consoles us within ourselves, and the conspicuous effects that emerge from them gloriously excuse us before the public.

At the same time, I sent Pomponne[12] to Sweden with orders to negotiate there for the affairs of Poland and of Germany, for I wanted to form some connection with that country before my enemies could.

I also maintained a secret contact with Count Zrinyi[13] in order to create some commotion in Hungary in case of war against the Emperor. There was a Theatine monk at my court, sent by the Duchess of Bavaria with the consent of her husband, to make me some proposals, to which I believed I should listen favorably so as to detach him from the house of Austria. I also listened to proposals from the Electors of Mainz and of Cologne for a treaty that they wanted to conclude immediately between the Emperor and myself for the partition of the domains of the King of Spain, for although the thing did not appear very feasible to me, I wanted to let all the difficulties accumulate so that all the blame for the rejection of this plan would be directed against him.

The Dukes George William and John Frederick of Brunswick having fallen into some differences, I believed that it was in my interest for them to be settled through my intercession, and I had

12. Simon Arnauld (1618–1699), Sieur de Pomponne, was the minister for foreign affairs from 1671 to 1679 and a minister again from 1691 to 1699. Louis also refers to him as d'Andilly or Andilly.
13. Count Péter Zrinyi (1621–1671).

them concluded by De Lumbres,[14] who was then returning from Poland, where he had just served as my ambassador. I was also an arbiter, along with the crown of Sweden, in a dispute between the Elector of Mainz and the Palatine[15] concerning the right of *Wildfang*, but I would not allow the Emperor to be recognized as final arbiter in case of a diversity of opinion.

A rumor then began to circulate that the Bishop of Münster had expressly dispatched a man to me with proposals for a settlement, apparently convinced that neither he nor his friends would be capable of withstanding my power for long; and this did not seem too farfetched, for the few troops that I had sent against him distressed his men so much that they hardly ventured from their quarters any longer, where their unbearable discomfort caused continual desertion among them.

A few days before this rumor had begun to circulate, a German colonel with eight hundred troops of this Bishop having thrust himself into Oudenbosch and begun to fortify himself there, he was so actively pressed in this post that he was compelled to surrender with all his men; and the good fortune of this undertaking could only be attributed to France, not merely because La Vallière[16] and my troops under his command were primarily responsible for it, but because even those of the States of Holland were led by Frenchmen.

The recent failure of this Bishop in his undertaking against Daelhem and Willemstad should have taught him another costly lesson about the valor of the French troops, for these two strongholds being more than thirty leagues from the scene of the fighting appeared to him all the more easy to surprise in that they believed they had nothing to fear, and the connivance of the Spanish, who are always maliciously trying to harm the United Provinces,

14. George William of Brunswick-Lüneburg (1624–1705), Duke of Zell. Louis indiscriminately refers to him as the Duke of Brunswick or the Duke of Lüneburg. John Frederick of Brunswick-Lüneburg (1625–1679), Duke of Hanover. Antoine de Lumbres (d. 1676).

15. Charles Louis von Simmern (1617–1680), Elector Palatine since 1632, but dispossessed until the Treaty of Westphalia, where he received only the Upper Palatinate. He claimed the right of *Wildfang*, to the effect that he had jurisdiction over all foreigners who settled in the states on his borders.

16. Jean-François de La Baume Le Blanc (1642–1676), Marquis de La Vallière, brother of Louis' mistress.

seemed to guarantee his success; and indeed, they pretended to dismiss some regiments from their nearby strongholds in order to thrust them by surprise into these two cities in the name of the Bishop of Münster, but a small number of Frenchmen defeated these disguised regiments and made a shambles out of the Spanish trickery.

However, I was not content for my troops to be useful to my allies; I did not want them to disturb them, and with this thought, not merely was I careful to maintain them under strict discipline in that country and to furnish their pay in advance, but fearing that it would not be sufficient with the dearness of victuals in the area, I increased it by one *sol* per infantryman and by three per cavalryman.

At the beginning of this year, I furnished a considerable sum to the King of Poland, so that he could wage the war against his rebellious subjects, and I paid pensions to some of the most powerful nobles of the kingdom in order to facilitate the execution of my plans for it.

I had ordered my ambassador to distribute money to the principal deputies and even in the individual cities of the United Provinces, in order to gain control over their deliberations and over the choice of their magistrates, believing it in my interest to exclude from all public offices the faction of the Prince of Orange, whom I knew to be entirely devoted to the King of England.

I sent a present to the Queen of Sweden, and knowing that the Grand Chancellor had the greatest influence in that state,[17] I thought that I should win him over through my liberality. I also made similar presents to the Queen of Denmark and to the Electress of Brandenburg, having no doubt that these Princesses would consider themselves honored at my efforts to acquire their friendship and that they might for this reason enter more willingly into my interests. But in order to engage this Electress even more firmly, I subsequently gave her a necklace of great value, and I also had my envoy attempt the same methods on the Prince of Anhalt and on the Count von Schwerin,[18] who had the most influence in the councils of that court, so that in return for twenty-two

17. Magnus de La Gardie (1622–1686).
18. John George (1627–1693), Prince of Anhalt, brother-in-law of the Elector. Otto (1616–1679) Count von Schwerin, prime minister.

thousand *écus* divided between them they have served me most successfully ever since.

All these individual expenditures came to a very considerable capital, particularly at a time when the new troops that I had levied, the ships that I had equipped, the strongholds that I had provisioned, and the sums disbursed in the other negotiations that I have described to you might have made me use a little more restraint. But if it is useful for princes to know how to spare their money when the peaceful state of their affairs permits it, it is no less important for them to know how to spend it wisely for the advantage of their crown. Kings, whom Heaven has made the sovereign trustees of the public fortune, assuredly do very badly by their duty when they squander the wealth of their subjects in superfluous expenditures, but they do even worse, perhaps, when they refuse to provide for the defense of their people.

Meager sums spent with judgment often save states from infinitely greater losses. For lack of a vote that could have been acquired cheaply, one recklessly draws entire nations upon himself. A neighbor whom we could have made a friend at slight expense sometimes costs us dearly when he becomes our enemy. The smallest army that might invade our lands takes more from us in one day than it would have cost us to maintain a contact for ten years, and the reckless administrators who do not understand these maxims sooner or later find punishment for their miserly behavior in the devastation of their provinces, the stopping of their revenues, the exhaustion of their treasuries, the desertion of their allies, the scorn and aversion of their people.

Far from hesitating to disburse money for public needs, it is only in order to meet them that we must collect it. Loving money for its own sake is a passion of which great souls are incapable. They never consider it as the object of their desires, but merely as an instrument for the execution of their plans. The wise prince and the private miser are entirely opposite in their conduct. The miser always seeks money with avidity, collects it with extreme pleasure, saves it without discrimination, retains it with concern, and cannot disburse a bit of it without unbearable vexation, whereas a virtuous prince taxes only with restraint, demands only with compassion, spares only from duty, reserves only from prudence, and never spends it without some special satisfaction, because he does it only to increase his glory, to enlarge his state, or to benefit his subjects.

The edicts that I had issued toward the end of the year, and particularly the one on the reduction of the price of offices, caused vexation to all the officials. I was informed that the *Enquêtes* of the *Parlement* was demanding an assembly of the chambers, where they intended, under various pretexts, to resume indirectly their deliberations on this subject and that the first president, convinced that he was rendering me a service, was carefully practicing various delays, as if there could still be something dangerous about the assemblies of the chambers.[19] But to show that they counted for very little in my mind, I myself ordered him to assemble the *Parlement* to say merely that I did not want any more discussion of any kind about edicts verified in my presence; for indeed, I wanted to take this opportunity to make a conspicuous example, either of the entire subjection of this court or of my just severity in punishing its assaults. It chose the best course for itself and, separating without daring to try anything, clearly showed that these bodies are not to be feared. After this example, the most distant *parlements* verified the edict on the price of offices within their jurisdictions, which was very clear proof of the perfect restoration of royal authority, since the very ones who deliberated being both judges and participants would not have acted directly against their own interests without powerful feelings of respect.

The last throes of the illness of the Queen my mother and the dreadful incident of her death caught me in the midst of these occupations and attached me for some days to the sole consideration of her loss, for although I have just told you that a prince must sacrifice all private emotions for the good of his state, there are instances when this maxim cannot be practiced immediately. One might even say that if it were ever proper to depart from it, it would be on just such an occasion.

Nature had formed the first bonds between me and the Queen my mother, but spiritual connections are far more difficult to break than mere blood ties. In order to explain to you both the

19. The *Chambre des Enquêtes,* or Inquests, was one of the Chambers of the *Parlement* of Paris. Assemblies of all the Chambers had been a threat to royal authority during the Fronde.

extent and the justice of my grief, I would have to relate to you here all the merits of this Princess, which would be a difficult undertaking. The most eloquent men of the age, whom I have set to work on this subject, have been hard put to exhaust it, and for all their efforts, the simple account by history of the actions of this Princess will always far surpass their praises.

I who knew better than anyone the vigor with which this Princess had sustained my dignity when I could not defend it myself, could not see her die without overwhelming sorrow, since not even her former enemies could refrain from mourning her then and from confessing that there had never been piety more sincere, firmness more intrepid, kindness more generous. But the best evidence that I can furnish you of my agony at her death is to call your attention to my attachment to her during her life, for the respects that I have always paid to her were not pure formalities dictated merely by propriety. My usual habit of living under the same roof and eating at the same table with her, my diligence in visiting her several times a day, in spite of my most pressing affairs, was not a rule that I had made for reasons of state, but an indication of the pleasure that I took in her company; for indeed, her willing surrender of sovereign power had made it so clear that I had nothing to fear from her ambition that I was not obliged to restrain it through any affected attachment.

After this misfortune, being no longer able to endure the sight of the place where it had happened, I left Paris immediately and withdrew first to Versailles, where I could have the most privacy, and some days later to Saint-Germain. The first moments when I could force myself into some effort were spent in performing the duty that this incident imposed upon me. The obligation of informing all the princes of Europe cost me more than could be imagined, and particularly the letters to the Emperor, to the King of Spain, and to the King of England, which I was obliged to write in my own hand.

Meanwhile, having learned the last wishes of this Princess from her testament, I commanded that they be executed scrupulously, except for her order against any ceremony at her funeral; for finding no other relase from my grief than in the honors accorded to her memory, I commanded that everything be done just as she herself had ordained at the death of the late King my father.

With all the corporations that had to be assembled for the public services, it was hard to avoid some problems over rank, but the most hotly contested one was whether the first honors would be rendered to the clergy, which was then assembled, or to the *Parlement*. I decided the question in favor of the clergy, and the decision was executed for the first time at Saint–Denis, to the great disgruntlement of the *Parlement*, which, anticipating the same humiliation at Notre Dame in Paris, tried to parry this blow by delegating the *gens du roi*[20] to me. They came to see me at Versailles, where I had gone that day, and, Talon acting as their spokesman, protested that their corporation possessed the right to be greeted before the clergy. His speech was a little long, because he hesitated to come to their proposal that I permit the *Parlement* not to attend the ceremony; and he was quite right in thinking that these sorts of arrangements could not be made with me, but although I was not pleased with this proposal, I still replied immediately and with my usual coolness to all the points in his speech, and I even gave him a longer explanation than I had intended, since having already rendered judgment against this court in some other disputes, it was desirable to show it that I decided nothing lightly, and that it should not presume to think that I had a special interest in belittling it. But finally, I replied to their proposal by saying positively that I wanted them to be present, and that meant everybody; and I was scrupulously obeyed.

Among the occupations produced by the death of the Queen my mother, I have not described to you the division of her property because it was effected so quickly and so effortlessly between me and my brother that it was not worth mentioning, but I should perhaps have related to you a conversation that we had in the deepest throes of our common sorrow, which might be worthy of note owing to the pressing expressions of friendship that we exchanged at that moment.

The most important thing that transpired in it was that I promised him not to diminish any of the familiarity in which we had lived during the lifetime of the Queen my mother, even assuring

---

20. The *gens du roi*, or the agents of the king in the *Parlement*, were the *procureur général*, Achille II Harlay (d. 1671) and the *avocats généraux* Denis Talon (1628–1697) and Jérôme II Bignon (1627–1697). Louis also refers to them as *gens du parquet*.

him that I intended to extend it to his children, that I would have his son raised and taught by the same governor and the same tutor as you, and that he would always find me as warmly attached to his just interests as to my own.

The time I said these things and the way I said them could leave no doubt that my attachment alone had inspired them, but I can tell you in passing that even if I had meditated on this speech in full clarity of mind, I could have thought of nothing more subtle than to give my brother an honor for which he should have felt obligated, while taking the most precious token that he could give me as security for his conduct; for it must be agreed that there is nothing more useful to the public good, nothing more necessary to the greatness of the state, nothing more advantageous to all the members of the royal family than to preserve their connection with its head. I could make you realize this truth by calling to your attention that the factious, seeing these princes too committed, make no further attempt to seduce them, and fearing to see the failure or even the punishment of their criminal undertakings, they are forced to remain silent; that the malcontents, having no rallying point, are compelled to stomach their vexation in the privacy of their homes, and that foreigners, deprived of the connections which alone could have given them some advantage in this state, are more restrained in their designs. I could tell you that if such measures had always been taken, so many rich ornaments of this crown would not have been plucked by the very hands which should have been the most concerned to preserve them, and that France would long ago have been the mistress of the world if disunity among her children had not exposed her to the jealous frenzy of her enemies.

But leaving aside these purely public reasons and considering nothing but the interest of princes as private individuals, I intend merely to show you here that it befits the fatherly love of a king for all those of his house to protect them as much as possible from the evil counsels of those who want to advance themselves at their expense, for aside from the wrong they do themselves in dimming the brilliance of a diadem from which they derive all their greatness and in devastating a heritage which they or their descendants may legitimately possess one day, the mere idea of what they must tolerate even during their rage shows that crime and punishment are closely united on this point and leads one to wonder how so many have wanted to rush into such discomforts.

When a prince becomes the leader of rebels, for a single master whom he flees, he acquires an infinite number of comrades who do not even live on very good terms with him. Since they see in him only a borrowed power, he receives very little deference from them. What his people lack is immediately blamed on him, and if he chances to be in a position to grant some important grace, for a single person whom he barely satisfies, he alienates all the others. If he may have some good fortune, each one of them claims the credit for it, and if he should meet with some disaster, there isn't a one who does not think of leaving him. If he is at all enlightened, his suspicions are indescribable, for it cannot take him long to realize that his principal adherents, having followed him only out of interest, are always ready to abandon him once it is to their advantage. He learns that each one is negotiating privately; the number of his commanders and soldiers constantly diminishes, and those who remain at his side, becoming haughtier with his weakness and with his need of them, make him pay dearly for their services by their bluster. They speak to him arrogantly, they murmur freely, and they often even lose their esteem for him along with their respect, because his false move makes them suspect him of weakness.

But then, truly, what consideration could those who have already lost him as their legitimate lord preserve for him as the leader of a rebellion; and if he has himself given an example of disobedience toward the one whom the laws of the state and the rights of descent had made his sovereign, what must he expect from those whom crime alone rallies to his banners?

But if the soldiers act toward him in this manner, the people of the cities and the principal bourgeois are even more insolent toward him. There is no magistrate whom he is not obliged to flatter and who does not immediately expect to become his prime minister, no captain of a quarter who does not obey him only as he sees fit, no inhabitant who does not take the liberty of saying and even doing whatever comes into his head in front of him, and no one, finally, who does not desire to make a separate peace once he must bear the slightest tax for the maintenance of the war, so that soon lacking in all necessities after having exhausted the wealth of his house and the fortune of his most faithful servants, he is often fortunate if he can return to his duty on worse terms than he had left it.

The subject matter, to which I am adhering here more often than the chronological order, has prevented me from telling you that I had been afraid at the beginning of the year that, with the plague continuing in England, what remained of our commerce with the inhabitants of this island would cause us more prejudice than going to war against them, particularly since the disease had already reached our coasts. But in order to extinguish it early, I sent Talon, secretary of my cabinet, to the most exposed areas, with orders that succeeded so well that they very quickly safeguarded France from the misfortunes of her neighbors.

I should also have indicated to you that the *Grands Jours* having expired in the month of January before they could conclude a good part of their work, I extended them for a month, after which I allowed the commissioners to return and expressed my satisfaction with their services.

There was some difficulty, however, over certain articles, but not wanting to quash them openly, lest this detract from the merit of the rest or humiliate people whom I knew to be well-intentioned, I issued a new regulation on my own authority, which included the things I approved and omitted the others without mention.

A short time later, on hearing that a great many appeals were accumulating in the courts owing to the bankruptcy of the receivers, so that a good part of the funds that might have been left to the creditors were being consumed in useless expenses, I referred the whole matter to the *Grande Chambre* of the *Parlement* of Paris.

Meanwhile, I continued to work on certain set days at the general restoration and reform of the ordinances on justice, having decided that whenever I had assembled a sufficient number of articles I would send them to be verified in the courts, in order to give the public a clear indication of my concern for its relief and to show it that the tumult of arms and my preparations against foreigners were not capable of diverting my attention from restoring the purity of the laws and the general discipline in my state.

But since these universal concerns produced more things for me to do, I believed that I should give more time to them, so I most often worked three times a day. The morning was still devoted to the regular councils of justice, of commerce, of finance, and of correspondence, the afternoon to the current affairs of the state, and in the evening, instead of amusing myself as I was accustomed to do, I would return to my chamber to work either on the details of the war with Louvois,[21] who was in charge of them, or on other affairs that I had resolved to examine privately; and if I had a few moments left after this, I spent them on the *mémoires* that you are now reading.

My brother, who undoubtedly under the circumstances could not have had such pressing things to do, but who did not even seem much disposed to adopt any of the useful and pleasant occupations to which he might have devoted his time, decided in his leisure to make me the request that his wife should have a chair with a back in the presence of the Queen.

My friendship for him would have made me wish never to have to refuse him anything, but in view of the importance of this, I explained to him immediately, as gently as possible, that I could not satisfy him, that I would always be pleased to do anything that might serve to raise him above my other subjects, but that I did not believe I should ever permit anything that might seem to approximate him to me; and so that he would not pursue this thought I tried to show him, by many good reasons, how careful I had to be of my rank, how ill-founded was his claim, and how useless it would be for him to persevere in it.

But nothing I could tell him would convince either him or my sister, and my brother then began acting toward me in such a way as to make me afraid of the consequences if I had not basically been very sure of the mold of his heart. His passion even led him to say that the Queen my mother had resolved to speak to me of this affair before she died, presuming to use the name of this Princess and my respect for her memory in order to compel me to do as he desired, or rather, to strengthen his claim in the eyes of others; for as for me, I knew too well that the Queen my

21. François-Michel Le Tellier (1641–1691), Marquis de Louvois, son of Michel Le Tellier, had been acting secretary of state since 1662 and became full secretary of state in 1666. He was destined to become one of Louis' most influential ministers.

mother would never have been capable either of making or of condoning such a proposal, because she had shown too much esteem for royalty in the course of her life for anyone to believe that she had wanted to lessen its principal advantages at her death; for indeed, there is no doubt that we must guard nothing more jealously than the pre-eminence that embellishes our post. Everything that indicates it or preserves it must be infinitely precious to us. It does not merely involve our own interest. It is a possession for which we are accountable to the public and to our successors. We cannot dispose of it as we see fit, and we can have no doubt that it is among those rights of the crown that cannot be legally alienated.

Those who imagine that claims of this kind are only questions of ceremony are sadly mistaken. There is nothing in this matter that is unimportant or inconsequential. Since our subjects cannot penetrate into things, they usually judge by appearances, and it is most often on amenities and on ranks that they base their respects and their obedience. As important as it is for the public to be governed only by a single person, it is just as important for the one who performs this function to be raised so far above the others that no one else may be confused or compared with him, and one cannot deprive the head of state of the slightest marks of superiority without harming the entire body.

But remember, however, my son, that the pre-eminence that you must seek most and that will give you the greatest distinction must come from your own personal qualities. Loftiness of rank is never more solid than when it is sustained by uniqueness of merit, and this is undoubtedly what has led some to believe that it might be advantageous to a ruler for the conduct of his closest relatives to be in sharp contrast with his own. His virtue creates a great gap between them that presents him in a better light and with greater brilliance before the eyes of the whole earth. The loftiness and strength of his character draws entirely new luster from the mediocrity of those around him. The greatness and firmness of his soul is emphasized by contrast with their flabbiness, and his love for work and for true glory is infinitely more glowing when elsewhere there is only profound lethargy or attachment to trifles. With such a difference, all eyes are fixed on him alone. It is to him alone that all appeals are made; he alone is the recipient of all respects; he alone is the object of all hopes; nothing is pursued, nothing is anticipated, nothing is ever done except through him. His good graces are regarded as the sole source of all favors. The only way to advance oneself is by growing in his personal esteem. All else is fleeting, all else is powerless, all else is barrenness, and one might even say that his brilliance spreads like wildfire into foreign lands. The glowing image of his greatness travels everywhere on the wings of his renown. Just as he is the admiration of his subjects, he soon becomes the wonder of neighboring nations, and if he only knows how to use this advantage, there is nothing, either within or outside his dominions, that he cannot eventually accomplish.

But although these seem like rather plausible reasons, and that the manner in which I have just explained them to you may lead you to believe that they are not remote from my own opinion, don't imagine, nevertheless, that if you should one day have any brothers, I would work blindly in my affection for you to give you all the advantages over them that I have just described. On the contrary, I shall try to give you all the same lessons and the same examples, but it is up to you to distinguish yourself from the others. My care shall be to raise them as well as you, but yours must be to rise above them and to show the whole earth that you actually have the virtue to merit the rank that might be attributed only to your order of birth.

The envoy from the Bishop of Münster, whom I heard about in the month of February, arrived at the beginning of March with what were undoubtedly very fair and very convenient proposals for me. But I could only reply to his compliment that, not being personally at war with his master, it was not me whom he had to approach about making peace. I offered, however, to do my utmost to facilitate it, in case they wanted to negotiate it with the States of Holland, whom I immediately informed of what had transpired.

I had done similarly with them a short time previously, in an instance of no less importance, for the Portuguese ambassador to England, who was then here, convinced that it was to his master's advantage for there to be peace between the two crowns from which he obtained his principal support and wanting to initiate a negotiation on this subject, I would not let the matter go any further without communicating it to the resident of the United Provinces at my court. I could, of course, have gained some very important personal advantages on each of these occasions, for I could see that by listening to the proposals of peace with England, I could have saved enough at sea to put large armies to much better use on land, and by accepting the offers of the Bishop of Münster, aside from my being free to recall the troops that I had sent against him, he was also prepared to place his own troops at my entire disposal. But even more important, I saw the Marquis of Brandenburg, one of the most powerful princes in Germany, entirely disposed to join with me in attacking the Low Countries, and I was informed by Colbert that while he had been at the court of this Elector on my behalf, he had heard him say, apparently intending to be overheard, that if I had some claims on Brabant, he also had some on the Duchy of Guelderland.

However, determined in spite of these strong considerations not to try anything new until I had secured an acceptable peace for my allies, I merely replied courteously to the proposals of these princes in order to retain their good will.

The United Provinces, in whose favor I was making these decisions, were immediately informed of them and did not fail to thank me profusely for my frank behavior. Time will furnish more solid proofs of their actual gratitude, but whatever the outcome, I shall always enjoy the entire satisfaction of a magnanimous soul that has acted virtuously. For all the virtues, my son, have their own rewards, independently of the actions that they direct. Whether or not fate crowns their plans with success, whether or not men are grateful for their many favors, one can always derive private satisfaction from the secret consciousness of their own integrity, and one might even say that they rarely fail to receive the public praise that is due to them.

But honesty or good faith, the one that I mean to discuss with you here, has special characteristics of its own that make it recognizable to the least enlightened, and powerful charms that make it beloved to the whole earth. As corrupt as the world is, it still holds it in such veneration that those least inclined to practice it are obliged to feign it every day so as not to be entirely excluded from society. The most brilliant qualities in those who reject it soon arouse the most suspicion, whereas everything its followers do is taken in good spirit, and their greatest faults are almost always excused. It is the only virtue on which men pride themselves in every instance. There are many people who are well aware that magnificence is not for them. There are times and situations where good sense shows clemency to be out of place. There are professions in which valor is not felt to be necessary. There are ages and countries where even those who are considered as the most upstanding people vaunt their intemperance, but there is no time, no place, no condition, in which anyone even wants to be suspected of dishonesty. It may thus be said that this virtue is not esteemed without reason, since it is through it that the world receives all of its mildness and its comfort. It establishes relations among nations, it associates citizens, it keeps families united, and finally, it nourishes love and confidence between princes and subjects.

But in regard to me personally, it must be agreed that all Europe then became entirely convinced of how scrupulously I kept my word; and the Spanish gave rather good evidence of this when they resolved to entrust me with what seemed, as things then stood, to be the most precious possession and the most delicate responsibility in the world: I mean the person of the Empress,[22] for whom they requested access to my ports in case she needed it on her way to Germany; which I granted most willingly, ordering that wherever this Princess might land she be received with the same honors that would have been paid to my own person.

Meanwhile, I was still prepared to compel the house of Austria to render me justice once I was in a position to do so properly, and I was constantly aiming toward this end.

The States of Holland had followed my advice and begun to confer with the Bishop of Münster in Germany, and I had sent Colbert there on my behalf to try to facilitate this peace, which was concluded a short time later.

On the other hand, the Queen of England, displeased at seeing two crowns for which she was equally concerned divided almost without cause, seemed eager to reconcile them.

22. Margarita Maria of Spain (1651–1673), the bride of Leopold I.

The Swedes had explicitly declared to Pomponne that they would never do anything against my interests, and the arrival of Saint-Romain at the court of the King of Portugal had entirely disrupted the treaty between this Prince and the Spanish.

I had even seen a major consequence of this break soon thereafter. The marriage of Mademoiselle de Nemours having been entirely arranged, she came to say good-bye to me at Versailles just before setting sail for Portugal. Her voyage, however, was postponed until the month of June, and it was decided not to hold the marriage until she was on board ship, in order to avoid the ceremonies. But it is patent that this marriage could only be of great advantage in regard to me, since it created a new obstacle to the reconciliation of the Spanish and the Portuguese, who were already naturally full of hate for each other.

Moreover, I had a manifesto all prepared in order to inform the public of the rights of the Queen over Brabant and over some other provinces,[23] and I was levying good troops in order to enforce my reasons upon those who would not hear them peaceably.

But it was not enough to have ordered these levies; I knew that it was necessary to see how they were being executed; and so that those to whom my commissions had been issued would work harder at it, I had wanted them to be warned right away that I would check on them very closely. This is why I had declared publicly that I would each month hold a review of all the troops that could conveniently be assembled. I had even set the date of the first one for January 19, but all the orders having been issued for the troops to march to Breteuil, and my household having already departed in order to arrive there before me, I was stopped unexpectedly by the bad turn in the illness of the Queen my mother, for although the doctors did not consider the matter to be as serious as it proved to be later, a secret foreboding about things, or rather, a natural feeling of attachment would not allow me to leave the Queen in such a condition, so that I was compelled to send M. de Turenne[24] and Louvois, who had the department

23. *Le Traité des Droits de la Reine Marie-Thérèse sur divers États de la Monarchie Espagnole* (Paris, 1667).

24. Henri de La Tour d'Auvergne (1611–1675), Vicomte de Turenne, the renowned Marshal of France.

of war, in my place to Breteuil, charging them with giving me an exact report on all the troops that were to be there, which was actually so good that I could hardly have learned more about them if I had viewed them myself.

The month of February, during which I had resolved to view my troops for a second time, passed in expediting the pressing affairs that I have described to you in their proper place, so that I was obliged to wait until the month of March. But in the meanwhile, I lost no opportunity to put my troops in good condition, and not content with directing most of the activity of my councils toward this end, I did the same with my most ordinary amusements. I found most pleasure in praising commanders who took good care of their units, in investigating personally what transpired in each quarter, or in issuing instructions on this matter.

I then reduced what I customarily spent each year for furniture, for jewelry, for paintings, and for other things of a similar nature, finding no better way to spend my money than for armaments and for the comfort of the soldiers, and instead of amusing myself with hunting and with promenading, I often spent my leisure time in having one or several units drill before me.

It is a very great and very unique advantage to be able to find our satisfaction in things that contribute to our greatness and to learn how to take a kind of pleasure in the requirements of our calling. There is assuredly no one stupid enough to argue with this, but there are few people wise enough to put it into practice, and this is perhaps more true of sovereigns than of private individuals; for truly, the ease with which princes become accustomed to commanding renders any sort of subjection more difficult for them, and being raised above the ordinary laws, they need more strength and more intelligence than others in order to impose new rules upon themselves. Private individuals seem to find a well-beaten path to wisdom by observing the public ordinances. The prudence of the law, the consent of an entire people, the fear of punishment, and the hope of reward are constant aids to them in their weakness, of which we are deprived in our brilliance.

Perhaps there are many good subjects who would make very bad princes. It is much easier to obey one's superior than to command oneself, and when one can do anything he wants, it is not easy to want only what he should. Think about it early then, my son, and if you feel some reluctance now about submitting to the orders of those whom I have instituted over your conduct, consider how you will one day heed the counsels of reason when it will speak to you directly and when there will no longer be anyone at your side who has the right to defend her interests. Take care to profit from the precepts that I am having you taught while you can do so, and since in the post that awaits you, you can no longer without shame be led by any other insights or compelled by any other authority, get accustomed from now on to watching over your own actions and to testing often upon yourself the sovereign power that you are to exercise over others.

The thirteenth of March, I left Saint-Germain and arrived at Mouchy on the fourteenth in order to begin the second review the following day. I might well have taken up residence in Compiègne because it was closer to where I had resolved to view the troops and more convenient for my entire court, which then included a great many ladies because the Queen had wanted to accompany me. But considering that only the city of Compiègne could accommodate six thousand foot soldiers who would assuredly have been less orderly if spread about the countryside, I believed that it was necessary just this once to disregard my usual indulgence for the ladies and that it was better to let them complain about my strictness for two or three days than to cause the inhabitants of the area a loss that could not quickly be repaired.

My intention of carefully reviewing the great number of men I had assembled there made me devote three whole days to this occupation, which were still only barely sufficient for my purposes although I was on horseback from morning till evening. On the first day, I viewed all the troops together and, after having put them in battle formation, I began a particular inspection of the infantry regiment that bore my name[25] and had it drill in my presence. The two other days were employed in viewing each of the units, each of the companies, as well as each of the men separately; and in my count, I found [c. 200] companies of infantry and [c. 160] troops of cavalry; with [c. 10,000] foot soldiers and [c. 8,000] horse, almost all of whom were so handsome and so well-equipped that they could have passed for commanders elsewhere. I expressed my satisfaction by distributing gratuities to

25. The *Régiment du Roi*.

a good number of captains as a reward for their special dedication to my service, and I felt well rewarded for my own cares by the good results that they were beginning to produce.

But this was not enough, for aside from the troops that I had brought in there, there were a great many others that I could not view so quickly, either because they were needed for guarding strongholds or because they were so far away that I could only have brought them in at great expense; and yet I was well aware that it would be difficult to restore them to their proper condition without constant surveillance. I knew how easily captains and commanders who believed themselves out of my sight could relent on their duties and how their own interest could lead them to conspire against my service. This is why I sent special agents everywhere, with orders to catch the troops by surprise initially in order to check innocently on their condition, warning the commanders to put things in better order promptly and making it clear that they would return as often as they deemed it necessary—a most useful practice, for the captains, seeing that they were closely observed, were obliged to maintain their companies constantly at full strength, and the commissioners could no longer exaggerate the number of troops they were reviewing, having no doubt that the discrepancies would immediately be discovered, for my investigators gave me an exact oral and written report on their return so that I could see at leisure to those things that required my authority.

I also went to the trouble of distributing even the most minor offices in the infantry as well as in the cavalry myself, something that my predecessors had never done, having always relied on the superior officers for this, so that this function had become associated with their dignity. Finally, I assigned quarters to the troops, I settled differences between units and between mere officers, and believed that I had to make sure of everything myself. So must you be entirely convinced that our dedication to the public welfare or to the good of our service is the only means of satisfactorily achieving them; and as for me, I cannot understand how princes who neglect their own affairs can imagine that those to whom they entrust them should take better care of them than they.

It is usual for subjects to imitate their monarch in every way they can, but they are never quicker to follow his example than in his neglect of his own interests. When private individuals discover that the prince lacks dedication, that whatever good and evil they may do go equally unnoticed, that in either case they will be equally treated, and that he who has so many people working for him at once will not go to a moment's trouble to see how he is being served, they gradually develop a cowardly indifference that makes their courage fail, their vigor slacken, their mind soften, and even their body grow heavy. They quickly lose their love of duty, their esteem for their master, their shame at public criticism, their love of glory, and even their idea of virtue, so that they perform their functions in the manner that is most convenient to them, which is usually the worst, for perfection is hardly ever achieved without some difficulty.

But when, on the contrary, a prince is always seeking what is best for his service, when it is realized that nothing escapes his attention, that he discerns everything, that he weighs everything, and that sooner or later he punishes and rewards everything, this cannot help but make him both better obeyed and more highly esteemed. His dedication seems to descend from rank to rank down to the lowliest officer of his troops; each one who is at fault fears, each one who has served well hopes, and all constantly strive to do their duty as the only means of making their fortune; for we cannot expect, however able we may be, to correct the natural inclination of all men to seek their own interest, but it would still be sufficiently glorious for us to arrange so that they can only find it in honest practices, in meritorious actions, and in observing the rules of their profession.

I did not want, however, the expense of the reviews that I have described to you to fall exclusively upon the area where they were held, but since they were for the general benefit of the state, I also arranged for the entire expense to be assumed by the general treasury; and therefore I sent special agents into each of the villages through which the troops were to pass, in order to buy provisions for the soldiers at the current price for distribution to them later at a rate proportionate to their pay, so that the troops would lack nothing and the peasants would not be cheated—an arrangement that worked so well that there was hardly any complaint either from the soldiers or from the peasants.

My subsequent regulation on desertion was more difficult to devise and was no less necessary to implement. It had always been recognized that the liberty to desert produced losses to the captains, weakening of the troops, and libertinage among the soldiers, and yet no one had ever been able to do anything about it. This is why, convinced that it would be worth my while to remedy so many evils at once, I consulted those whom I believed most capable of giving me their advice on it, and after carefully examining their proposals, I issued a lengthy ordinance, in which I took every possible precaution against this abuse, whether by prescribing rules to commanders for identifying new men who had served in some other unit, or by imposing severe penalties against captains or soldiers who committed or condoned subterfuges in this matter.

It was no less important nor less hard to establish order and discipline among the troops in their quarters. I had above all wanted them to be billeted only in closed cities or towns, where my regulations could be more strictly enforced, but since the cost of provisions naturally rises with an increase in the number of consumers, their pay in many places was insufficient to support them comfortably, and they were often reduced to the necessity of suffering themselves or of inflicting great suffering upon their hosts.

But what contributed most to the disorder was that there being no precise limit to the allowance that they were to be furnished on the spot, this was extended or contracted arbitrarily, for in the quarters where the soldiers were stronger or bolder, they usually and insolently took more than was due them; and where the inhabitants were more numerous and more ill-disposed, they would often not furnish a reasonable amount, so that there were always complaints from one of the parties. This is why I believed that the only way to establish good order was to have a common law for all my dominions. Thus I set the rate for the soldiers everywhere at eighteen *deniers* per infantryman and three *sous* per cavalryman; but so as to distribute the burden, I ordered that each inhabitant should personally bear only a third, while the other two thirds would be divided between the entire town and the whole *élection*.[26]

26. An *élection* was a tax district in the *pays d'élection*.

I had also been informed that certain commanders sometimes abused their marching orders by collecting contributions for their own profit from the towns and villages through which they were to pass, under the pretext of exempting them from the billeting and the stay of their men; and I believed that it was necessary to put a stop to this. This is why, wanting to make it known at the outset with what severity I would punish such extortions, I cashiered a captain of the Auvergne regiment at the time of the review for having taken three hundred *livres* from the inhabitants of Rethel to exempt them from a stay in their city, although he was otherwise a rather good subject and had many friends at court. But I was resolved to stop at nothing in order to re-establish perfect discipline among my troops.

I was well aware, of course, that most people are usually attracted to the military profession by a spirit of libertinage and that there have been commanders even in our time who have exploited this maxim so effectively that they have maintained large armies over long periods by giving them no other pay than the license to pillage everywhere. But I have never believed that this example was to be imitated, except by those who, having nothing more to lose, also have nothing more to spare, for any prince who values his reputation at all can have no doubt that it is just as committed to defending the possessions of his subjects from pillage by his own troops as by those of his enemies; and if he knows his affairs, he will not fail to notice that whatever he allows to be taken from his people in any way at all is always taken at his expense; for indeed, the more exhausted the provinces are by the soldiers or by anything else, the less capable they are of contributing to the other public burdens.

It is a great error for princes to appropriate certain things and certain persons as if they were theirs in a different fashion from the rest of their empire. The money in our coffers, what remains in the hands of our treasurers, and what we leave in circulation among our people must be equally spared by us. The troops under our name[27] no more belong to us for this than those whom we have given particular commanders; and likewise, those who follow the profession of arms are neither more loyal, nor more

27. That is, "under our direct orders".

committed, nor more useful to our service than the rest of our subjects. Each profession contributes in its own way to sustaining the monarchy, and each has its own functions which the others would undoubtedly have a great deal of difficulty in doing without. The peasant by his work furnishes nourishment to this whole great body, the artisan by his craft provides everything for the convenience of the public, and the merchant by his cares assembles from a thousand different places all the useful and pleasant products of the world in order to furnish them to each individual whenever he needs them; the financier by collecting the public money helps to support the state, the judges by enforcing the law maintain security among men, and the clergy by instructing the people in religion acquire the blessings of Heaven and preserve peace on earth. This is why, far from scorning any of these conditions or raising one at the expense of the others, we must take care to make them all, if possible, exactly what they should be. We must be firmly convinced that we have no interest in favoring one at the expense of the others, but that whichever one we would unjustly reward will not be more grateful or esteem us more for it, while all the others will begin to complain and to murmur about it, so that the only way to reign in all hearts at once is to be the incorruptible judge and common father of all.

If, however, in spite of these reasons, my son, you can still not resist that secret inclination of most magnanimous souls for arms and for those in this profession, watch out that this particular goodwill never leads you to tolerate their excesses and that you display your affection for them by caring for their fortunes rather than by corrupting their morals.

But I did not occupy myself entirely with affairs of war; the administration of a state constantly requires cares of a different nature, and he who wants to encompass it worthily must be prepared to conquer new difficulties every day.

The unforeseen death of the Prince de Conti[28] at the end of February created a serious problem for me at the beginning of March in appointing to the governorship of Languedoc, for my

28. Armand de Bourbon (1629–1666), Prince de Conti, brother of the Prince de Condé.

brother immediately concluded that since my late uncle[29] had occupied it, he had a right to this post, and he came to tell me so himself; but I could not agree with him, convinced, after all the disorders this has caused in the kingdom, that it would be utterly reckless to place governorships of provinces into the hands of sons of France, who, for the good of the state, must have no other refuge than the court nor any other stronghold than the heart of their elder.

The example of my uncle, which seemed to be the principal title of my brother, had been a great lesson to me, and what had happened during my minority obliged me to be more careful about what might happen in yours, if it was my misfortune to abandon you in that state; to which it may be added that having resolved, after considerations that you have read, to give out governorships for only three years, it did not seem desirable to place them in the hands of persons whom one would hesitate to remove upon expiration of their term; at which my brother and my sister, who did not enter into these considerations and who were perhaps embittered even more by the speeches of some troublemakers, expressed great dissatisfaction. But, for my part, without seeming to notice anything, I gave them ample time to reconsider; and indeed, they returned by themselves a short time later and both apologized for their anger.

Meanwhile, I had awarded the governship to the Duke de Verneuil,[30] my uncle, because he had never departed from his loyalty to me and was returning from my service in England; and I was all the more certain about it since I had put intendants in that province to help him to administer its affairs according to my intentions.

But after having in this manner made my brother abandon his claim, I had many difficulties to settle with my neighbors that were no less complicated.

Although Saint-Romain had arrived just in time to disrupt the already well-advanced negotiation between the English ambassador in Spain and the King of Portugal, this could not be accomplished without leading this Prince to hope that aside from the

29. Gaston de France (1608–1660), Duke d'Orléans, brother of Louis XIII, had been governor of Languedoc from 1643 to 1660 and had participated in the Fronde.
30. Gaston-Henri (1601–1682), illegitimate son of Henry IV.

indirect aid I offered him immediately in the name of M. de Turenne, I would soon be in a position to assist him openly, and since these proposals were immensely pleasing to him, he did not fail to press constantly for their execution, even utilizing for this purpose their ambassador to England, who was then at my court for the marriage of his master. But not being prepared to comply with his desires so quickly, I worked merely to maintain his hopes, without having to change my plans prematurely. I had another problem to the north that was no easier to disentangle.

I have told you how the Swedes had initially led me to understand, through Pomponne, that they would not take sides against me; and yet they subsequently declared to me that seeing all their neighbors armed, and particularly the Danes, they could not alone remain unarmed, nor even refrain from fighting the King of Denmark if he fought the King of England.

At this surprising news, considering how much France had always esteemed the Swedes and the consequences of breaking such an old connection, or wondering rather whether the friendship of the Swedes, which might then have been lost, would not be more useful and more certain for me in the future than that of the Dutch, who were causing all the commotion, I had some difficulty in deciding what to do; but finally, not wanting to abandon my first moves, I merely ordered my ambassador to do what he could to stop the first movements of this nation, whether by displaying some initial firmness, or by being a little conciliatory, or even by proposing as a final compromise that the Danish ships would not join with our fleets and would fight the English only in the Baltic Sea. But it was not necessary to come to this, because the Swedes relented a short time later, as you shall see in its place, when they sent me an embassy.

Meanwhile the King of Denmark, alarmed by the preparations that the Swedes were making against him, had sent me Hannibal Sehested,[31] his Grand Treasurer, to press me to declare for him against Sweden, and the States of Holland, extremely pleased at this opportunity of making me break with my allies, were making continual appeals to me for the King of Denmark; while on the other hand, the Swedes were protesting to me that seeing all their

31. Hannibal Sehested (1609–1666).

neighbors armed, they could not alone remain unarmed, and that they could not even refrain from fighting the King of Denmark if he declared against England, denying any intention of doing anything against my interests. The situation was assuredly delicate, for to declare against Sweden in order to please the King of Denmark and the Dutch meant breaking with powerful allies who had been very useful to France and to leave the Swedes free to attack Denmark meant depriving myself of all the benefits of my recent treaty with this Prince. This is why, without granting either party exactly what it desired, I sought to find some compromise solutions, while furnishing the one hundred thousand *écus* that I had to pay the King of Denmark in a single payment rather than in two installments; but I eventually found a means of settling the matter, and I even obtained the assurance of the Swedes that they would not attack Denmark; which may well raise the question of whether a prince needs more strength to defend himself against the different pretensions of his allies, of his subjects, and even of his own family than he does to resist the attacks of his enemies.

And indeed, whoever considers the desires, the importunities, the murmurs to which kings are continually exposed might perhaps feel less superior to those who are confused by such commotion and might feel greater esteem for those who have retained their composure through it all. It takes a great deal of strength to keep the scale in constant balance when everyone is trying at once to tip it in favor of himself.

Out of so many neighbors who surround us, out of so many subjects who obey us, out of so many men who court us, there is not one, perhaps, without his claim; and since each one of them is entirely dedicated to giving his demand every appearance of justice, it is not always easy for the prince alone, who has so many other things to think about, to distinguish the good from the bad. With the variety of matters that arise every day, it is difficult to furnish precise rules to you on this, but there are, however, certain maxims about which you should know.

The first is that however you try, you cannot please everybody, because whatever satisfies one always displeases many others.

The second, that a claim cannot be judged by the eagerness

with which it is advanced, because passion and interest are naturally more impetuous than reason.

The third, that those who are closest to you, or whose advice you procure on the claims of others, are those on whose claims you must reflect the most yourself, or procure the counsel of people of different rank, lest although they may not otherwise be friends, they favor their colleague with the thought that his rise might set an example for themselves.

And the third,[32] that the wise monarch must always consider the consequences of a request rather than the merit of the person who makes it, because the general good must be dearer to him than the satisfaction of private individuals, and that no state in the world could last very long if its ruler were prepared to grant everything to people of merit.

It is true that a prince always displeases those whom he refuses and that the malcontents never fail to attribute any rejection of their request to the bad disposition or to the bad judgment of the sovereign. Furthermore, it is certain that it is always distressing to refuse and it is naturally more pleasant to receive thanks than complaints, but on this point, we are obliged to sacrifice our inclinations for the good of our calling; and what is worse is that this sacrifice, which usually costs us a great deal, is hardly ever appreciated; for indeed, most of those who distribute praise often appreciate only those virtues that are useful to them, and in their public compliments they seldom ignore their private interest.

The Queen of England continuing to express her ardent desire for peace, I wanted to use her as a means of defending myself against the claim of the King of Great Britain, who maintained that since I had declared war against him first, I should also send off to his domains first to negotiate the peace; for I protested to him that the lodging of this Princess should be considered as neutral ground by us, that the respect owing to her dignity should immediately suppress all those preliminary questions that are usually more troublesome than the substance of the treaties themselves, that this Queen's affection for peace would constantly furnish her with solutions for whatever difficulties might arise,

---

32. Périgny scribbled the previous maxim hastily on the margin and then neglected to renumber this one accordingly.

and that, finally, since she had made the proposal, it was only reasonable to work on it in her presence, in order not to deprive her of the honor of its success. But my principal reason for favoring this place was its advantage for constantly instructing my ministers in the course of the negotiation.

The King of England, who seemed initially to see through my plan, argued for some time against it, but he finally became more tractable and empowered Lord Holles,[33] his ambassador, as his agent, who arrived at the Queen of England's on April [26], where Lionne was present on my behalf, and where the States of Holland were represented by Van Beuningen,[34] their envoy. They began with many compliments and many expressions of good will on both sides, but when they entered into matters, the English ambassador seeing that he was not being proposed anything new, announced that he could not come to terms and received orders a few days later to withdraw from my court, where he had remained notwithstanding the war. Meanwhile, the Queen of England having to leave for the waters before this, she had asked me not to let her absence interrupt the negotiations.

But while these dealings with our neighbors were disrupted, there were others to conclude with more distant nations.

The inhabitants of Tunis, tired of the continual threat of my ships, had desired to make peace with me, and the Algerians, inspired by this same desire, went even further, offering to serve me with their own forces against England, against which I could now use all my ships, having no other enemies to fight at sea.

But truly, my strongest reason for entering into these negotiations was that their success would be glorious for this state and useful to all Christendom, whose merchants could henceforth use the French flag to protect their persons and their goods from the barbarous frenzy of these pirates, aside from the considerable number of captives that I then delivered through these treaties, for whom I felt such compassion that the moment an agreement was reached merely with the Tunisians, I sent off Du Molin[35] to free them from the hands of these infidels.

About the same time, the Pope, who desired to see the full

33. Denzil Holles (1599–1680).
34. Coenraad van Beuningen (1622–1693).
35. J. du Molin (or Dumolin), a naval officer.

execution in this state of his bulls on the doctrine of Jansen, was pressing me for the trial of the four bishops who had refused to sign the formulary that I have already described to you,[36] but the matter appeared too delicate to me to be resolved without thorough deliberation. On the one hand, I desired to satisfy His Holiness, but on the other, I feared to attenuate the prerogatives of this kingdom. I did not fail to consider how important it is to extinguish all religious novelties early, but I also knew how dangerous it is to furnish the court of Rome with examples of jurisdiction that it can later exploit; and not wanting to do anything lightly, I decided to consult my councillors through the medium of my Chancellor, the *Parlement* in the persons of the first president and the *gens du parquet*, and the clergy itself by secretly asking the opinions of a number of bishops, wanting first of all to see if any of them could furnish me with a solution that would please the Pope without disturbing the rights of my state.

The Queen of Spain[37] took fewer precautions in her reply to a proposal that I had charged the Archbishop of Embrun to make to her concerning Portugal. Knowing that the King of England was making a continual effort to revive negotiations between the Spanish and the Portuguese, I had believed that the best means to disrupt his plans for this was to have myself accepted as mediator; and although, in the final analysis, I had no doubt that the Spanish would raise some objection to this plan, I believed that I should still try it since I had nothing to lose by doing so. Thus I informed my ambassador of how best to present this matter to the regent, which actually succeeded so well that she immediately accepted my proposal. But it is true that she has not wanted to remember it since, perhaps because she had committed herself too lightly.

It is certain that there is nothing more dishonest than to go back on one's promise. Remember, my son, that the only means of

36. Alexander VII had issued a new bull against the Jansenists on February 15, 1665, but a number of French bishops, ultimately reduced to four, accepted it only with qualifications. When Louis directed this text, he had previously mentioned the formulary (see p. 25, n. 3) in the first text for 1661, where, as here, he was still for pressing the Jansenists, but he had not yet supervised the subsequent revisions for 1661, which do not mention this item.

37. Maria Anna of Austria (1634–1696), widow of Philip IV and regent for Charles II.

keeping one's word is never to give it without a great deal of thought. Recklessness is almost always followed by regret and by bad faith, and it is difficult to adhere faithfully to a foolish promise.

To deliberate calmly on all important matters and to procure the counsel of various people on them is not, as idiots imagine, a sign of weakness or of dependence, but rather a mark of prudence and of strength. Surprising as the maxim may seem, those who want to show that they are their own masters by not procuring any counsel hardly ever accomplish anything, because as soon as their ill-conceived decisions come to light they meet with so many obstacles and they are shown to be so absurd that they are themselves compelled to retract them, thus justly acquiring that very reputation for weakness and for incompetence that they had expected to guard against.

We don't have to follow any counsels that don't appear reasonable to us. Rather than dividing or weakening our authority, they very often furnish us with the means to enhance it, and we need not ever fear that they will in any way diminish the merit of our actions, since all sensible people agree that the wisdom of the prince is always at the basis of everything that is good in the administration of the state.

The difference between the wise monarch and the misguided one is that the latter will almost always be served badly even by those who are considered upstanding people in the world, whereas the former can very often obtain good service and good advice even from those whose integrity may be suspect; for indeed, it can be established as a general principle of human conduct that there is hardly anyone who does not have some natural and secret inclination toward his personal advantage and that the virtue of the most upstanding people is hardly capable of defending them against their own interests if it is not occasionally sustained by fear or by hope, so that the misguided monarch who does not know how to play on these great springs and who, without distinguishing the good from the bad, behaves equally toward all those in positions, is almost bound to corrupt even those who had joined him with the best intentions in the world, whereas with an intelligent prince, even the most unscrupulous do not dare to depart ever so slightly from the right path, because their greatest fear is to lose the confidence of their master. The desire to please him and the fear of arousing his suspicions oblige them to be very careful of themselves. They take no liberties because they believe that nothing will remain hidden, they spare no effort because they know that no merit will go unrewarded, and they are firmly convinced that they cannot make the slightest move without its affecting their reputation.

Their entirely natural feelings of self-esteem are cultivated by the wise monarch with all the skill at his command. Now he tries to impress them by his capacity to penetrate into the most hidden feelings of men and by his singular qualities, now he attaches them to his interests with unexpected graces or by acceding easily to their just desires, and now he makes them realize that it would not be safe for them to depart from their duty and that no secrets can withstand his insights for long. Indeed, he finds a means of profiting from their good qualities without tolerating any of their bad ones. He can utilize them for his affairs without burdening his subjects, he can include them in his graces without filling them with pomp or with vanity, he can give them his confidence without abandoning his authority to them, he can become intimate with them without ever ceasing to be their master; after which I am sure that you will no longer be surprised if I maintain that whatever they may contribute to his service must be attributed entirely to him, and that you will easily agree now that it is neither good counsels nor good councillors who inspire prudence in a prince, but that this prudence alone produces good ministers and provides him with all the good counsels that he receives.

I continued my usual cares in regard to religion.

At the same time that I sent Saint-Romain to the King of Portugal for my affairs, I also transferred the abbé de Bourzeys to that court in the service of God, ordering him to try in every way possible to convert Schomberg,[38] who certainly merited that special care be taken for his fortune and for his salvation, because he was a man of extraordinary merit.

A short time later, on hearing of the terrible scandal committed in Holland against a chaplain of my ambassador, I obliged

38. Friedrich Hermann (1619–1690), Count von Schomberg, German Protestant in the service of France, was unofficially providing military aid to the Portuguese. He was to die defending the English "Glorious" Revolution at the Battle of the Boyne.

the States to make full amends for this insult and to insure that it would never happen again.

Moreover, I charged Cardinal de Retz with seeking ways in Rome to settle the problems of the Sorbonne, believing that since he was himself one of its doctors, he would be the most likely to find some suitable solutions in this matter, for frankly, I wished it to be concluded as quickly as possible, convinced that with the important occupations that were awaiting me everywhere, it was better for this court to favor me.

With this same idea, I was more inclined to accept the apologies of Cardinal Orsini, who had come to offer me his excuses, and after he had expressed sincere regret for his misconduct in the affair of the Duke de Créqui, I restored the co-protectorship to him before his departure.[39]

I intended a short time later to settle a dispute over a speech by Talon, my attorney, in the affair of the Bishop of Alet,[40] for some clergymen, having been unhappy with what he had said on this occasion, had waited for the Assembly of the Clergy in order to express their resentment more forcibly; and there having proceeded to examine his plea, perhaps with a little more severity than may have been necessary, they pronounced a kind of censure against the author, from which he desired to be relieved.

I had initially tried to settle the matter by commanding Talon to make me some kind of apology with which I could satisfy the deputies of the clergy, but seeing that the assembly insisted on discussing the terms of this apology, so that there would have been no end to it, and knowing that they even demanded the removal of the plea from the records of the *Parlement*, even though they had already been published throughout the kingdom, I believed that the best thing was to let them write whatever they pleased in their so-called records, which were truly only inconsequential private *mémoires*.

39. Charles de Créqui (1623–1687) was the French ambassador insulted by the Pope's Corsican guards in 1662. When the Duke angrily withdrew from Rome, Cardinal Virginio Orsini (1615–1676), Co-protector of French Affairs, had neglected to follow suit.

40. Nicolas Pavillon (1597–1677), the Bishop of Alet, had written to Louis in August, 1664, criticizing his efforts to enforce the formulary. Talon had replied in the *Parlement* on December 12 of the same year, claiming that kings could judge dogmas.

At the end of the month of March, desiring to put an end soon to this assembly, which had been lasting since the beginning of June, I wanted it to decree promptly the special grant that it gives me only every five years and that it always makes as small as possible. This time, however, it was brought to eight hundred thousand *livres*, but this may have been partly due to my own efforts, such as on the day before their last session. Seeing quite a good number of deputies at my mass, I told them as I was leaving that I knew that they would be dealing on the following day with a matter that related to me, and that it was in just such instances that I could discover who was truly devoted to my service.

I have never failed to call to your attention, whenever the occasion has arisen, how much respect we must have for religion and how much deference we must have for its ministers, particularly in regard to their mission, that is, in the celebration of the sacred mysteries and in the preaching of the Gospel. But since clergymen tend to be a little presumptuous about the privileges of their state and since they seem to want to use them sometimes in order to escape their most legitimate duties, I feel obliged to explain to you here briefly what you should know about this matter, and which might prove useful to you, whether for making your decisions more confidently or for enforcing them more easily.

You should therefore first rest assured that kings are absolute lords and naturally have free and full disposition of all the goods possessed by clergymen as well as by laymen, in order to use them at any time as wise administrators, that is, according to the general need of their state.

In the second place, you should learn that these mysterious names of freedoms and liberties of the Church, with which they may try to dazzle you, regard all the faithful equally, whether lay or tonsured, who are all equally sons of this common mother who, however, exempts none of them from submission to sovereigns, which the Gospel itself specifically enjoins.

Thirdly, all this talk about the special purpose of the property of the Church and about the intentions of the founders is only a forced scruple, for the founders of benefices could not free their donations from the restrictions and obligations that were naturally attached to them, nor can their possessors claim to hold them with more rights and privileges than the donors themselves.

Fourthly, if the clergy have been permitted to fix their contribution in their assemblies, they cannot attribute this custom to any special privilege, since this is even practiced with the laity in most of our provinces, and it was practiced everywhere in the honesty of the early days; for indeed, at that time the mere spirit of justice sufficed to inspire each individual to give according to his means, which would never happen today; and yet all this has never prevented the compulsion of both the laity and the clergy when they have refused to perform their duty voluntarily.

But in the last place, if anyone under our dominion should put all his possessions at our disposal, it would undoubtedly be those who, holding their benefices only by our appointment, are bound to this duty not merely by their birth like most of our subjects, but also by special motives of gratitude. The taxes that are laid on them are as old as the benefices, and we have titles to them that go back to the beginning of the monarchy. Even the popes who have tried to deprive sovereigns of this power in order to take it over themselves have established our right in trying to weaken it, since they have been compelled to retract their claims specifically with regard to this crown.[41]

But there is no need here of history, of titles, or of examples; natural equity alone suffices to prove my point. Is it fair that the nobility should work and bleed for the defense of the kingdom and so often consume its wealth in the positions that it is given, that the people who have so many mouths to feed and provide so many soldiers should still pay all the regular taxes in spite of their poverty, while the clergy, who are dispensed by their profession from the dangers of war, from the costs of luxury, and from the burden of families should alone enjoy all the abundant public benefits without ever contributing anything to its needs?

The King of Poland, being still disturbed in the administration of his domains by the temerity of his rebellious subjects, the Queen his wife had so often in the course of the previous year pressed me to aid him that I had decided to do it, particularly since I had no great occupations at that time and I was given hope of placing this crown soon into the hands of a prince of my house.

41. Boniface VIII. Louis alludes to the fact that this Pope's successors had retracted his claim. See François de Mézeray, *Histoire de France* (Paris, 1643–1651), I, 700–707.

This is why I had then intended to send M. le Prince to Poland this spring with five hundred horse and six thousand foot soldiers, declaring, however, to those who were urging me to it, that I would only execute this plan if the state of my affairs still permitted it.

But a short time later, having been compelled to declare war against the English, foreseeing the difficulties that would inevitably arise over the passage of my troops, knowing that I already had a large body of them occupied in Holland, informed that the Swedes would not commit themselves as I had been led to hope, and that the Queen of Poland herself was not positive about the election that she had promised us, I believed that I should not have to overcome so many obstacles all by myself; and yet, so as not to give the Queen of Poland any grounds to complain that I had uselessly continued to flatter her hopes, I had written her a letter in the month of January to inform her of all the difficulties in her request and not to expect anything that year. But a short time later, I could not refrain, in spite of my pressing affairs, from furnishing her with two hundred thousand francs in her need, although I was under no obligation to do so.

Peace having been made between the Bishop of Münster and the Dutch, everything appeared peaceful in Germany, and since this Prince no longer needed his troops, he offered to furnish me with five thousand horse to use where and when I would please. I assuredly had reasons to accept his offer, for I could have no doubt that if I refused it, as he could no longer afford his men, they would immediately join the ranks of one of my neighbors or enemies. I knew that Castel-Rodrigo,[42] the governor of the Low Countries, wished for nothing better than to take them into his service, and I even had cause to believe that the Emperor would have been quite inclined to employ them. But still, in my position, seeing the peace negotiation with England broken, having no idea when I could use my own troops, fearing that these would add even more to the suspicions of Europe regarding my intentions, obliged to incur great expenses at sea, and not wanting to increase the burden on my people in any way, I believed that I should not commit myself prematurely to maintaining these foreigners. Thus

42. Francisco de Moura (1621–1675), Marquis de Castel-Rodrigo.

I resolved not to do anything for the present, except to thank the Bishop courteously so as to remain in a position to revive the negotiation in case of a sudden change in affairs.

Meanwhile, Count Wilhelm von Fürstenberg, having returned from Germany, had reported to me on the success of his mission and had informed me that all the princes neighboring Flanders were prepared to unite immediately in order to prevent the Emperor from transferring any troops there if I would furnish the funds to maintain the men, but because this amounted to two million four hundred thousand *livres*, I felt, for the same reasons that I have described to you in the preceding article, that I should not rush into anything and that it sufficed for the time being to advance about four hundred thousand *livres* with which to begin the levies, waiting to decide in my own good time, according to the circumstances, if it would be desirable to postpone or to advance this affair.

Meanwhile, the commotion caused to the north by the apparent decision of the Swedes to arm against Denmark had inspired the States of Holland, the Marquis of Brandenburg, and the Duke of Lüneburg to form a private league among themselves in order to prevent any new undertakings in Germany. The moment I heard of it, I had no doubt that although this connection was made with another idea, it might inconvenience me if it lasted too long; for I knew how closely the States of Holland and most of their neighboring princes were watching my actions and how frightened they were of my becoming the master of Flanders; but I did not believe I should, on the basis of uncertain speculations about the future, strive to ruin a league that was most useful to me at the present, since the Swedes, threatened by so many other powers, were obviously obliged to cultivate my friendship more carefully. Thus I merely did what I could to alleviate the suspicions of these princes regarding my plan by appearing to concentrate entirely on the affairs of England, and to remove their fear of the rise of my power by constantly giving them new tokens of my affection; without excluding, however, the possibility of disrupting this league once it had served my purposes—or at least when it could cause me some notable prejudice—for indeed, the able prince must regulate his demands and his actions according to the difference in circumstances.

There are moments when, requiring only our valor in order to succeed, we do not need any other means, but there are others when prudence being the only way to achieve our goal, it seems as if we should suspend the use of all our other virtues for its sake. There are instances when we are obliged to make a brilliant exhibition of all our power in order to terrorize our enemies, but there are others, on the contrary, when we must display moderation and restraint in order not to arouse the envy of our friends. The wisdom lies in choosing the proper policy at the proper time, and nothing renders the fortunes of a prince more stable and less changing, perhaps, than his ability to change his tone, his expression, his bearing, and his direction when necessary.

A full understanding of this maxim can teach you to distinguish, by the behavior of each prince, those who are truly able from those who merely have the good fortune to appear so, although they actually are not, for you can have no doubt that many of them have acquired their reputation for ability in the world solely from the advantage of being born in times when the general state of public affairs corresponded to their disposition, so that what they did naturally was what prudence would have dictated, and these men might perhaps have appeared extremely stupid if there had been the slightest change in their affairs or if they had been born at a time that required behavior contrary to their natural inclination; for indeed, it is no easy thing to adapt constantly to the situation. Since most men are accustomed to act emotionally rather than rationally and since they are most often guided by their disposition and by their passions, their disposition, which remains the same, almost always maintains them on the same course. Whatever disorder they may see in their affairs, whatever misfortune may befall them, they don't have enough good sense to seek its cause in their conduct. They attribute the entire thing solely to the caprice of fortune and do not consider that if, on feeling its first blows, they would have devised a new way of dealing with it, they would assuredly have guarded against the worst cruelty, for it is certain that one of the best remedies against these changes is to change with them, and you must not think, my son, that the firmness that I have sometimes mentioned to you before is opposed to the maxim that I am establishing here.

The virtue does not always lie in doing the same thing, but in always aiming at the same end; and although this end, which is none other than our glory and the greatness of our state, may actually always be the same, the means to attain it, however, are not. Those who are useful at one time may often be harmful at another. The world in which we live is subject to so many changes that we cannot possibly continue the same policy for long. The able monarch, just like the wise pilot, can sail with every wind, and experience has repeatedly shown two entirely opposite ways of acting perfectly reconciled by the difference in the times and both of them eventually producing the same happy effect.

Having learned toward the end of January that the English had entered the Mediterranean, I resolved immediately either to fight them there or to drive them out. With this intention, toward the beginning of February, I ordered the Duke de Beaufort to arm what ships he could collect as soon as possible, so as to seek out the enemy; but since many things are involved in equipping a naval expedition, the entire month of March passed before my men were ready to leave, while the English, well aware that they could not be attacked for a while, were continually blustering, boasting everywhere that as soon as my admiral left port, they would themselves seek him out and engage him in battle.

Meanwhile, I had work continue with all possible haste in order to be in a position to test their bravery and, if possible, to test it successfully. But the Duke de Beaufort having raised anchor in the month of April, the English were no longer so valiant, and as if they were content with the marvels that they had announced without bothering to perform them, they hastily left the Mediterranean Sea.

It was undoubtedly rather glorious to begin this naval campaign by compelling people who consider themselves masters of the sea to flee before those whom they had threatened, but not wanting it to end there, I resolved to have them followed soon into the Ocean Sea. It is true that I had initially resolved to reinforce my limited number of ships with the eight that were at La Rochelle for the passage of the Queen of Portugal, and I had already ordered them to be sent out, intending, however, to have them return promptly on June 15, which was the time set for the departure of this Princess; but the Portuguese ambassador indicating to me that he was distressed to see the departure of ships destined for his passage and informing me that he hoped to put out to sea any day, I did not want to delay his embarkation in any way, convinced, moreover, that although this left the Duke de Beaufort with only thirty-two ships, they would still suffice to defend themselves against any attacker. But the English having in the meanwhile returned to their ports, they would not come out again without the bulk of their fleet, without making any effort to challenge my passage.

They put out to sea again on the second of June with their full might of eighty-six ships, and so proudly that it seemed as if nothing on earth would have been capable of resisting them. The Dutch had raised anchor at the same time in almost equal strength, but although their fleet was very well equipped, it appeared so contemptible to our common enemy that they felt assured of complete victory if they could only draw them into battle.

It was apparently with this thought that Prince Rupert,[43] with twenty-three of the largest and most heavily armed ships, broke away from the rest of his men, saying that he was going out to meet the Duke de Beaufort, having no doubt that the rest of the English ships would more than suffice to destroy the Dutch.

The entire island eagerly awaited the news of this double victory; the commanders had promised it, the King felt sure of it, the people were already celebrating it. On this assumption, they had broken off all negotiations, and they had no doubt that our defeat would soon establish them in all those honors that they claim with such vanity; but their success failed to respond to their great expectations. After four days of stubborn fighting, the English were, so to speak, defeated four times, and Prince Rupert, attempting to restore the fortunes of his country with the twenty-three ships that he had detached, was himself finally compelled to retreat like the others, so that I had the entire satisfaction at that moment of seeing fortune smile upon my ally and give the States of Holland the victory after initially refusing it; yet so full and so complete that, after losing many ships, the islanders were unable to continue the battle and were compelled to run for cover to the banks of the Thames, where they could learn at leisure not

43. Rupert von Simmern (1619–1682), Count Palatine of the Rhine, the famous royalist cavalry leader of the English Civil War. The battle took place June 11–14.

to be so quick with their idle boasts; and the most remarkable thing about it was that they had to defend their exploit at home, and lest the people, whom they had flattered with the hope of victory, react violently at the news of the defeat, they were compelled to announce throughout the kingdom that they had returned victorious and even to order fires of joy for it—fires whose ridiculous merriment showed only too clearly before the eyes of all Europe the sad plight of a state where the prince could only preserve a semblance of authority by rejoicing at his own losses and by blatantly misleading his subjects in order to prevent them from breaking into open rebellion.

As for you, my son, the lesson that you must derive from the vanity and from the humiliation of the English is to observe the foolishness of those who boast about things that are beyond their control.

He who promises nothing himself makes his achievements appear even greater. Good news is most pleasantly received when it is least expected. Whoever boasts too soon about the future, whatever praise he may earn later, takes all the novelty out of his actions, because the world is prepared by his words not to be surprised by his deeds. This vain behavior usually begins pleasantly and gaily enough, but it usually ends in great sorrow and shame. Initially, he who is full of his own illusions feels gently flattered by the acclaim of the people and by the caresses of the prince, and he is secure in the thought that his blustering will dazzle his enemy. But these imaginary joys quickly vanish once it comes to blows. His men, supremely confident of an easy victory, are taken aback by unexpected resistance, whereas the enemy, ired rather than alarmed by his threats, intensify their efforts against him. He returns defeated and confused instead of triumphant. The empty and premature praises of the vulgar become taunts and imprecations, and the prince whose confidence and favor he has so unworthily captured, ired at having been taken in so easily, has only hate and scorn for him, so that all he has gained by his unfortunate vanity is the regret of having deluded himself, the shame of having misled others, and continual remorse for having precipitated his own demise.

But if individual commanders commit a great error when they become infatuated with their conduct or with their good fortune, the prince makes an even greater one when he is taken in by the vain speeches of these fops; and yet there are some every day who make decisions of war and peace on the basis of these uncertain promises and who try to use these imaginary triumphs to support their wildest claims.

The best way to avoid this problem is not to believe anyone lightly about important things and to believe even less those who are so quick with their promises, because the most capable are usually the least inclined to make promises. But the most critical question we must ask ourselves in this matter is whether what causes us to believe in these fine promises is not our own excessive self-esteem or our own excessive self-interest and whether what makes others so ready to deceive us is not their knowledge that we have already deceived ourselves.

While the events that I have just described to you were transpiring in the Ocean, although my ships had left the Mediterranean, my galleys alone were still able to uphold the glory of the French name there.

The inhabitants of Algiers, who, struck by the same considerations as the Tunisians, had like them made a proposal of peace to me, had then agreed to the terms of the treaty, which were the best ever to have been obtained from these barbarous nations; and one of its principal benefits for me was that I delivered more than three thousand French slaves from their chains in return for a very meager sum, which I believed I could without reluctance levy upon my states, it being impossible for France to put her money to better use than to free so many of her inhabitants from such miserable servitude.

Meanwhile, my galleys patrolling this sea without finding either enemies or competitors, met seven one day of the King of Spain's, only two of which were armed. Vivonne initially commanded them to lower their standard, according to my general order, but the Spanish galleys having from the eccentricity of their commander determined to let themselves be captured rather than to obey, Vivonne believed that it would be shameful for him to defeat two galleys with the twelve under his command, so that pardoning the rashness of the Spanish out of consideration for their weakness, he allowed them to pass, warning them that he would secure better obedience when they were stronger, merely ordering them, as a mark of his superiority, to sail downwind for one of their ports.

It is true that there was still another reason that might have prevented him from treating these galleys with full rigor, for they protested to him that they were carrying the belongings of the Empress, in whose favor he knew that I had issued very specific orders along my coasts, from which he undoubtedly concluded that I did not want my subjects to mistreat anyone serving her in her passage.

But in the meanwhile, thinking of the ships that I had lent to the Queen of Portugal and considering that they had to guard against two sorts of enemies, that is, the English and the Spanish, I was rather hard put to take adequate precautions against both; and nonetheless, I finally found a solution for everything. First, I placed this squadron under the command of Ruvigny,[44] a man in whom I had the highest confidence, even giving him the rank of lieutenant-general, so that his orders would not be challenged by any of his officers; then I found an excellent means of protecting myself against the English armada, without, however, appearing to have anything to do with it, by having the Queen of Portugal herself request a passport from the King of England for the voyage and return of her ships, which this Prince was so quick to grant that he did not even think of insuring himself against an advantage that I could easily have taken of this; for it is certain that if my ships had met a stronger English force on their return, they could have used their passports, and if they had met a weaker one, they were free to attack them.

But if I had enough sense to see that the English had not been prudent to ignore such an easily foreseeable eventuality, I was too magnanimous to profit from their error, not wanting to take any action even against my enemy that could ever so slightly disturb my perfect good faith.

In regard to the Spanish, the remedy was more difficult to find, because I had heard that they kept eighteen warships off the coast of Lisbon, and I could have no doubt that my ships would be fair game for them whether going or returning; for if they considered

44. Henri de Massué (c. 1605–1689), Marquis de Ruvigny, a leading French Protestant.

them as carrying the wife of the King of Portugal, they had every right to take them, since this Prince was their open enemy, and if they regarded them as belonging to me, I had no grounds to reclaim them, since I had a special treaty with Spain by which, on their frequent complaints that the French were aiding Portugal, I had consented to their taking all the ships they might find within fifty miles of the coast of Portugal. Thus the only solution I could find in order to safeguard mine from this peril was to order the Duke de Beaufort to wait for them at the Lisbon River, so as to assure their arrival and return.

But since this could delay the junction of my fleet with that of the Dutch, I sent them a courier a few days later to prevent them from raising anchor, showing them that there was no need for them to risk fighting the English fleet alone, since with the shortest wait they could be reinforced by my ships or by those of Denmark; that after their junction with both, our victory would be assured and that there was no point in taking unnecessary chances; and that in the final analysis there would not even be any need to fight the English, that if they were merely left to consume their provisions uselessly, they would be reduced to desperate straits, since they could hardly obtain more funds for putting out to sea again without causing a great deal of commotion in that unruly island.

My advice, however, was without effect, for the Dutch had already set sail when my courier arrived, and the hope of winning without our aid had even made them risk their successful battle, as you have seen in the previous sheaf.[45]

But without stopping at events whose outcome depends on the will of Heaven, it is certain that within the limits of human reason the advice that I was giving them was the best, because it was entirely without danger.

Whatever the goal may be, the surest path to it is always the one to follow. The Dutch might well have hoped to be victorious, since they actually were that time, but they had much more reason to expect victory from prudence than from the uncertain outcome of battle. Hope of victory usually draws both sides into the fight, and yet one of them is always defeated. The States of Holland, who

---

45. Périgny was in the habit of dividing the manuscripts into *cahiers*, or sheaves.

had been beaten in the previous year, might well have been once again; and perhaps if they were in good faith, they might even confess that there had been many moments on this occasion when the enemy fleet would have gained the advantage over them if some mysterious fate had not intervened to prevent it. The time to rely on good fortune is when there is no other alternative, but when we can adopt a safer course, it is a great error not to do so.

Hope is very flattering, but it is also very misleading. It inspires us to the most glorious things, but it makes us undertake many that turn against us, and I think that it would be very difficult to decide whether hope produces more good than harm in the ordinary course of human affairs. The imaginary pleasures that it makes men relish are sometimes followed by great actual sorrows. Its power to lift them beyond themselves most often serves only to worsen their fall, and since nothing is more necessary for the rise of their fortune and of their reputation than to be struck by some fine hope, there is no part of their conduct where they appear more wild and less reasonable than in their hopes.

No one can judge this matter as well as we, who see so many different hopes before us every day and who can thereby easily recognize how unwarranted they are and how much time is wasted upon them. But the best lesson that we can derive from this reflection is to examine our own more carefully, because as we now judge those of others, posterity will some day judge ours; and if we can expect that our deeds will live in her memory, we must not neglect her authority.

Just as the King of Denmark was feeling most threatened by the Swedes, the latter had sent Königsmark to me in the capacity of ambassador extraordinary, with instructions to pay me all sorts of compliments and subsequently to request my financial aid in their undertaking against Bremen.[46] I accepted his compliments most courteously, but I believed I should take advantage of this request to make them explain their commitments toward England; and in order to oblige Königsmark to clarify this matter for me, I replied to him that I could hardly be expected to aid the

---

46. Otto Wilhelm (1639–1688), Count von Königsmark. Sweden had received the Duchy of Bremen at the Treaty of Westphalia, but the city itself claimed that this cession did not apply to it.

crown of Sweden while I had such doubts as to what side it had taken.

Since these were strong words, the ambassador was obliged to reply that Sweden had always been much too happy with its alliance with France ever to want to break away from it, that in regard to her recent moves against Denmark in favor of the King of England, she had only made them under the impression that I would be taking the same side, and that she had based this assumption both on my close alliance with the King of England and on certain statements of my ambassadors to Swedish ministers concerning this subject, but that nevertheless, whatever commitments this crown may have had toward him, it was so incapable of doing anything against my interests that it was immediately offering me its mediation for the settlement of our quarrel.

This offer appeared truly too important for me to ignore, for since the Swedes could not be both judges and participants, to accept them as mediators at least meant depriving the King of England of their aid; but in order to derive the full benefit from their proposal and to insure that the Swedes, while appearing to remain neutral, did not attempt to harm me indirectly by fighting against the King of Denmark, I told their ambassador that in regard to me personally I would be very happy to accept the mediation of the Swedish crown, but that not being able to enter into any treaty in this affair without including the King of Denmark and the Dutch, I inquired of him whether Sweden intended to offer its mediation to them as well.

The ambassador had made it sufficiently clear during our conference that he intended to offer the mediation to the States of Holland, but having no authority to promise anything in regard to Denmark, he was obliged to write home for further instructions.

Meanwhile, the King of Denmark finding some cause for reassurance in the way things were going, the States of Holland intimated to me that he might be easily persuaded to join his ships to ours and that with this reinforcement we could keep the English entirely blockaded in their ports, but that this Prince having no such obligation by our treaty, he would have to be furnished some compensation for the expenses of the trip and for maintaining his ships in our seas instead of at the entrance of the Baltic, to which they believed I should contribute for the good of the common cause. But I replied to them that having for my part already spent so much on the construction and equipment of ships, being already engaged by a treaty to furnish large sums to the King of Denmark and having even paid them in advance at their urging, there could hardly be any doubt of my enthusiasm for the common cause, but that they had only to consider that a prince with as much affection for his state and for his subjects as I had was not about to distribute his most liquid funds abroad when he needed them for so many other things.

While this was being negotiated at my court, it was taken amiss in Vienna that the Chevalier de Grémonville,[47] my resident, would not attend the celebrations in honor of the wedding of the Emperor, and he was even requested to do so on behalf of this Prince. Grémonville, who was not at all certain that this festivity would be pleasing to me, defended himself against this proposal by replying that the Queen my mother having died so recently, he would have felt it against propriety and against his duty to participate so soon in public celebrations. But when the matter came to my attention, I was willing to extend this courtesy to the Emperor, and I instructed Grémonville to quit his mourning as soon as possible, even sending him a sum of money so that he could do it more conveniently.

The Duchies of Oppeln and of Ratibor, which Emperor Ferdinand II had ceded to Sigismund Casimir to reimburse him for money spent in his service during the war against the Swedes, having recently been given by the King and Queen of Poland to the Duke d'Enghien as a wedding present, this Prince asked the Emperor to invest him with it or to reimburse him for it; but although his demand was reasonable, he did not believe he had enough influence of his own to overcome the difficulties that the Emperor was raising against it, and he had recourse to my authority in order to obtain justice.

I thought that I should not refuse this assistance to a prince of my house; and having exerted myself vigorously on his behalf, for these two distant duchies which gave him only thirty-five thousand *livres* in income, the Emperor reimbursed him in France with sixteen hundred thousand *livres*, aside from one hundred

47. Jacques Bretel (d. 1686).

thousand *écus* retained by his [minister][48] for having arranged such a favorable settlement, so that the two repurchased lands came to nineteen hundred thousand *livres*, that is, sixteen hundred thousand *livres* for the Duke d'Enghien and three hundred for the minister to whom the Emperor had entrusted his interests.

There are very few corrupt ministers bold enough to rob their master openly and to appropriate his wealth directly, because their crime would too easily be detected and too inevitably be punished, but the manner of stealing that they find most convenient and most difficult to trace is to profit through others. Their tricks for doing this are of so many different kinds that I shall not attempt to explain them in detail, but I shall tell you merely that they all have this in common: they almost always increase the theft that they are meant to hide; for indeed, there is no doubt that the individual whom the minister uses for his own profit would never become involved in this transaction without finding some advantage in it for himself, so that in one way or another the prince is bearing both the illegal profit of the minister and the gain of his accomplice in the larceny. But it is certain, furthermore, that of all these fraudulent agreements, none is so prejudicial to a prince as those with foreigners, not merely because the money leaves his state, but because they destroy his reputation among his neighbors, who see in this all too clearly his neglect or his ignorance of his own affairs.

And this consideration alone seems of such weight to me that it should assuredly restrain those who engage in such transactions, but at least it must teach the prince not merely to examine men before placing them in positions, but to observe them even more carefully once they are actually handling affairs, because they are then more free to follow their own inclination to the detriment of the affairs or of the reputation of their master. This continual observation will insure that by recognizing the weaknesses of all his servants, he can dismiss them if their faults are too great; or if he finds redeeming qualities in them, he can at least guard against the prejudice that they might cause him, because knowing them as he does, he can easily distinguish which of their proposals are in his interest and which ones are in theirs.

48. Franz Ulrich (1634–1699); Count Kinski was the culprit.

Although it might appear from what I have already described to you in the course of this year that I had no lack of things to do, I was still constantly preparing for new occupations in the future.

The island of Jersey, long possessed by the English, appeared advantageously situated to me both for war and for commerce; and considering it easy to defend because of its proximity to Brittany, I thought of means to seize it at the first opportunity; but actually, this was not my principal concern then, for convinced by the initial success of the Dutch alone against England that it could not long resist our combined forces, I was already beginning to give more attention to my original designs on Flanders.

I had recently received the plans for all the strongholds in that country, but lest they were inaccurate, I had sent a new engineer into the area with orders to verify the first report. I had even given particular instructions for the careful reconnaissance of the Bouchain, with which I had intended to begin, because I did not believe I should undertake the siege of a larger stronghold at the end of the summer, aside from the fact that this one seemed to give me excellent access into the country by opening a passage on the Scheldt.

But while waiting to execute this plan, knowing how reluctant the Dutch were to see me invade the Low Countries and not wanting to have this republic as an enemy, I was always trying to think of ways to bring them around to my sentiments. I saw clearly that the only thing that made this people afraid of my arms was their concern over the proximity of such a powerful prince; but although the cause of the trouble was easy to see, the remedy was no less difficult to find, for their fright was so deep that it was almost impossible to eradicate; and what seemed to give it some basis was that I had the most right to those areas that were closest to them, some of which they even possessed. Thus I believed that if anything could lessen their fear, it would be to show them that I was willing to indemnify myself with places more distant from their lands instead of attacking those that could cause them suspicion.

But because this matter had to be handled carefully, I brought it up on purpose during a conference with Van Beuningen, in which I found an opportunity to tell him in another connection that suspicions between allies could only cause great prejudice both to their common affairs and to their private interests; at which the Dutchman, echoing the opinions of his countrymen, did not fail to reply that the only possible cause of dispute between me and the States was the undertaking against Flanders, to which I retorted that sometimes failure to reach an agreement loses important advantages for both sides; that even though I had very strong rights to their neighboring provinces, I was not incapable of fixing upon another place, giving them to understand, furthermore, that they could turn the opportunity to their own advantage and that, for my part, I would never be jealous of their rise.

Although these things were said only casually, I put them in such a way that I had no doubt that Van Beuningen would inform the States of them, and it seemed to me that this might even begin to dispose them to consider a treaty on this subject at some future time.

Meanwhile, I was preparing with all possible haste to put this plan into effect, without disclosing it to the public; for under the pretext of the English war, I had collected great stores of victuals and munitions along my coasts, and particularly in Picardy, so as to serve me for two purposes, that is, at sea against the English and on land against the Spanish, in case I should undertake an expedition against them toward the end of the campaign; and in order to convince foreigners that this preparation was destined solely for the maritime war, I had issued orders everywhere to supply the Dutch ships as if they were my very own.

I was also in a position to amass a great deal of wheat without its being observed, because I was having it collected in separate locations under the pretext of feeding my troops at my own expense during the winter. In the guise of a pleasure encampment for the amusement of the ladies, I had found a means of having tents made for my entire household cavalry as well as for some infantry units, and I had distributed the troops in the garrisons so that I could assemble [c. 32,000] foot soldiers and [c. 18,000] horse in less than [c. 15] days, without depleting any of my frontiers. Not that I was entirely neglecting the naval war, for although the English appeared too weak then to cause me any concern for a while, I was still preparing to construct and to arm new ships.

For more than two years, I had been having cannons cast thoughout the kingdom; and although during this time at least sixteen hundred pieces had been finished, half of bronze and half of iron, I was not content with this, and I had ordered many more up north, which although finished, could still not safely be transported to my ports; and finally, because my other naval stores had been exhausted, I was having them replenished as if there had been some imminent danger, a precaution that proved to be useful, because fortune having soon thereafter seemed to abandon Holland for England, I should have been ready to resist my enemies alone if they had the temerity to attack me.

They say that kings are long-handed, but it is also important for them to be farsighted and for them to foresee events long before they happen; for whether or not we want certain things to happen, it is always useful to anticipate them. What comes from us is much more complete when we have had the time to reflect upon it, and what comes from our enemies is much weaker when we are prepared for it. All our setbacks, whether in attack or in defense, are almost always attributable to lack of foresight or to insufficient reflection.

Mediocre minds must be excused for not thinking about the future, because they have more than enough cares to occupy them in the present, but greater and loftier intellects who can easily administer their ordinary affairs must use the rest of their time to look constantly beyond them, because the farther ahead they can see into things, the longer they have to think of how to react to them and are never reduced to the unfortunate necessity of making hasty decisions.

Impatience and haste are always either giving us bad counsels or are depriving us of the means to execute good ones, whereas foresight and reflection, on the contrary, prevent evils before they arise, or at least always find some way to mitigate those that cannot be prevented. Whatever opinion we may have of ourselves, it must be agreed that no statesman is so great that he could not learn more about an affair if he had a longer time to think about it. Since all things in the world are different, they must be examined carefully in order to be understood, and even the most elusive solutions to the greatest difficulties will usually occur to us if we have an opportunity to think about them.

I am well aware that it might be objected to this that plans that are executed immediately have no time to become known and are more likely to catch the enemy off balance; but far from agreeing that this maxim is always true, I am convinced that the contrary is more often the case. Since excessive haste creates a great deal of commotion, our enemy cannot fail to get wind of something and immediately looks to his safety, and if he was initially in a poor position to defend himself, it is certain that we would then be in a poor position to attack him; whereas plans that are devised long before can be handled so subtly and hidden under so many pretexts that in spite of all the warnings and all the suspicions about them, they still hardly ever fail to cause surprise. The most successful plans have almost always been the best-laid.

Important plans almost always become known with the first moves to execute them, for aside from the treason or the indiscretion of those who are employed in the preparations, mere common knowledge of the most apparent interests of princes insures that out of a thousand wild conjectures, someone chances to suspect the truth. This someone with his innocent statement convinces many others who immediately recognize its likelihood. A vague rumor quickly starts. But if one has the prudence to ignore it and the patience to wait, it passes as easily as it arose. When we do not immediately execute our plan, it is generally assumed to have been misunderstood, and aside from everything that we can do ourselves to remove suspicions about it, time itself never fails to produce contrary conjectures. While our plan matures in our mind, it gradually fades in the minds of others. Our adversaries, after their first excited preparations, eventually get tired of remaining uselessly on their guard. Their vigilance decreases each day with their fear, and indeed, when we are in the best position to attack them, they are sometimes least prepared to resist us.

Toward the end of the previous year, I had sent La Haye the younger to Turkey, and I could not, apparently, have chosen a more suitable person for this position, since none of my subjects was better acquainted with the customs of this uncivilized nation, with which he had already long been dealing under the direction of his father.[49] I had even taken the precaution to ask before

49. Denis de La Haye-Vantelet (1633–1722), son of Jean.

sending him if the Grand Vizier had any objection to his person.[50]
But in his great desire to see a French ambassador at the Porte
again, this Ottoman minister had not raised any difficulty, hiding
his aversion for La Haye so effectively as to give no grounds for
the least suspicion about it.

However, he could not always contain himself so well, for the
moment this ambassador arrived, he created difficulties over all
his requests and seemed to go out of his way to show him his
hatred. It was, however, of rather long standing. The father of
the Grand Vizier having held the same office while La Haye the
elder was ambassador, there had been some squabbles between
them, which the present Grand Vizier remembered only too well.
He even claimed that La Haye the younger had been involved in
an intrigue with the Venetians, which had led him to imagine this
man to be such a mortal enemy of the entire Ottoman nation that
it was only through his counsels that I had sent my troops into
Hungary[51] and that I had for some time permitted French
corsairs to make raids in the archipelago, raids which had greatly
disturbed the commerce of this sea.

Such being the sentiments of the Vizier, and my ambassador
constantly feeling their effects, it should not be astonishing if the
first conference between these two ministers was not very friendly
and if, things continuing to deteriorate between them, they finally
exploded at their second interview. The main point at issue between them was that an ambassador from Germany who had
arrived a few months before having received great honors from
this Vizier, mine rightly claimed that he should receive even
greater ones; to which the malevolent Grand Vizier raised such
objections and used such abusive language that La Haye, struck
to the quick on my behalf—or rather on his own, for he was well
aware that this was all due to his private quarrel—became so
enraged that not merely did he threaten to withdraw to my court,
but he threw down his roll of capitulations[52] so close to the
Grand Vizier that he claimed to have been struck by them.

This minister, who publicly performing all the sovereign

50. Ahmed Kiuprili (1635–1676), Grand Vizier since 1661, son of Mohammed.
51. See p. 113, n. 23.
52. The capitulations were commercial and extraterritorial privileges granted by
the Ottoman Empire to the French. La Haye was seeking their renewal.

functions, also receives all the honors of a sovereign in his country, was extremely shocked at this action, and taking offense both for his master, whose seal had been thrown on the floor, and for himself as the recipient of the blow, he had La Haye detained at the end of the conference in one of the apartments of the house where it had been held.

But immediately thereafter, reflecting more seriously about the consequences of his action, on the capacity of La Haye, and on my reputation in the world, he became afraid that his countrymen would hold him responsible for the effects of my displeasure. He was even confirmed in this fear both by the growing concern of the Grand Seigneur[53] on this subject and by what was said openly in Constantinople to the effect that this minister was having enough trouble in defending the Ottoman empire against a band of fishermen,[54] without rashly getting embroiled with a prince such as myself; so that in his general alarm he believed that he should patch up this affair as quickly as possible, and the first thing he tried was to send a request to Guitry,[55] master of my wardrobe, who was then in that country out of simple curiosity, to assume the negotiation of my affairs in place of the ambassador, promising him that he would be treated in such a manner that the whole earth would soon know that the sole difficulty was over La Haye and not over the rank of the prince who had sent him. But Guitry not having deemed it appropriate to interfere without orders in a matter of this nature, the Vizier was obliged to seek other solutions, and after consulting with his friends and with his family, he finally decided to send the first pasha, his brother-in-law, to pacify my ambassador with very full apologies, immediately after which he himself also paid him all the honors that he had been refusing him.

But since the most important thing to them was to arrange that I could not be displeased at what had gone on, they tried to gloss it over by sending word to me that they had acted thus only to prevent La Haye from suddenly returning to me in his anger and inspiring me to abandon the long-standing capitulations between France and the Porte.

53. Mohammed IV (1641–1687), Sultan since 1648.
54. The Venetians.
55. Guy de Chaumont (d. 1672), Marquis de Guitry.

This is what Guitry himself, who had seen this squabble with his own eyes, reported to me soon thereafter and what was also confirmed by various letters of La Haye, so that in all fairness I believed I had reason to be satisfied at the consideration that the Grand Vizier had finally shown me, which appeared all the more remarkable in view of his violent aversion for my ambassador, since he had suppressed his natural feelings for my sake and had treated his hated enemy as honorably as if he had been his esteemed friend, not to speak of the fact that these people do not usually relent so easily in their undertakings, and particularly when they believe they are sustaining their prerogatives over other nations.

However, this event did not fail to be turned against us by those who were not our friends, and particularly by the Republic of Genoa, which had recently undertaken to negotiate separate treaties with the Porte, to maintain her own ambassadors there, and to trade with it under her own flag, contrary to the ancient custom of Christendom, which had always traded under the French flag in the lands of the Turk.

But the moment I heard about this novelty, I resolved to oppose it, for even though it did not appear in itself to be very important for my other affairs, because it somehow concerned the glory of the French name and the increase of the commerce of this kingdom, to which I was then very dedicated, I felt obliged to make every effort against it that the distance and the intractable character of this nation would permit. What I decided to do was to order my ambassador to insist on the execution of the long-standing capitulations and, if this was not granted, to threaten openly to return, but not to do so, however, without waiting for new orders, under the pretext of wanting one of my ships for his passage.

It was about this time that I decided to conclude the matter of the reform of the Cistercian Order. This undertaking was begun in the year 1633. Cardinal de La Rochefoucauld,[56] a very well-intentioned man, had then worked on it zealously, but his efforts had done more to divide this order than to regulate it. The differences that had resulted from them had already exhausted every jurisdiction in the kingdom, and even Rome had already heard

56. Cardinal François de La Rochefoucauld (1558–1645).

about them repeatedly when I resolved to take them upon myself, after considering the fame of this order in my state as well as its diffusion in foreign countries, that the tumult of its latest disputes had been a public scandal, and that the kings my predecessors had often successfully assumed such functions, so that it seemed like a praiseworthy effort for me to restore such a famous order to its original saintliness.

It is true that knowing at the start how complicated this affair was, I believed that in the midst of my great occupations I should not attempt to undertake the first and most difficult discussion myself, and I referred this care to the Pope, who undoubtedly has more experience than anyone else in disputes of this type, reserving the right to enforce his bulls insofar as I found his opinion in keeping with reason and with the ancient liberties of this monarchy. But truly, this solution did not save me very much trouble, for even though the Pope responded to my request by doing everything possible to study the matter thoroughly and that he had actually met with an assembly of the most learned cardinals to settle things in keeping with the original character of this order, it seemed as if the sight of his brief rekindled all the disputes, some wanting the immediate implementation of the bull as it was and others demanding an entirely different one.

The former, who appeared the most sincere, were supported by the authority of their general and actually seemed to desire nothing more than to reunite all the members under the authority of their true head. The latter, who wanted to appear the most zealous, but who perhaps were only the most factious, were led by some individual abbots and warmly demanded a more austere reform, apparently expecting to disguise by this specious pretext their conspiracy to free themselves from the jurisdiction of their general. Thus I was obliged to have the entire affair considered in my presence, and with the great number of arguments or of advocates the parties had collected, my council was even divided in its opinion, so that I was reduced to the necessity of deciding the matter myself, which rarely ever happened; for although my decisions did not actually need to be authorized by numbers, I was always quite willing to go along with the majority.

My judgment was in favor of the bull and of the general, for aside from factual reasons that would be tedious to relate to you,

I considered that it was advantageous for the state to retain under the obedience of the head of this order all the foreigners who offered to submit to it under the conditions of the brief, that after having referred this dispute to the Pope, who had actually discussed it very carefully, there was no reason to insult him by ignoring his judgment, and finally, that it was about time to recall this religious community to the authority of its superior.

But to come to the special lesson that we can derive from this, know that on such occasions your maxim must always be, like mine, to establish insofar as possible the authority of those in command against those who strive by conspiracy and by sedition to escape from their control. Both public and private affairs can only be maintained in their regular course through this general subordination of the different persons in a state.

Since it is certain that kings cannot give orders directly in every place where they hold power, nor watch with their own eyes over all the subjects under their dominion, there is no doubt that in order to maintain public discipline they must lend vigorous aid to those who administer their authority. The same spirit of sedition that leads a subordinate to act against his superior would assuredly lead him to conspire against ourselves if he were in a position to do so. The example of authorized libertinage is the most dangerous in the world. It is unjust to allow the weak to be oppressed, but it is perilous to sustain the temerity of rebels. A subordinate who is persecuted by his superior must always find a secure refuge in the supreme authority of kings, but those who hope to advance themselves by meddling in things that are beyond them or want to weaken the reputation of the people who are instituted over them must be met with scorn and punishments rather than with hospitality and rewards.

I am well aware that some princes have not shared these sentiments and have even taken pleasure in secretly turning people of low extraction against their lawful superiors, undoubtedly expecting to derive useful insights from these interested parties. But aside from considering this method to be unworthy of noble souls, I am convinced, furthermore, that it very rarely succeeds. The reports that we get from this sort of people in the guise of zeal for our service are so corrupted by self-interest and by passion that it is impossible to be certain about them. The prince is more often confused than enlightened by them. They are infinitely more trouble than they are worth, and unless this so-called information concerns matters of the utmost importance, it is best and most proper to ignore it.

A short time after declaring war against the English, having no doubt that there would be violent hostilities in the islands that my subjects occupied jointly with them, I had promptly embarked eight hundred men, even drawing them from the strongholds nearest to the sea so that they could come to the aid of their countrymen more quickly; but I learned a short time later that for all their haste, my wishes and my good fortune had preceded them to the defense of these colonies.

It just so happened that the French and the English on the island of Saint-Christophe had learned of the declaration of war at the same time, but since the state of their affairs was very different, so also were their decisions. The French, who numbered no more than six hundred on the entire island, had concluded that it would be more advantageous to maintain the peace than to come to blows and had even made an unsuccessful overture about this to the English, who, numbering at least six thousand and having no doubt that they were the stronger, had immediately resolved to put all the French in the area to the sword, and they had even been commanded to do so by their viceroy, the original order having been found in the pocket of one of the dead after the fight. But this decision was easier to make than to execute, for the French, spurred by the greatness of the peril, acted with such valor and haste that, having fought four different battles in a single day against various enemy troops, they defeated them in every instance, killing a thousand of the most valiant; and finally exhausted and without powder, they nevertheless displayed such determination that they compelled the rest of the enemy to capitulate on conditions that were shameful for people who were still three times stronger than we were. The principal ones were that they would immediately surrender all their forts and that they would either leave the island or lend me their oath of fidelity. Faced with this choice, most preferred to leave, selling their goods to the French at a pittance and peacefully withdrawing to the nearby islands. After this success, with the eight hundred men whom I have already mentioned to you also arriving to reinforce these French colonies, I could have no more doubt about the security of this island.

Thus the news of war abroad did not prevent me from letting my people at home enjoy all the advantages of peace, for aside from continuing to expand the commercial and manufacturing establishments that I had begun, I also sought to open new ports or improve the existing ones, both on the Ocean and on the Mediterranean. I even devised the more unique and more important plan of joining the two seas together; and this undertaking appeared all the more glorious to me since it had so often been contemplated in past times without ever having been fully realized. But I was not content to procure all sorts of benefits for my subjects; I also took care to safeguard them from all the misfortunes that could threaten them.

Having learned that the plague was beginning to break out along my frontiers, such as at Dunkirk and at Gravelines, I spared no effort, in my paternal affection for my people, to aid those who were there. But since the most important thing was to prevent the infection from spreading to the other provinces of the kingdom, I did not merely issue the customary orders for such occasions, but I even commanded that the pay of each soldier in the infested areas be increased by two *sols* per day, so that this inducement would discourage the garrisons from deserting and from infesting the nearby areas.

With the same thought, when I decided to recall the troops that I had sent to Germany for the service of the Dutch, I ordered Pradel,[57] their commander, to take all possible precautions to prevent their bringing back some infection from the contagious diseases that were infecting all our neighbors, which he did very scrupulously.

When this Pradel arrived at my court, I gave him a private audience in order to learn more from him about his voyage, wanting to know confidentially in what manner my troops and my officers had acted, how our allies had treated them, the strengths and weaknesses of the men and strongholds that he had seen, and finally, whatever might contribute to my affairs or to the discipline of my troops.

57. François de Pradel (d. 1690).

My care for those who served at my side was such that most young French gentlemen wished eagerly to come to learn their profession there and even many retired officers were eager for service that brought them into such close contact with me, so that I was under constant pressure to give out posts in my body-guard; and certainly, for my part, I would have been most happy to oblige them, but the number of posts always being filled to overflowing and the great expenses of the state making me hesitate to increase them prematurely, for everyone to whom I had the pleasure of granting this grace, I had the vexation of refusing it to one hundred. This is why I then resolved to make some increase there, although as sparingly as possible.

Meanwhile, there arose a dispute among my allies that might have been harmful to our common interests if it had not been pacified promptly. The last battle between the Dutch and English fleets having gone against the Dutch, their principal commanders were disputing about the responsibility for the misfortune; and although, actually, Vice-Admiral Tromp was at fault for having undertaken an unsuccessful action without orders from his superior,[58] his reputation for valor among his countrymen had created a kind of party for him, from which some disorders were to be feared. This is why I carefully intervened to soothe things on both sides, and if I could not entirely prevent this republic from giving Tromp some token of its displeasure, I at least had the satisfaction of seeing this affair settled quietly.

On the other hand, seeing that the quarrel between the Electors of Mainz and the Palatine over the right of *Wildfang*, about which I have already told you something, was already reaching the point where it could exhaust the strength of these two princes, I sent them Courtin,[59] one of my masters of requests, to try to reconcile them.

I had recently concluded a less important dispute that concerned me more directly. Immediately after the marriage of the Duke of Savoy, there had arisen some difficulty over the treatment that my ambassador was to receive from the Duchess his wife; and

58. Cornelis Tromp (1629–1691), Rear Admiral of Holland, was serving under Michiel Adrianszoon de Ruyter (1607–1676). The battle took place on August 4.
59. Honoré Courtin (1626–1703).

the cause of this dispute was that this Princess demanded exactly
the same honors as the Duchess my aunt. But I submitted to the
Duke of Savoy that even though his wife bore the same title as
his mother in his domains, he could not expect them to be considered as persons of equal rank in the rest of the world; that the
character of daughter of France carried certain prerogatives that
no other princess had the right to assume; that originally they
even preserved the hereditary title of queen, whatever prince they
might marry; and that if they had been deprived of this title in
recent times, they had nevertheless been left with most of its distinctions, so that the respects that were paid to them for this
reason could not set a precedent; and the Duke finally found these
arguments so convincing that he abandoned the claim of his
wife.

The Duchess of Mantua and the Pope having subsequently had
some squabble over an inquisitor and each of the two parties
having taken care to inform me of its claims, I had resolved to
employ my mediation in concluding this affair when it was settled
by itself.

Moreover, I followed the same policy with my own subjects as
I did toward my neighbors, letting no dispute develop between
persons of standing without trying to pacify it immediately,
either by reason or by authority; for as for me, I have never believed in the maxim that the art of reigning consists principally of
spreading division and disorder everywhere. The quarrels between our allies, by engaging us to take sides sooner or later,
create problems all the more serious for us in that they divert us
from our own, and the squabbles between our principal subjects,
by obliging each side to strengthen itself against its enemy, divert
them both from serving us.

I am well aware that there are weak and shaky princes who, not
being able to sustain themselves with their own strength, expect
their aid from private animosities and who, not being capable of
securing obedience by authority, try at least to become necessary
by intrigue, but I cannot agree with any of their reasoning. Their
subtlety in creating differences to arbitrate between their subjects
may actually secure extraordinary deference for them at certain
times, but it cannot fail to produce very dangerous consequences
for them sooner or later. Once two men of quality have fallen out,

they have friends on both sides to take up their quarrel. There is not a person in the state who does not offer himself to one of them. Each side holds its councils and its assemblies. Their common interests unite them more closely every day. The prince cannot speak to anyone who will not try to influence him in one way or the other. His council is most often divided, and what is more, he is often obliged to divide himself and to take from one to give to the other, so that there being nothing sure or consistent about his conduct, he can never do anything useful or glorious.

Moreover, if there arises some internal disorder, the rebels, always favored by one or the other of the conspiracies, already find well-known leaders, organized councils, and places of assembly among them. And if there is an external enemy, the weaker of the two factions is always capable of seeking to obtain his support; for indeed, after hating its adversaries for so long, it will adopt any means it can of harming them, and fearing nothing so much as having to yield to them, it prefers to work toward the devastation of its own country rather than see it flourish under their authority; as we have discovered so clearly from the example of Navarre, which Ferdinand could never have usurped in almost a single day if the feud between the Gramonts and the Beaumonts had not safely and easily put him in possession of the entire country.[60] And although truly, my son, you seem destined for too much power to have to fear such problems, it is always wonderful, however, to accede to the maxims that I am teaching you, if only for the glory of practicing them and for the sake of your allies and of your subjects.

A short time before, I had learned of the rather extraordinary action that La Feuillade[61] had taken without telling me in the very heart of Spain, for knowing that Saint-Aunay, a stubborn man who had angrily withdrawn from my kingdom, had written to Le Tellier in terms that could not be pleasing to me, and hearing that he had subsequently even adopted a most insolent emblem, he went secretly to Madrid to oblige him either to fight or to retract; at which the surprised Saint-Aunay immediately gave him a note in his own hand disclaiming the emblem. But this did

60. See Mézeray, *op. cit.,* II, 78–79, 350.
61. François d'Aubusson (d. 1691), Count de La Feuillade, a sycophant of the first order, brother of the Archbishop of Embrun.

not entirely conclude the affair, for Saint-Aunay having subsequently attempted to explain away the writing, still more Frenchmen returned to Madrid without my leave to make him speak more explicitly; and indeed, they intimidated him so badly that he immediately rendered me submissions that I in no way desired of him. With such zeal common to all my subjects, I learned that commanders everywhere sought to please me by keeping their troops in good condition, so that some even maintained a greater number of men than I was paying them to maintain.

It was at this time that Queen Christina,[62] having resolved to approach Sweden to plead for her interests there, asked me to support her with my good offices, and I obliged her by ordering my ambassador to do this on the spot. But to be of even greater service to her, I decided to speak personally about them to the ambassador of the crown of Sweden at my court, who was instructed to assure me that this Queen would be favored in everything that was not contrary to the good of the state.

However, I had more important matters to negotiate with this crown, on which its ministers were not so precise, but in order to expedite their deliberation, I also postponed my reply on what they wanted most from me: financial aid for the undertaking against Bremen, and delayed payment from day to day on a sum of one hundred thousand *écus* that were owed to them from some previous treaties, because I had no doubt that their interest in these affairs would influence them more than anything else I could do. And indeed, they authorized me soon thereafter to assure the King of Denmark that they would not attack his domains, which was undoubtedly doing great violence to themselves for my sake, because aside from their conflicting commitment to England, their assurances obliged them to request that I obtain similar ones from the Danish crown, as shameful as they considered it to deal on equal terms with a weaker power.

This point settled, I paid them the hundred thousand *écus* that I owed; but in order to keep them interested in the articles that still remained to be resolved between us, I continued to withhold my decision on their request for aid against Bremen, without,

62. Christina of Sweden (1626–1689), eccentric daughter of Gustavus Adolphus, was Queen from 1632 to 1654, then abdicated, converted to Catholicism, and settled in Rome.

however, giving them any cause for complaint against me; for I pointed out to them that the season already appeared too far advanced to execute anything important; that any delay was owing entirely to them; that for my part, I had done my utmost to press their ministers to conclude our treaty, which could naturally have included this article; that they had not even presented my deputies with their claims, which I would not have known if it had not been for the special courtesy of their ambassador in recently providing me with a copy, to which I had immediately replied so as to save my agents from having to send me a formal request for it, so that the crown of Sweden had only itself to blame for the slow progress of this affair.

I was then beginning, of course, to see the Swedes much disposed to accommodate me on the most important point, for they had made it sufficiently clear that they were willing to ally with me against the house of Austria. They had already sent word to me through their ministers that they desired nothing better than to see my armies in the Low Countries, so that they could for their part invade Germany; and that it was for this purpose that they were working so hard to make peace between us and England and that they had sent an ambassador to the King of Great Britain so as to offer him their mediation as they had offered it to us. But the mood in this island was still not very receptive to such offers, for although they talked as if they wanted to accept them, they placed the difficult condition upon them that the negotiation take place on their soil.

The Swedes uselessly portrayed to him that this affair having to be negotiated with me, it was useless to make such a proposal to me, for the English maliciously circulated that this not being my quarrel but merely that of the States, they felt fully justified in claiming this prerogative over them. But the actual cause of this chicanery was that the King of Great Britain was then secretly angry at the Swedes, whom he could still not accept as mediators, having so recently hoped to have them as allies.

Sweden had, however, excused her failure to execute their treaty by maintaining that it had engaged to aid them against Denmark only if she had no other problems elsewhere, and that this obligation did not hold then because she was about to be attacked by the Muscovites any day and could not sacrifice her own defense to that of her neighbors; but the excuse about the Muscovites appeared so obviously contrived that even though the English had no alternative but to accept it, they still harbored a deep vexation for having been left in the lurch.

This example shows two things, my son: one, that giving their word will not restrain those who are naturally in bad faith; and the other, that in executing our plans we can take full confidence only in our own strength. Even though the honest prince will always keep his word, he would not be prudent to rely entirely on that of others, and although he may not feel capable of misleading anyone, it does not follow that he is not capable of being misled.

Once one has resolved to go back on his word, it is easy to find the pretext. No clause is so precise that it is not subject to some interpretation. Each one speaks in treaties according to his present interests, but most try to explain their words later according to whatever new circumstances arise; and when the reason for making a promise no longer holds, there are few persons who will hold to their promises. But it may be added here for your special instruction that this conduct is more typical of states that are directed by many heads than of those that are governed by a single person.

Princes, in whom a brilliant birth and a proper upbringing usually produce only noble and magnanimous sentiments, can never entirely eradicate these good principles from their character. As dim as their idea of virtue may be, it always gives even the worst of them a kind of repugnance for vice. Their hearts, trained from an early age in sentiments of honor, become so accustomed to them that they cannot entirely corrupt it, and their constant desire for glory makes them disregard their own interest in many cases, so that they are afraid of nothing as much as to be blamed for an obvious breach of faith. But it is not the same with these people of middling condition who govern aristocratic states. The decisions of their councils are based exclusively on the principle of utility. The many heads who make up these bodies have no heart that can be stirred by the fire of beautiful passions. When the joy of doing right, the blame for behaving shamefully, gratitude for favors, and the memory of services are divided among so many persons, they lose all their effect, and it is interest alone, whether private or of the state, that guides their conduct. You must not draw the conclusion from this, my son, that there should be no alliances at all with such states, for on the contrary, I hold that an able prince must use every means in order to achieve his purposes, but you should know merely that our agreements with republics or with other states that resemble them must be based on the assumption that whatever good or harm we may do to them, they will never fail to court us whenever we make it worth their while, and they will never hesitate to abandon us once it seems the safer course.

While I was pressing, as I have told you, for the conclusion of my treaty with the King of Sweden, expecting it to create a powerful diversion to the aid that Flanders could receive from the Emperor, I was making another for the same purpose with all the German princes whose lands bordered on the Low Countries; and it was already signed by some of the most powerful and about to be signed by the others. The principal article was not to allow any troops to pass from the lands of the Emperor to those of the Spanish in Flanders.

But these thoughts were somewhat interrupted by the outcome of the second battle between Holland and England, for after the victorious Dutch had virtually blockaded the English on the banks of the Thames during the entire month of July, the English were finally compelled by the murmurs of their entire island to put out to sea and to venture a new battle in which they were more fortunate than the first time. The sole cause of their success was that Vice Admiral Tromp attempted to pursue an English squadron too far and thoughtlessly took a good part of the Dutch fleet with him, so that Admiral Ruyter was much weaker in number than the enemy and was compelled to withdraw before them. His retreat, of course, had been orderly, and he had caused almost as much damage to the enemy as they had inflicted on him, but most of his ships had been so badly mauled that they required a good deal of time for repairs, during which the English remained the unchallenged masters of the entire Channel.

But while this event seemed to prevent us from combining in order to attack them openly, I sought to find secret ways of weakening them. On the one hand, I encouraged the remainder of the Cromwell faction to create some new disturbances in London; and on the other hand, I maintained contacts with the Irish

Catholics, who, always extremely dissatisfied with their condition, always seemed prepared to make an effort to ameliorate it.

With these thoughts, I listened to the proposals of Sidney,[63] an English gentleman, who promised me that for one hundred thousand *écus* he could produce an uprising soon, but I felt that this was a little too much to risk on the unsubstantiated word of a fugitive. This is why I merely offered him twenty thousand *écus* in cash, with the promise to send the rebels all the aid they would need, as soon as they could put it to good use.

It was at that time that I sent Trubert back to negotiate with the Tripolitanians and with the King of Tafilet,[64] who, having recently defeated Gaysland, the new ally of the English of Tangiers, seemed to me quite capable of becoming my ally against them in Africa.

Meanwhile, the great and continual expenses involved in these various plans, combined with other necessary ones on land and sea, obliged me to economize carefully wherever I could. With this idea, I reduced the allowance of infantrymen from one *sol* to six *deniers*, and I set that of the cavalrymen at two *sous* instead of three.[65] I abolished most of the commissioners of war, who, through past mismanagement, had been multiplied needlessly. I even postponed building on the Louvre, and when my galleys returned at the end of the month of August, I decided not to go to the expense of re-equipping them, seeing no pressing need for it.

There arrived at my court a gentleman dispatched by the King of Poland[66] to ask me for more aid, to whom, in view of the difficulties in his request, he had issued two commissions; one as mere envoy under the pretext of offering me condolences on the death of the Queen my mother, the other as ambassador extraordinary in order to make me the aforementioned request, leaving the bearer free to use either one, depending on his hopes for the negotiation. When I was informed of these details, not

63. Algernon Sidney (1622–1683).

64. André-François Trubert (d. 1699), Commissioner of the Navy. Mulei-Archi (d. 1672), King of Tafilet and Fez.

65. Actually, the allowance of infantrymen had been one *sol* six *deniers*, or 18 *deniers*, as correctly indicated on p. 153.

66. Wladyslaw Rey, Palatine of Lublin and Chancellor of the Queen.

wanting the King of Poland to declare an embassy for nothing, I had his minister counseled to appear before me only as an envoy; but whether to satisfy his personal vanity by a loftier title, or to gain some unknown advantages for his king, he would not follow my advice and immediately assumed the title of ambassador.

I received him, for my part, with all the customary honors, and although I had initially resolved not to fulfill his request, I could not, nevertheless, refrain from immediately granting him a rather large sum, for the Bishop of Béziers,[67] my ambassador, had informed me that the Lithuanian army, the only force and authority remaining to the King of Poland, being on the verge of mutiny, he had believed he should, even without my orders, engage to pay it a quintal, that is, a certain portion of its pay; and I confess that I could not disavow a promise made for such a good reason, and truly, I soon had occasion to be pleased about it, because the continued devotion of this army to the service of its prince immediately forced his rebellious subjects to return to their obedience.

At that time, I also paid twenty-five thousand *écus* in arrears on pensions to some nobles of that kingdom, who might one day be useful to me in placing the Polish crown into the hands of a prince of my blood.

The time, however, did not yet seem very ripe for this plan, for the Estates of Poland, stirred by various factions, were extremely reluctant to elect a successor to their king while he was still alive, so that their ambassador extraordinary suddenly asked me a question during one of our conferences that might have embarrassed a less competent prince. He wanted to know whether or not I still insisted on the election. The proposal was delicate in itself, but what seemed to make it even more so was the disposition of its author, for I was reliably informed that he was a difficult person. This is why, thinking that I could not speak too carefully, I simply told him that I saw no way of pursuing this plan at present, but that if, as I hoped, things would change someday, I might also change my mind; and it seems to me that this is precisely what I should have replied to him, since if I had said more, I would have given this troublemaker a means of getting me embroiled with the

67. Pierre de Bonzi (1631–1703), Florentine in the diplomatic service of France.

Estates of Poland, and if I had said less, I would too easily have renounced all my important moves to advance this claim, whereas the way I spoke could disturb neither the sensibilities of this nation nor the honor of France.

And with this example I shall take the opportunity of calling to your attention how much weight the words of princes carry in the outcome of their affairs; for although I am always telling you about my conferences with foreign ministers, I would not counsel just any sovereign to put himself to this test, and I hold that those of limited intelligence should abstain from this function rather than display their weakness before all their neighbors. A great many monarchs might be capable of conducting themselves wisely if they have the time to procure counsel, although they might not suffice in handling their affairs by themselves against able and experienced men who never approach them unprepared and who are always seeking the advantage of their masters. Whatever general notion we may have been given of the subject under consideration, a foreign minister can always catch you by surprise, and what is worse is that a sovereign cannot then disavow his mistakes as he would those of a minister, but that in an instance of this nature he must either suffer in silence for what he has rashly promised or retract it shamefully and confess his own incompetence before the whole world.

But it is not merely in important negotiations that princes must watch what they say: this is also true of their most intimate and most ordinary conversations. Unpleasant as this restraint may be, it is absolutely necessary for those in our position to speak of nothing lightly. Because a sovereign has the authority to do everything, he is not free to say everything. On the contrary, the greater and more respected he is, the more circumspect he must be. Things that would be meaningless in the mouth of a private individual often become important when spoken by a prince. He cannot show the slightest disdain toward anyone without wounding him to the heart. What may console someone for a stinging mockery or a disdainful comment is either the expectation of soon repaying it in kind or the conviction that the words had not made any impression; but whoever has been insulted by his sovereign feels his affliction all the more keenly in that he has none of these consolations, for indeed he may well speak badly of the prince in return, but he would have to do so in secret and cannot let him know about it, which is the sole delight of vengeance, nor can he believe that the words had fallen on deaf ears, becuase he knows with what acclaim all the sentiments of those in authority are greeted.

And kings must not delude themselves on this matter into thinking that these sorts of injuries are forgotten by their recipients or that they can remain unknown to them. We have said elsewhere that whatever they do or say is always known sooner or later, but it may be specified that the very persons to whom they speak and who pretend to approve their mockery are often offended privately, particularly when the prince directs it against people who are devoted to his service, because they are afraid of receiving the same treatment.

One of the best solutions for this is to do more listening than talking, because it is very hard to talk a great deal without saying too much. Even a pleasant conversation about seemingly unimportant things will sometimes lead into the most hidden ones, and there are some people who simply don't know how to stop. Little harm has ever come from not having said enough, because what has been omitted from the first conversation can almost always be included in the second, but infinite misfortunes have resulted from having said too much, because what is once said cannot be unsaid.

Indeed, there can be no doubt that one of the most dangerous habits for princes to develop is that of talking too much, since the success of their greatest plans usually depends on secrecy, whereas those who surround them are continually trying to penetrate their decisions, on which depend both the fate of individuals and the fortunes of the public; for although respect prevents them from being asked direct questions, no subtle trick is left unused in order to make them disclose their thoughts, and they can only guard against this pitfall by exercising extreme restraint in speaking. But it will not be difficult for you to acquire this restraint if you consider how much respect excessive liberty can lose for us; for indeed, it is evident that great talkers often talk great nonsense and that many people who might appear very sensible if they did not speak, destroy themselves by making outrageous statements, undoubtedly a greater drawback for a prince than for a private individual, because the sovereign must do every-thing to preserve or even to increase everyone's esteem for him.

The Empress finding favorable weather for going to Finale, she made it there without having to drop anchor on our coasts, where I had ordered, however, that she be given every welcome.

Not that the conduct of the Spanish obligated me in any way to do this. I was always receiving complaints of ill treatment from my subjects who had business in Flanders, and there was no doubt that this involved some secret order of Castel-Rodrigo, its governor, for Frenchmen were robbed or murdered without anything ever being done about it. But after having employed every possible means to put a stop to this mistreatment, I also allowed some of the Spanish couriers passing through France to be robbed; and yet, in cases of such reprisals, I commanded my officials to proceed against the thieves according to law, but since they were never clearly identified, they could not be punished.

At the same time, well aware that an offensive and defensive league was under negotiation between the Spanish and the English, and knowing how much prejudice it could cause to my affairs, it occurred to me that I might delay its conclusion by mak-ing a most unlikely proposal which at least could do no harm. This was to offer the Spanish a similar league and on even better terms, because I also included Portugal in it. I could see clearly, of course, that no sensible person would take this overture seriously, because it was in no way consistent with my true inter-ests, but I thought that it could at least entertain the more simple members of the council for the time being—and this succeeded so well that not merely did it divide the Spanish council for several days, but there were even some people in Madrid who took it upon themselves to write long disquisitions on whether it was better for their prince to ally with me or with the King of Great Britain.

In the meanwhile, the Duke de Beaufort appeared with my fleet at the entrance of the Lisbon River, where he found eighteen Spanish ships that lowered their pennant as soon as they saw him and saluted him with their cannon at his command. The Duke replied with his artillery, but as for the pennant, he would neither lower it like them nor even dip it, which the Spanish could hardly have liked, although they did not dare to show it. They even did something else in their astonishment, for they immediately abandoned the Berlengas, which are two islands they had seized at the mouth of that river,[68] although my admiral had not made the slightest move to attack them, and that on the contrary, he had positively refused the suggestions of the Portuguese that he do so, correctly maintaining that he had no orders from me to engage in hostilities against the subjects of the Catholic King. However, my fleet was received most honorably and joyfully in Portugal, and truly, I was not displeased in letting that country see that England was not alone in being capable of putting ships out to sea. My admiral remained there for a while, because I had ordered him not to return until the Queen of Portugal had arrived, wanting to see not merely the conclusion of the marriage of this Princess, but also the safe return of the ships that I had lent to her.

Meanwhile, I had to contend with the Dutch, who were continually pressing me to bring up my fleet, which I would undoubtedly have hesitated to do before the arrival of the new Queen if necessity had not forced my hand; but the Duke de Beaufort having consumed his victuals during the long voyage of this Princess and the Portuguese offering him none of good quality, he was compelled to raise anchor on the twenty-second of July and make for La Rochelle, where he arrived on the twenty-third of the following month. Now although truly, as you see, this return had not been advanced for the States of Holland, I believed, however, that I could gain some merit with them for it, and actually I even tried to make it useful to them. For this reason, when I heard about it, I had them informed of it by special courier; and so as to join them more quickly, I had my ships replenished promptly by boats that had long been loaded for this purpose.

I also reversed, in their favor, my decision not to bring up my fleet beyond Brest or Belle Isle and commanded it to sail directly to meet our allies, which it did so faithfully that when the squadron that had taken the Queen of Portugal returned depleted in the course of this voyage, they would not even wait to resupply it and drew the necessary provisions from the other ships. Finally, to eliminate any cause for delay, I had taken the precaution of

68. Actually, c. 50 miles to the northwest.

settling all questions concerning the junction and what each party was to do in every eventuality.

This negotiation having been initiated through letters, I had subsequently sent Bellefonds[69] to Holland to continue it; and by the time that the Duke de Beaufort had reached my ports there was nothing more to settle except for the salute that he was to receive from the Dutch fleet. Admiral Ruyter insisted that after having made the first salute, he was to be answered in the same manner, but this did not pose any problem with people in no position to challenge my rank. Moreover, in order to please them in every way I could, I had ordered my ports to be opened to their merchant fleet, which they were then eagerly awaiting, even sending some small boats out to inform it so that it could come to anchor there with greater confidence; and in short, I had left no stone unturned either for the particular advantage of the Dutch or for the good of the common cause.

It was for this same reason that I sent Bellefonds, who had drawn up the terms of the junction with them, to inform the Duke de Beaufort of the details, and I ordered him, furthermore, to remain at his side instead of Terron[70] during this entire campaign; for although Terron had already served with distinction as an intendant on my ships, I did not want to reassign him to them, because the Duke de Beaufort had taken a dislike to him, this being no time for squabbles that could divert their attention from my service.

I had at the same time issued orders for all my maritime strongholds to send out small boats constantly for news of the enemy and to inform my admiral promptly of what they might learn, so that he could always know from shipboard what was going on in the Channel; and on the other hand, to prevent the enemy from being informed of his voyage, I had closed all my ports at the moment of his departure, but I revoked this order soon thereafter, because it appeared too prejudicial to me for commerce.

A little earlier, having cause to think that we would inevitably be fighting the English fleet, I had designated six hundred men of my household for service on my ships, and I had ordered the

69. Bernardin Gigault (c. 1630–1694), Marquis de Bellefonds.
70. Charles Colbert du Terron (d. 1684), first cousin of Jean-Baptiste Colbert.

Duke de Beaufort to pick them up at Dieppe; but he would have been obliged to embark a much larger number if I had not restrained most of my nobility, who immediately asked my leave to go along. There were even some who, seeing that I refused all such requests, ventured to leave without letting me know, thinking that I would easily accept the accomplished fact; and although basically I saw clearly that they had acted only out of a laudable desire to serve me and to distinguish themselves, I did not believe that I should tolerate their disobedience. Thus I sent two couriers after them, one of whom had the Chevalier de Lorraine and the Marquis de Villeroi arrested at Peronne on their way to join the Dutch fleet; word of the other carrying orders to my ships for the imprisonment of the Duke de Foix, the Count de Sault, and the Marquis de Ragny made them return to Paris, where they were put in the Bastille for two weeks.[71]

Meanwhile, I was impatient for news of the junction, for I had heard from various sources that my ships had entered the Channel, but I was told first that the English and the Dutch were fighting, at which news I immediately warned the Duke de Beaufort to advance with caution and to watch out that if the enemy got the upper hand they did not fall upon him with all their might; but this report proved to be false the following day and was followed by a much more disturbing one, for I learned that although the two fleets had come very close to each other, they had nevertheless separated without a battle, the English having stationed themselves at the Isle of Wight, right at the entrance of the Channel, while on the other hand, the Dutch had withdrawn more than thirty leagues. This news was all the more astonishing since it was the last thing that could have been expected after my recent agreements with the States of Holland.

I immediately sent off various couriers to inform the Duke de Beaufort of this surprising event, but as he could apparently not receive my orders in time and was threatened with defeat if he fell alone and unsuspecting into the hands of the stronger English,

71. Philippe d'Armagnac (1643–1702), Chevalier de Lorraine, a gay blade. François de Neufville (1644–1730), Marquis de Villeroi, son of the Duke, became Marshal of France in 1693. Henri-François (1640–1740), Duke de Foix, François-Emmanuel de Bonne-Créqui (d. 1681), Count de Sault, and Charles-Nicolas de Bonne-Créqui (d. 1674), Marquis de Ragny, were all military officers.

I sent La Feuillade to try to recall the Dutch to their obligations.

And truly, it is hard to imagine a more flagrant violation of our agreements, which stipulated that the States would make all possible haste to meet the Duke de Beaufort before the enemy could come between them, and that if the English still managed to do so, the Dutch fleet would follow close upon their heels and prevent them from using their numerical advantage over my ships; whereas the States had done the exact opposite, for although they had put out to sea several days before the English and they could consequently have made such progress toward my fleet that the enemy could not possibly have prevented their junction, they let the English fleet get in front of them, and they immediately turned back for home when they saw it going toward us, as if they had wanted to leave them perfectly free to attack us.

La Feuillade, encountering the Dutch near Boulogne, did his best to make them change their mind, but it was to no avail, for the illness of Ruyter, their general, had made them lose all their confidence and had thrown them into such deep despair that they did not even feel safe where they were, raising anchor in front of my envoy in order to withdraw closer to home. Villequier, captain of my guards, whom I had subsequently sent for this same purpose, had no better luck with them.

But in the meanwhile, although I had issued orders for all my maritime strongholds to keep my admiral informed of whatever might transpire and that I had, for my part, dispatched several couriers to him, I learned that he had unsuspectingly sailed right past the Isle of Wight and had arrived at Dieppe to pick up my men-at-arms as originally ordered.

I was certainly pleased that my small fleet had sailed past such powerful enemies without their venturing to attack it, but on the other hand, I was justifiably concerned that as soon as the English came to realize their advantage they would certainly try to exploit it. I saw that from the roadstead of Dieppe my ships could not get to the Dutch fleet without the English arriving long before us at the Pas de Calais; but I also knew that my fleet had no port on this coast and that it would be constantly exposed where it was to the caprice of the sea and to the insults of the enemy, who could safely lie in wait for a favorable wind in order to pounce upon my ships.

I resolved this pressing dilemma by instructing the Duke de Beaufort to raise anchor as soon as possible, and depending on what he might have heard of the enemy, make either for Holland or for Brest, but this Duke not having been able to learn anything, he fortunately made the right choice and returned safely to the coast of Brittany, whereas some Dutch ships which had persisted in taking the opposite route fell into the hands of the enemy, while others could only save themselves by beaching themselves on my coasts. Seven of mine which had not been able to follow their admiral found themselves in great danger, but two of the best sailers reached Holland safely, four others having fallen in with the English "white pennant" squadron, which they had taken for my armada, fought their way free and so badly mauled the pursuing frigates that they finally abandoned the chase; and the last, the *Ruby*, commanded by Captain La Roche, having advanced too far to withdraw, decided to sell itself dearly and fired a broadside into the admiral of this squadron before finally surrendering; so that after so much risk and concern, France lost only one ship and gained the unique distinction of having gone to the aid of its allies by sailing past the entire English fleet, outnumbered and unopposed.

It is true that most of those who are jealous of the reputation of this crown have wanted to attribute this success to the conflagration that happened to strike London at the same time and that lasted three whole days,[72] consuming three quarters of this great city; but since these two events are not very closely related, I don't see why they should be considered together. The fire actually did, of course, produce tremendous dismay in England, and the misfortune appeared so great to me that in spite of my war with the King of Great Britain, I felt obliged to express my regrets when I visited the Queen his mother two days later. I told her in substance that whatever might transpire between her son and myself, I would always distinguish between the interests of our states and those of his person or his fortune, and that for all our differences, I would always hold him in the highest esteem.

But in terms of politics, there was no doubt that this incident would be advantageous for the French state, since it weakened a

---

72. Actually, September 2 to 6.

nation that had always been its enemy. Her commerce and her manufactures could not help but suffer greatly from the losses of the merchants and from the inactivity of the workers, which seemed all the more ruinous for this island since it is naturally obliged to purchase many necessities abroad. But it seems to me that the King himself also stood to lose by it, not merely because such a great number of unemployed workers were a source of trouble, but because a great quantity of ammunition had been destroyed in London and the impoverishment of this city deprived him of his only recourse in his pressing need.

You will tell me, perhaps, that this affair may have its advantages as well as its disadvantages, that heavily populated cities have had their drawbacks, that the very one in question was a ghastly case in point, and that it was no great misfortune for the King of England to witness the ruin of a city that could ruin him just as it had ruined his father.

But my reply to this is that if we want to deprive ourselves of anything that may hurt us, we would soon be without not merely everything that makes for our greatness and our comfort, but even our most basic needs. The same foods that nourish man may sometimes choke him, the most salutary medicines are immensely harmful when improperly administered, the most prudent laws often create new abuses, and religion, which should be the object of our most profound respect, is itself subject to terrible desecration; and yet no one would argue against the use of meats, of medicines, of laws, and of religion.

God has given us reason and prudence to aid us in making good use of all His other gifts. A prince who, lacking in intelligence or in courage, can neither conduct himself nor govern others, might perhaps be just as easily disconcerted by a rebellion of peasants as by the revolt of his biggest cities, whereas a wise and vigorous one remains calm through every peril, and his reputation alone often spares him from suppressing uprisings by preventing them from arising. He does not differentiate between the stronger and the weaker in his state, because their submission to him is the same, and his cities could never be too rich nor his provinces too populated, because he knows how to use the number and the wealth of his subjects for his glory and for the good of his kingdom.

But to end this reflection with something that fits the purpose

of this work even better, note, my son, from the sudden conflagration of such a great and proud city, which this King sees
perish in the midst of his state, how insubstantial are even our
surest possessions and how extraordinary are the ways of Heaven
to humble our greatest pride!

In my continuing review of everything that went on within
my kingdom and within my household, I saw that in spite of how
much my great stable cost me each year, it had fallen into such
pitiful decay that it was no longer fit for a gentleman to enter; for
not merely was it short of horses, but pages of all conditions had
been appointed by means of influence and upon payment of small
bribes to the minor officials under the pretext of entry fees. Since
such conditions were unbecoming to the greatness of a household
like mine, I felt it necessary to remedy them as soon as possible,
and I thought that it would be wonderful to train a greater number
of gentlemen there who could later serve me elsewhere, aside
from the fact that I was always in need of horses for the war. Thus
I resolved to maintain one hundred riding horses, to choose fifty
pages from among the best families, and to provide them with
excellent squires and masters who would draw their salaries from
me. And knowing that what had previously facilitated the entry
into these posts of people who did not merit it was that they very
rarely came into contact with me, because the small stable alone
was entitled to serve me under ordinary circumstances, I decided
that in the future the pages of the great and small stable would
both serve me on the same basis.

At the same time, reflecting that the immense sums spent each
year by my subjects for laces from Genoa, Venice, Flanders, and
other places were virtually lost to France, I believed that it was
important to establish factories for these within the kingdom, so
that my people could gain rather than foreigners; but I could
easily foresee that the merchants who had long been trading in
these products would do their utmost to obstruct my plan, finding
imported goods of uncertain value more to their advantage than
domestic ones manufactured in public. This is why I felt it necessary to override their opposition; and yet, to give them no cause
for complaint, I announced this decision in the month of June
and at the same time prohibited all traffic in these foreign goods
within my domains.

But since many of the merchants did not believe that these factories would be ready for a while, they thought that they could always find a way to distribute the prohibited goods secretly and continued to bring them in from abroad; but they were sadly mistaken, for my overseers of this establishment made such good time that the stores being filled by the following September, I ordered them to be opened in October, and I immediately confiscated everything the merchants had brought in since my prohibition, and indeed, it was only fair to do this not merely as punishment for such obvious disobedience, but also as protection for those who, at my command, had invested in this trade.

At the same time, other no less necessary manufactures and works were established throughout my kingdom, such as tapestry, glass, silk stockings, crystals, and various other things which, by preventing a sum of more than four millions a year from leaving France, cannot but eventually produce great prosperity within it; aside from the fact that this was an excellent means to occupy my unemployed subjects and to relieve them from an idleness which could not but corrupt their morals as well as impoverish them.

But while I was considering this matter, I observed that the gradual and steady increase in the number of church holidays was causing considerable prejudice to the workers, not merely since they did not earn anything on such days but since they often spent more on them than they could earn during the others; for indeed, it was most obvious that these days which had originally been instituted for prayers and for acts of piety only provided persons of this type with an occasion for debauchery, in which they constantly wasted the fruits of their labor. This is why I believed that it was all to the good of private individuals, to the advantage of the public, and even to the service of God to abolish as many as possible, and I expressed this thought to the Archbishop of Paris, exhorting him, as the pastor of the capital of my kingdom, to set the example for his colleagues, and he soon thereafter followed my suggestion.

Meanwhile, the long history of sacrileges and other crimes in the Vivarais and in the Cévennes made me think of holding the *Grands Jours* there, as I had done in Auvergne, and I issued a declaration about this, appointing commissioners from the

Parlement of Toulouse, in whose jurisdiction these places were located. I immediately had a little difficulty, however, with the mixed chamber of Castres,[73] which protested with some justification that it should have been employed, as this tribunal would undoubtedly deal with many matters of great concern to people of the supposedly reformed religion; and although I could have regarded this difficulty more lightly at another time, it seemed more important then, since it was desirable, while at war against the English, not to make it appear to the Huguenots as if I wanted to attenuate their privileges under the edicts of pacification. And yet I found a way of gradually circumventing their claim without explicitly rejecting it, for I kept finding new pretexts for postponing a decision on their proposal until such time as the affair was concluded without them.

Dumolin, whom I have already told you about, had then fortunately returned from Africa with a great number of Christian slaves delivered at my expense from the hands of the Barbary pirates, in execution of the peace that the terror of my arms had made them desire; for although between the conclusion of this treaty and its execution the King of Tunis had been poisoned by his opponents, who consequently had an interest in reversing his policies, they still honored our agreement.

But I had also recently decided to work in France itself on a point of no less importance to religion, for I had intended to complete the extirpation of the Jansenist sect, and after holding various councils for this purpose and procuring the best advice I could find on such matters in the kingdom, I had finally requested His Holiness to appoint commissioners to try the four bishops who had refused to comply with his bull and my declaration, in keeping with the traditional privileges of this kingdom.

And truly, I would never have expected that the Pope, who should be concerned about affairs of this nature, would have hesitated over this request; nevertheless I learned that this proposal had met with grave difficulties on his part, and I finally discovered that the court of Rome, imagining that I was extremely concerned by the threat of Jansenism, had concluded that it could

73. A court established under the provisions of the Edict of Nantes, composed both of Catholic and of Protestant judges.

sell me the issuances that I desired at its own price, even insinuating that I should reciprocate by allowing the demolition of the pyramid that it had been obliged to erect for me as reparation for the crime of the Corsicans.[74] But to show the court of Rome that I had no other interest in this matter than that of the Church itself and that, in regard to my authority, I was not at all afraid of the Jansenists, I simply ordered the Duke de Chaulnes[75] to tell them that after having formally requested His Holiness to act in this matter, I believed that I had done my duty and that it would now be up to the Pope to do his whenever he would please.

This Duke had arrived in Rome some months previously and had been received very honorably, because the Pope was then in poor health and his relatives, worried about the outcome of his illness, had lost some of their usual pride. But when the Pope regained his health, things returned to normal.

It is a rather usual fault of those who are not born to greatness to be stunned by it when they attain it and to be able to sustain neither the brilliance that adorns it nor the storms that can threaten it. Since it is a novelty for them to be great, they don't know how to go about it. Wishing to compensate for their lowly birth with excessive pride, they do everything with such bad grace that they even alienate those whose friendship they seek, and being able to conduct themselves neither according to their present nor according to their former position, they usually earn the contempt of those whose friendship they desire. Lacking both naturalness and breeding in all their actions, they always advance or retreat at the wrong time. They never fail to do too much or too little, and the most uniform and constant thing about their vacillating behavior is that they always become excessively proud in the midst of good fortune and fall into extreme despair the moment it turns against them.

But princes must assuredly be completely free from this failing, because deriving their principal greatness from their merit or from their birth, the ups and downs of fortune should affect neither their bearing nor their feelings. They must take advantage of times of prosperity, not to become inflated with foolish vanity,

74. See note 39.
75. Charles d'Albert d'Ailly (1625–1698), Duke de Chaulnes.

but to become more useful for their subjects. They must rely on their own courage in times of adversity to persevere without despair and to do or tolerate nothing that is unworthy of their status—and this is undoubtedly a better way, my son, to distinguish princes from other men than by the crowd that follows them and by the commotion that surrounds them, so that I think I am doing more for you when I attempt through my lessons to inspire you with these thoughts than when I shall try by force of arms to extend our heritage.

My fleet fortunately arrived at Brest on [September 29], and a few days later I ordered it to be disarmed. I resolved, however, to maintain a squadron of twelve ships throughout the winter in order to wage war upon the subjects of England, and I also gave the Duke de Vendôme permission to arm two more at his expense.

But on hearing that the English were to send twenty frigates to escort certain merchant ships to Tangiers and to bring back still others that had been waiting for them there in order to return to England, I informed the States General that if they would also be willing, for their part, to arm a sizable squadron, we could easily combine to surprise the enemy in passage or compel them to remain in their ports, which would always have very useful consequences; for indeed, there was no doubt that if we had been able to obstruct the commerce of the English, we would soon have reduced them to desperate straits, and there would have been new rebellions in that divided state. But whether the Dutch were exhausted from the previous campaign or wanted to be well prepared for the following one, they would not go along with this; and truly, they had most recently given me a rather singular token of their intention to live on good terms with me, for they had condemned Dubuat, a gentleman of the Prince of Orange, to death for having tried to arrange a settlement with the English in which I was not included.

As for me, I was preparing to make a great effort the following year either to compel England to make peace or to make it endure the ravages of war, and I was constantly devising great new plans for this purpose. Among others, I had long been interested in seizing the Isle of Wight, which is well situated to survey the entire entrance to the Channel, so that my ships could constantly give chase to those leaving the English ports. In order to create a diversion, I had already embarked four hundred men, with orders to land in Ireland as soon as the Catholic faction could receive them, and was prepared to give them more aid if they needed it.

Meanwhile, so that my fleet could put out to sea more promptly for the following campaign, I resolved to have the troops who served on it take up winter quarters right there, as well as to maintain all the available naval officers and good sailors during the winter. I even tried to attach them more firmly to my service by issuing a regulation on a matter of great importance to them.

They had been complaining for ages that the ship captains retained a part of their pay and for this reason did not want to be paid by them any longer; but the captains, on the contrary, maintained that both the dignity of their office and the good of my service required that they themselves pay the sailors under their command; and indeed, those whose advice I sought on this were not all of one mind; but as for me, seeing that the sailors were justified in their complaints and knowing that, in the final analysis, I needed them more than anyone else for the naval war, I ordered them to be paid at the bank. As for the soldiers, since I was prepared to put many more ships out to sea the following spring than I had the previous year, I had intended to use my land-based troops if I did not need them elsewhere, which gave me the double advantage of accustoming some of my troops to serving at sea and of saving the cost of feeding them in the provinces.

In the meanwhile, learning that the English were constantly pressing the King of Portugal to make peace with Spain, I ordered Saint-Romain to obstruct this negotiation by every possible means and even to try to penetrate the sentiments of the prime minister on this point, so that if he proved to favor a settlement, the Queen could promptly be informed and could use all her influence against it. This Princess lent me her enthusiastic support, for I learned soon thereafter that she had quarreled with the minister of the King her husband.

It was around this time that I was informed of the good fortune of my arms in Canada and that I learned how much cause I had to be satisfied with the zeal of those whom I had sent there, for the hardships they had endured were even greater than those of the military expeditions of antiquity.

In a single year, they had made three different marches, each of more than three hundred leagues, carrying their provisions and their equipment through wild and uninhabited places, marching through the snow all day and sleeping in the open at night; but they were well rewarded for their hardships, because the pride of the Iroquois, the only enemies of France and of religion in that area, was completely humbled, since they believed their country to be inaccessible. Thus, after having seen my men burning their villages, taking their grain, and removing their children from their most hidden refuges, they hastily appealed to my lieutenants for peace.

But while I was thus trying to procure some tranquillity for these distant colonies, I was informed that the lower classes in various provinces throughout my state were harassed by the avarice of some minor officials supported by the authority of the governors, and I immediately established able and loyal observers in each district to keep me well informed of whatever might go on.

I also learned toward the end of autumn that all those who were to enter the league of German princes that I have described to you had finally signed it; and moreover, knowing of the negotiation that was going on before Bremen, I sent Millet there as my representative to Wrangel, Constable of Sweden, who was handling this matter.[76] His principal order was to observe this negotiation and the nearby princes, not merely for my information, but so that Pomponne in Sweden and the Bishop of Béziers in Poland could make their plans with greater assurance.

Nothing is so necessary for those who work on important affairs than to know what is really happening to their interests. Neither our ministers nor ourselves can deliberate with any assurance unless we have very exact knowledge of what goes on around us; and since reason itself, which governs all the other human faculties, cannot operate without the evidence of the senses, sovereigns cannot act in their councils without a constant flow of news from their agents.

Whoever is badly informed cannot refrain from reasoning badly, and if you will search past times for all the greatest faults

76. Guillaume Millet (c. 1617–1690), Sieur de Jeurs. Karl Gustaf Wrangel (1613–1676).

that are attributed to sovereigns, you will hardly find a single one that may not be referred to not knowing something that he should have known, so that among men in general the most common excuse is to say, "I did not know," or, "I did not think."[77]

Whenever we learn something new after having concluded an affair, we immediately note that if we had known about it sooner, we would have acted differently, so that in short, I believe that whoever is fully informed and fully conscious of everything will always do what he should.

But as for me, I carried my reflection even further, for I believed that it was not enough for a distinguished prince to know what goes on in his own time, but that he should even be informed about the most remote times. I considered that a knowledge of the great events of the past, digested by a mature and active mind, could strengthen his reasoning in important deliberations, that the example of the illustrious men and singular deeds of antiquity might possibly furnish some very useful insights in war and in peace, and that by contemplating the idea of so many brilliant virtues, a naturally great and magnanimous soul would be all the more inspired to practice them.

I had heard that all the heroes whose glory has come down to us were perfectly familiar with literature and that they owed some of their good qualities to reflecting upon their studies. But I was especially convinced that it detracted a little from the glory of my rank not to know what almost everyone knew, that it was better to learn it late than never, and I even remember seeing that one of my predecessors, who from the negligence or from the jealousy of his father did not even know how to read when he began to reign, was praised since he still did not neglect his studies.[78]

Finally, considering that by my past labors, I had put such precision into my affairs and had acquired such ease in handling them that I was then free to dispose of a good deal of my time, I believed that it would be both useful and glorious for me to take some time from my amusements in order to devote it to such useful knowledge, which should make you understand the importance of studying now that you have nothing better to do, for even

77. Compare with Cicero, *De Officiis,* Book I, Ch. XXIII.
78. Charles VIII, son of Louis XI. See Mézeray, *op. cit.,* II, 205.

in the midst of so many occupations I could not dispense with this one.

While one is a child, he considers studying as pure vexation; when he begins to enter into affairs, he regards it as a trifle; but when his reason reaches its maturity, he discovers only too late that he should have done it while he had the time.

As I was well aware that the greatest obstacle to my plans for the Kingdom of Poland had been and would be the conspiracy of Lubomirski, I resolved to make some private agreements with him for the purpose of winning his support.

It was partly with this same idea that I was more inclined to give the Swedes their subsidy for the undertaking against Bremen. Their ambassador extraordinary was still at my court, but wanting to settle this affair in conjunction with the negotiations up north and according to the actual financial need of this crown, I believed that it would be best to transmit my offers through D'Andilly, who was closer to things, than to settle them here myself with the Swedish ambassador. Thus I merely replied to this minister that I regretted not being in a position to conclude this affair with him, because I had no doubt that, for his part, he would have handled it most properly, but that I expected that the crown of Sweden would be pleased at what it would hear. And indeed, I immediately ordered Andilly to offer the Swedes one hundred thousand *écus* in cash, which, however, were to be deducted from the subsidies that I would grant them in our treaty of alliance, which was then well advanced. I had already replied to their claims and I saw them, moreover, quite disposed to favor mine; but what happened a short time later seemed to give added weight to this alliance, for with the conclusion of their agreement with Bremen, I was free to dispose of many of their troops, whether in their name or in mine, against the house of Austria or for the Polish election.

On the other hand, Ruvigny had by my orders maintained a secret contact with the Count of Saint-Alban[79] in England about the peace, which, to be frank, I desired passionately as a preliminary to my other plans. But the problem was that if I pressed too hard for it, the Spanish would be more on their guard, the

79. Henry Jermyn (c. 1601–1684).

English would demand better terms, and the States of Holland, especially, would fear to conclude it, because my eagerness would confirm their suspicions that I wanted to end this war in order to begin another one in their neighborhood.

This did not prevent me, however, from making secret preparations for this undertaking both in France and in foreign countries. I maintained contacts in Hungary in order to create problems for the Emperor if he meddled in mine. I had repeatedly consulted the best captains of my state about this undertaking. I was every day receiving new plans of the fortressses in Flanders, and I was particularly interested in the condition of Charleroi. As for my troops, I kept almost all of them poised on the frontier of the Low Countries, but I kept them in such order that even though there were more than fifty thousand men in one or two provinces, the inhabitants profited rather than suffered from it, in that the soldiers consumed in kind on the spot what these parishes would have had to pay me in money.

Meanwhile, to keep the public in the dark about my intentions, I often spoke of making a voyage to Brest in case the naval war should last, and I had even planned my itinerary and designated the troops that were to accompany me. I had considered that if I took my entire household on this march, I could not forage for less than fifteen leagues across, and that if I were to inspect my coasts on my return, this would make for a prodigious extent of country, whose inhabitants would be bound to suffer from the exactions of the soldiers in passage. Thus I had resolved to take only my gendarmerie with me, which could constantly camp at my doorstep or live in the large cities on provisions that I would have ready for this purpose, without the local inhabitants being obliged to furnish them either victuals or supplies. But actually, my hopes of not having to make this voyage were rising, because of news from England that the Count of Saint-Alban would be leaving there soon, and under the pretext of coming here to see the Queen his mistress, would bring full powers to conclude a peace between myself and the King of Great Britain.

However, the further this appeared to get, the more I attempted to hide it, and thus I still entertained the Spanish with the proposal of a league that I have described to you, and under one pretext or another, such as the English war, I was gradually strengthening my troops and making other important preparations. With this thought, I fixed my guards at eight hundred men, excluding officers, intending to keep them all on active service, with others all ready to replace them in case of any vacancy; and this unit was all the more impressive since with the exception of twenty cadets per company it was entirely composed of former officers or of veteran cavalry. And furthermore, as soon as I heard of the settlement of Bremen, I ordered Andilly to ask the Swedes for their surplus troops, intending to use them in Poland or in Germany, depending on the situation.

As I felt that the best way to achieve a great success was to catch the enemy by surprise with my invasion before they could offer any resistance, I gradually arranged everything in order to begin this campaign much earlier than was customary. Thus I amassed wheat, flour, hay, powder, bullets, cannons, and whatever might be needed at each location to expedite the march and the operations of my army. But I was especially careful to continue drilling the troops that were at my side, so that my example would lead individual commanders to do the same with theirs, which was certainly all the more necessary at that time, since after seven years of peace my soldiers had almost forgotten their trade. But this effort was even more important for the newly levied companies, which would have fared badly in combat if their continued training did not give them some idea of what to expect.

For indeed, these frequent trials that constitute a kind of sport in peacetime gradually accustom the mind and the body for war. Whatever qualities men may possess, they can hardly be held responsible for their initial reactions in the face of something new. The bravest may be startled by the unknown, whereas the most timid can become accustomed to remaining quite calm before the most terrifying sights. Habit is the best way to make things easy for ourselves. The most crushing labors become almost negligible to those who have long been engaged in them, and the most frightening perils have such little impact on those who are accustomed to them that they will often stand up to them without hesitation.

But if it were only a matter of training the troops to march well, it would well be worth the effort. The greatest captains now agree that many more battles are won by good order and by good bearing than by the sword and the musket. The assurance with which troops march can terrorize the enemy, and most often it is enough to appear brave for our adversary not to wait around to discover if we actually are.

Thus it is not without reason that the captain is often held to be entirely responsible for the outcome of a battle, because it usually depends on how well he has trained his troops. It is a great mistake to attribute the success or bravery of armies to climate or to race, because the same nations that were once the terror and wonder of the world have since become the most cowardly and scorned on earth.[80] The Macedonians, who were almost entirely unknown, attained by virtue of two great kings to the empire of the entire world, and the Romans, whose valor had conquered so many people, ultimately became the pawns of the barbarian nations. Thus as long as a prince has subjects, he should have soldiers, and whoever rules a populous state but lacks good troops has only himself to blame.

80. Compare with Jean Bodin, *Les Six Livres de la République,* Book V, Ch. I.

1667

THIS year began with the Queen going into labor a little prematurely, giving me good cause to be afraid for her, for I can say here that she merited all my cares and that never, perhaps, has Heaven endowed any woman with more virtue, more beauty, higher birth, more attachment for her children, more love and respect for her husband. But my fears finally vanished with the birth of a daughter.[1]

It was at the beginning of this same year that I had the finishing touches put in Germany on the treaty to prevent the passage of the Imperial troops.

I also had plans for one with the King of Portugal, in which he promised me not to deal with the Spanish for four years, but before we could sign it, we had occasion to make another one that I shall describe to you in its place.

Meanwhile, the Queen of Poland continued to ask for my aid, and especially since after the death of Lubomirski,[2] she was more optimistic than ever about restoring her affairs, she pressed me harder and dispatched Morstin,[3] her Grand Referendary, to me, who intimated that if, under the pretext of aiding her against the Turk, I would send her a body of French troops commanded by the Prince de Condé, she could pacify her kingdom and achieve the election of the Duke d'Enghien.

The proposal was glorious and well conceived, but I was in a difficult position to execute it. I was still at war with the English, I was about to begin one against the Spanish, I had no doubt about what side the Emperor would take; I knew how hostile the Dutch were to my rise; and I was still uncertain of Sweden, so that I had to rely entirely on my own forces for the success of my plans and hesitated to weaken them.

And yet, in my extreme desire to augment the glory of my

1. Marie-Thérèse de France (1667–1672).
2. January 3, 1667.
3. Jan Andrzej (1628–1693), Count Morsztyn (or Morstin), Grand Referendary of Poland since 1659.

crown, I agreed to it, and primarily because the war against the Turk was indeed a very fine pretext for transferring the Prince de Condé; that once the King of Poland, who was already ailing, died, his wife would be without power; that this Princess herself, who had recently been threatened by apoplexy, might not always be around; that the Swedes, for their part, then seemed to be disposed to assist her; but truly, the consideration that struck me most was that there would rarely be another opportunity to bestow a crown and to assure it for France.

After this decision, I had immediately asked the Elector of Brandenburg for passage and was preparing to send off my troops by land or sea, depending on whether I was at war or at peace with England. But soon thereafter, I learned from Germany that no passages were being granted, from Sweden that they wanted no part in this undertaking, and from Poland that the Queen did not believe she could propose the election, which made me think that I should not try to do everything all by myself.

Meanwhile, I combined internal with external cares. In order to remedy the usual disorders in Paris, I decided to re-establish its police, and after hearing the old ordinances on this subject, I found them so well considered that I merely revived many of their provisions, which the negligence of the magistrates had abolished; but I took some precautions in order to implement them better in the future, particularly on the bearing of arms, on the cleaning of streets, and on some other specific points by forming a special council for this purpose.

I also believed that it befitted the general discipline of my kingdom to diminish the great number of monastics, most of whom were useless to the Church and burdensome to the state. With this thought, I became convinced that since nothing contributed to filling the convents as much as the early age at which children were accepted, it would be desirable to postpone the vows in the future; that if the undecided did not find the door of the cloisters open so soon, they could, while waiting, serve the public in some other profession; that most would remain in this work and strengthen the state by having their own families; and that even the Church would find this to its advantage in that individuals who would have time to think before going into convents would lead a more exemplary life in them.

My council, to which I had referred this plan, had repeatedly confirmed me in it, but at the last moment I was stopped by those sentiments of respect that we must always have for the Church in what truly lies within its jurisdiction, and I resolved to settle this point only in cooperation with the Pope. And yet, while waiting to inform him, I wanted to prevent the disorder from spreading by every means at my own disposal. Thus I prohibited the establishment of any new monasteries, I saw to the closing of unauthorized ones, and I had my *procureur général* regulate the number of monastics that each convent could maintain.

In regard to the general regulation on justice about which I have already told you something, seeing a good many articles drawn up as I desired, I did not want to deprive the public of this relief any longer, but I believed I should not simply send them to the *Parlement* lest they engage in some distressing chicanery there, nor take them there initially myself lest they allege one day that they had been verified without due process. This is why I adopted the compromise solution of having the articles read at the Chancellor's in the presence of deputies from all the chambers and commissioners from my council; and if some reasonable difficulty arose during their conference, it was immediately brought to me for decision, after which I finally went in person to issue the edict.[4]

At the same time, I also reformed my own customary manner of rendering justice to those who sought it directly from me, for I did not find that my method of receiving their petitions had been convenient to any of us; and indeed, since most of the people with requests or complaints for me were in no position to obtain private audiences with me, they had difficulty in finding a suitable time to speak to me and often remained waiting several days for me, away from their families and from their functions. This is why I designated one day per week in which all those who wanted to speak to me or to give me *mémoires* were free to come to my chamber and would find me there, ready to listen to them.

But aside from these public cares, I lost no opportunity for rewarding private individuals justly.

4. See this edict, which was the principal result of the council of justice, in the *Recueil général des anciennes lois Françaises,* ed. François André Isambert (Paris, 1821–1833), XVIII, 103–182.

Having increased the size of my bodyguard, I took the opportunity of creating new offices in it for my good servants. Remembering what La Feuillade had accomplished in Hungary,[5] I consented to investing him with the title of Duke de Roannez, an estate that he had acquired through marriage, and I even gave him some money to facilitate the execution of the contract.

I permitted my *procureur général* to resign his post to his son, although it did not usually pass from father to son. I used my authority and my finances to relieve, insofar as I could, many merchants whose affairs had suffered from the maritime war. I also aided, by various means, those who had recently gone into receivership, and I settled a long and unpleasant dispute that had arisen between the Carmelite convents of Paris.

For their part, my subjects were each day displaying more and more ardor and eagerness for my service.

The long-standing neglect of the navy had sometimes made me afraid of not finding enough sailors for all my ships, but at my slightest bidding, there were more than I needed, entire provinces offering to abandon their homes and to leave their wives and children behind for my service.

At the first rumor of war in Flanders, my court was suddenly flooded with gentlemen requesting positions. The captains of all the old units sought my permission to recruit men at their own expense. Others requested only my simple commission for raising new troops, and all, in their various positions, vied with each other in showing me their zeal.

It is assuredly pleasant to receive such tokens of esteem and affection from one's subjects: all princes agree that this is the greatest treasure that they can ever possess; all esteem it, all desire it, but not all try hard enough to acquire it!

For in order to attain it, my son, we must direct all our actions and all our thoughts toward this end: we must prefer it to all other possessions and flee, as the greatest evil in the world, all that separates us from it. It is for ordinary men to limit themselves only to what they find useful and pleasant, but the first thought of kings in all their councils must be for what may or may not win

---

5. La Feuillade had been on Coligny's staff at the Battle of Saint-Gothard. See p. 113, n. 23.

them the acclaim of the public. Kings, who are born to possess everything and to command over everything, must not be ashamed to accede to renown. It is a possession that is avidly to be desired, that indeed can contribute more than any other to the success of our plans. A reputation can often do more by itself than the most powerful armies. All conquerors have gone further with their name than with their sword, and a thousand times, their sole presence has easily brought down ramparts capable of resisting all their forces.

But it is important to note that such a noble and precious possession is also the most fragile in the world, that it is not enough to have acquired it without constantly seeing to its preservation, and that this esteem which is formed only through a long succession of good actions can be destroyed in a moment by a single error.

And we don't even have to fail in order to be condemned! It is often enough if our fortunes decline for our reputation to suffer, and just as all the luck of the fortunate man is turned by the people to his glory, so also all the failures of the unfortunate are attributed to their lack of prudence.

The caprice of fate, or rather that wise Providence that rules supreme over our interests for purposes beyond our comprehension, chooses sometimes to deflate the pomp of the loftiest men in order to oblige them, in the midst of their greatest advantages, to recognize the source of all their blessings and to merit, through a continual avowal of their dependence, the assistance necessary for the success of their plans.

About the same time, the Venetians, threatened with the loss of Crete, ordered their ambassador to obtain the assistance of the papal nuncio in requesting my aid. But I could not give them a favorable reply, because my many commitments then did not permit me to give them a large body of troops, and I believed that to give them a weak one would have meant a useless loss of my men, for small bodies never return from these long voyages.

I would actually, of course, certainly have desired to assist them, for aside from the common interests of Christianity, I had personally been so unhappy with the Porte over the scheme of the Genoese that I had resolved to say no more of this affair, intending to get satisfaction from Genoa itself as soon as I had some time to think about it.

The news, at this time, of the extreme illness of the Pope made me order the French cardinals to be prepared to sail at any time in case the worst should happen, as indeed it did soon thereafter,[6] and my cares on this occasion assuredly contributed to filling this great post well.

Meanwhile, the Dutch were continually asking me to settle the article on the salute between our admirals, covering their eagerness with the best reasons in the world, although the only real one was their conviction that while the naval war lasted I might be more conciliatory with them, whereas after the peace I would be more firm in preserving my rights. But as I knew what they were thinking, I delayed them from day to day, fully aware that even at home they were under strong pressure to make peace.

Four of their provinces had already declared that they would no longer contribute to the expenses of the war, and the others were divided on this subject, because while the politicians, afraid of my rise, were opposed to the conclusion of the treaty, the people, on the contrary, who especially desired the restoration of their commerce, wanted the affair concluded; and this went so far that I feared the dissolution of the republic and was obliged to intercede in favor of moderation.

Besides, there was nothing more to settle except for a single article on the island of Polaroon.[7] The English claimed, for their part, that it had to be returned to them by the explicit terms of the Treaty of 1662, and the Dutch maintained, on the contrary, that they had then fully complied with this by surrendering the island, but that the English having abandoned it soon thereafter, they had a right to return to it as to a land without a lord. But in any case, it was of very little value: it did not seem that either side should make an issue out of it, so that peace already seemed inevitable.

Thus the house of Austria, not being able to think of any other way to disrupt it, proposed the mediation of the Emperor to me, hoping that its agents would perhaps find a way to incite some new dispute over the articles that still remained to be considered.

6. Alexander VII died on May 22. He was succeeded by Giulio Rospigliosi (1600–1669), elected Pope as Clement IX, who acceded to the shaky "Peace of the Church" with the Jansenists in 1668.

7. One of the Moluccas, or Spice Islands, in the East Indies.

But as the motive of this proposal was not difficult to penetrate, I did not fail to defend myself against it with the excuse that the Swedes had already been accepted as mediators by all the parties concerned in this treaty; and that after all that they had accomplished, it was not fair for anyone else to share in the glory of their success; to which the resident of the Emperor did not fail to retort, but I still ended by rejecting his offers most courteously.

The Spanish, in another effort to deter me from turning my arms against them, proposed a treaty of commerce to me; and still later, with the same intention, the Marquis de Fuentes in taking leave of me, told me the most ingratiating things on behalf of the Queen Regent, so as to evoke similar comments from me, of which he immediately tried to take advantage by intimating in public that I had definitely promised him not to break with the Spanish, apparently hoping that I would not disavow him. But actually, as I had paid him only some very general compliments, I ignored all his speeches, constantly preparing for war on sea and on land, depending on the situation.

For indeed, I always feared that in my great desire to achieve the peace with England, I was more likely than anyone to be misled by appearances, and I followed the maxim that when in doubt, one should always count on the worst.

It is only too natural for men to come to expect what they ardently desire, and we can guard against such a common fault only by distrusting our own thoughts about everything toward which we have too much inclination.

Nothing is more important or more difficult for a prince than to know how far to trust his own opinion. I have told you elsewhere, and it is true, that a sovereign may be sure of this about himself: that since his rank is above other men, he can also see things more clearly than they and he must rely on his own insights more than on reports from the outside; but I warn you here that this maxim is not equally applicable to all our different functions. There are undoubtedly some where taking, so to speak, the place of God, we seem to participate in His knowledge as well as in His authority, as for example in regard to discerning character, distributing positions, and dispensing graces, things that we can decide better ourselves than our councillors can, because in our higher sphere we are further removed from the petty interests that might lead us to be unjust. But it must be confessed in good faith that there are also other instances when leaving, so it seems, the independent role of sovereigns, we become as biased as, if not more than, the lowliest private individual, because the greater and the loftier the things to which we aspire, the more likely they are to disturb our judgment.

The fire of the most noble passions, as well as that of the most common, always produces enough smoke to obscure our reason. One often wonders how, out of many who see and hear the same thing, hardly two reports are ever the same; and yet this variety comes only from the different interests and passions of men, who unconsciously reconcile everything they see around them to their state of mind.

This is one of the strongest reasons that has always obliged princes to have councillors around them and that should even lead them to pay special heed to those who disagree with them. As long as we are in power, we shall never lack for people who strive to guess our thoughts and to seem in full agreement with them, but we must fear to lack for people who can contradict us, because our inclination is sometimes so obvious that the boldest fear to shock it; and yet it is desirable that there be some who can take this liberty. Insincere indulgence toward us on these occasions can be more harmful to us than the most stubborn contradiction. If we are mistaken in our opinion, he who agrees with us confirms us in our error, whereas even if we are right, he who contradicts us is still useful to us, if only by forcing us to meet his objections and by giving us the satisfaction of having examined all the arguments on both sides before acting.

In my settlement with England, the point that deterred me most was that the English absolutely insisted on the return of the Western Islands, for aside from their general interest to France, I took into particular consideration the new company that I had formed for this trade; but on the other hand, also considering the circumstances—Flanders depleted of money and of men, Spain governed by a foreign princess, the Emperor irresolute, the house of Austria divided into two parts, its forces exhausted by various wars, her supporters almost all lukewarm, and my subjects full of zeal for my service—I believed that I should not lose such a favorable opportunity for advancing my plans, nor compare the acquisition of these distant islands with the conquest of the Low Countries. This is why I made a private decision to grant their demand; and yet, in order not to disclose it without deriving some important benefit from this, I asked the King of Great Britain if, in return for my secret word to accept this article of the treaty, he would, for his part, also promise to assume no engagement against me for a year.

But while we were negotiating about this, he aroused my suspicion by proposing to the States without my knowledge to go treat the peace at The Hague. For since this city was very thickly populated and very easily stirred, I had no doubt that this choice was concerted with Spain, with the intention of having their ministers intrigue there either to re-establish the authority of the Prince of Orange, or to detach this republic from me.

But I circumvented their artifice by exposing it to the States, who at my suggestion replied to the King of England that they were willing to go treat in his kingdom, or that if he preferred to negotiate in their country, he could choose among Breda, Bois-le-Duc, and Maestricht, because, they said, an open city like The Hague did not provide enough security for the deputies.

But the King of Great Britain, who immediately realized the real cause for this reply, was so displeased to see his plan discovered that he would not accept any of the proposed places. And yet, he chose Breda soon thereafter, even claiming that he was making this concession out of consideration for me.

Thus our assembled agents began working openly at the peace, and I, for my part, resumed the secret negotiation in order to make sure about my own plan as soon as possible; for since I had no doubt that, with the various interests of the different parties, the disputes would drag on interminably, I believed that it was in my interest to divest myself of this affair so as not to lose precious time.

The principal obligation I undertook in this treaty was to return the Western Islands to the English, and for their part they promised that the article on the island of Polaroon would not prevent the general peace and that even if it were not concluded within a year, they would not obstruct my plans in any way. In order to keep the States of Holland from knowing about these agreements, they were stated only in private letters written in my hand and that of the King of England to my aunt his mother, who was to be our trustee. And this done, I began to prepare openly for the war in Flanders.

But so as to neglect nothing that would justify my behavior, I issued a manifesto establishing my rights and sent new orders to Spain to demand the territories that belonged to me and to declare that if they were refused I would take possession of them for myself, or at least of their equivalent. The Queen Regent replied that she could not disregard the testament of her late husband, which explicitly prohibited the alienation of any of his possessions. But Castel-Rodrigo, who was closer to me, did not display such firmness, for I had hardly left Saint-Germain before I received a letter from him, in which after some rather ill-conceived protests he proposed appointing some deputies, certain, he said, that the Queen his mistress would agree to a reasonable settlement. But as it was easy to see that he was only making this proposal out of fear of my arms, I gave this letter no other thought than to note the fright gripping the writer.

On May 19, I arrived at Amiens, where I had resolved to watch the assembling of my troops. And knowing that the Spanish were particularly short of soldiers, I wanted to threaten them on all sides so that they would be obliged to divide their limited forces among many garrisons.

With this intention, I had a unit under Marshal d'Aumont march toward the sea, the Marquis de Créqui[8] led another in the direction of Luxembourg, a third under Duras[9] was forming around La Fère, and I myself assembled a fourth near Amiens.

My first thought had always been to begin with Charleroi, since I wished to capture this important stronghold while the new fortifications were still easy to wreck, and although I was informed at Amiens that the Spanish were wrecking it, this did not alter my plan, because at the same time I learned that the demolition party had been in such a hurry to leave that they had left the outside standing.

8. François de Créqui (c. 1624–1687), brother of the ambassador to Rome, became Marshal of France in 1668.

9. Jacques-Henri de Durfort (1625–1704), Duke de Duras, became Marshal of France in 1675.

Thus I sent the Count de Sault with fifteen hundred infantrymen and Podwitz[10] with twelve hundred horse ahead to seize it, following immediately upon them with my army, so that the campaign opened with my profiting without bloodshed from two years' expense and care by Castel-Rodrigo in building this stronghold.

Meanwhile, Marshal d'Aumont, under orders to go to Bergues, took it without a blow; from where, moving immediately to Furnes, he met hardly any more resistance. Armentières and La Bassée having been abandoned before they could be attacked, I had sent three hundred men to seize the former because of its bridge over the Lys, but since I learned that its condition was such that I could always reoccupy it, I did not want to waste any men by leaving them there.

I had initially intended to go from Charleroi to Brussels, but seeing that my infantry, composed mostly of new soldiers, might be discouraged or shattered by a long siege, I later resolved to attack Tournai, which could be taken in much less time, and which was still a large and well-situated city. But the problem was that my cannon and my victuals having already gone in the direction of Brabant, it was necessary to issue new orders, so that my men would lack nothing either in their march over enemy country or during the subsequent siege.

For it is not enough, my son, to engage in vast undertakings without thinking of how to execute them. We may initially devise the most valorous plans in the world, but they are of little solidity unless they are sustained by the foresight to arrange at the same time for everything that must accompany them.

This point undoubtedly illustrates one of the principal differences between good and bad captains, for no able general ever undertakes a lengthy enterprise without knowing exactly where he will obtain all the necessities for the sustenance of his men. For the other disasters that may shatter an army, one can almost always blame either the cowardice of the soldiers or the cruelty of fate, but for the lack of victuals, the foresight of the general alone is to be blamed; for just as the soldier owes loyalty and

---

10. Heinrich (1615–1696) Count von Podwitz, German soldier in the service of France.

submission to his commander, the commander owes precautions and care for their sustenance to his troops. There is even something inhumane about putting good men in a danger from which their valor cannot safeguard them and where they have no consolation for death in any hope of glory.

But aside from these concerns common to all generals, the prince who commands in person must have some purely particular ones. Since the life of his subjects is his own possession, he must be even more careful to preserve it, and since he knows that they are endangering themselves in his service, he must provide with even more affection for all their needs.

Having nothing to do in my camp while the orders that I had issued on this subject were being executed, I took the occasion to return to my frontier, where the Queen came up to meet me.

In the meanwhile, the Duke of Lorraine was displaying great uncertainty about the troops he had promised me, for basically he was unwilling to keep his word to me and yet did not desire to break it. On the one hand, he imagined that being so close to the Emperor and having no more strongholds with which to oppose him, he would be entirely exposed to the resentment of this Prince, but on the other hand, he also saw the danger of going back on his commitment to me, as I was then in a better position than anyone else to retaliate, so that he always answered ambiguously without deciding one way or another. But since I knew the mold of his character, I was convinced that if I could just force him into a choice, he would not have the courage to displease me outright. Thus I sent word to him one day that it was necessary for his troops to leave his side promptly on the following day, because I had already made plans for them, with which he complied as I had foreseen.

After four days with the Queen, I returned to the camp at Charleroi and took a route in the midst of enemy country so as to threaten all their strongholds.

Meanwhile, my orders were issued to invest Tournai from three different sides. From the sea, Marshal d'Aumont marched there with his cavalry; the Lorranians, whom I had sent to Artois, were to arrive from that direction, and I came in person from the direction of Brussels—and our marches were so well coordinated that we all appeared there within a few hours of each other. On the way, I seized Ath, a small stronghold in truth, but well situated to facilitate the passage of my men into the country and to harass the Spanish cities surrounding it.

I did not believe I should build a circumvallation around Tournai, both because I was convinced that the siege would be of short duration and because I had some canals that were there connected with little effort; but I had two bridges built across the Scheldt for communication between the various quarters.

Thus, having arrived before the stronghold on June 21, I had the trench opened on the twenty-second. The night of the twenty-third to the twenty-fourth the inhabitants offered to capitulate. The city surrendered on the twenty-fifth and the garrison, withdrawn to the castle, left it on the twenty-sixth.

I marched to Courtrai on the same day, desiring my enemies to see in one day the loss of the first stronghold and the siege of the second, but I reflected on the way that this depleted stronghold did not merit my presence; and that moreover, Tournai being deep inside the country, it could not be preserved without some other city to connect it with the strongholds under my control.

Douai immediately appeared the most convenient to me for this purpose, and I believed that it was important to attack it before the Spanish grew suspicious about it, because if they had been able to thrust some troops inside and keep a very small unit in the country to resupply it, it would have been almost impossible to take it in view of the extent of circumvallation that would have to be guarded in order to enclose the city and the castle, which are a great distance from each other. Thus, considering the matter to be important, I hid my intentions from the enemy so successfully by pretending to go to Lille that, upon arriving at Douai, I found a garrison of only twenty-six horse and seven hundred infantrymen.

It is true that the number of inhabitants was infinitely greater and that they initially displayed every intention of putting up a stout resistance, firing more cannons than any other stronghold has ever fired in such a short time; but after three days of open trench, the Swiss having occupied the first ditch, the inhabitants capitulated, although there was still a second ditch to reach; and after the hostages had been surrendered, the Lyonnais and

Louvigny regiments having in another attack passed the first
ditch without knowing of the capitulation, the people of the city
grew alarmed and humbly begged me to have this work suspended. The fort, to which the garrison had retired, surrendered
eight hours later, so that the siege having lasted only four days
in all, I entered the stronghold on July 16.

My intention was to begin a new siege immediately, but M. de
Turenne protested to me that it was necessary to give my army
some rest while that of Marshal d'Aumont took Courtrai; and he
gave me such good reasons for this that I submitted to them,
convinced that whatever desire one may have to distinguish
himself, the best path to glory is always the most reasonable one.

Meanwhile, to avoid idleness, I took a trip to Compiègne,
where I was visited by the abbé Rospigliosi on behalf of the Pope
his uncle on the subject of his promotion.[11] But I refused to allow
the *Parlement* to offer me congratulatory speeches on my conquests, which still did not seem great enough to me for public
acclaim; after which, having expedited internal affairs, I also
wanted my voyage to facilitate the success of my arms abroad;
and therefore I brought the Queen back with me so as to show her
to the people of the newly conquered cities, for which they felt so
grateful that after having gone all out to give her a good reception,
they still expressed regret at not having had time to prepare for it.
I took her to the biggest cities, and it was a rather singular thing
to see ladies making this trip as safely as if it had been in the middle
of my kingdom.

However, I resolved to see if I could continue my advance
against the enemy by taking Dendermonde, which by its location
alone would have greatly disturbed them and would have given
me great advantages. On the way, I took Oudenarde, which
seemed useful for the success of this plan, and then Alost surrendered to me. From there, I had Duras, lieutenant-general,
advance with two thousand horse on the approaches to Brussels,
from where I expected that aid might come, and I went by another
route in order to reconnoiter the stronghold in person.

But since I could then see things more closely with my own
eyes, I found, on the one hand, that the Scheldt River was so wide

11. Giacomo Rospigliosi (d. 1684).

that without boats suitable for closing the entire channel it was absolutely impossible, however carefully the banks were guarded, to prevent passage down the middle with the wind or with the tide; and on the other hand, I learned that Duras had arrived six hours too late to prevent the Spanish from thrusting six hundred men into the stronghold.

These two considerations combined convinced me to discard my plan, and I don't believe that either in undertaking it or in abandoning it, I did anything that I could not offer you as an example on similar occasions; for on the one hand, hearing for certain that this stronghold was depleted of men, it was little enough to venture a few days' march against one of the biggest posts in the country; as on the contrary, learning subsequently that some aid had entered and seeing that more could enter at any time, I could not persist in besieging it without the risk of fruit-lessly consuming the rest of the campaign there.

I am well aware, of course, that my retreat has been interpreted in various ways, and I shall even tell you for your instruction that when I resolved upon it I saw everything that has been said about it since and scorned it as I should; for indeed, I was convinced that as soon as this affair was viewed rationally, it would be considered that human prudence does not always control events and that after having successfully accomplished so many things in so few days, it was no marvel that I should have desisted from a single one in order to occupy myself more usefully elsewhere; that it was not even possible to attribute any other motive to this action, since the whole earth knew that the enemy was not strong enough either then or during the rest of the campaign to force me to withdraw; and that, finally, since most men take pleasure in criticizing what is beyond them, the same men who would blame us for having left Dendermonde without attacking it would con-demn me with far better cause if I had attacked it unsuccessfully or if I had shattered my army in taking it.

From which you can conclude, my son, that there is no great need to be alarmed at the adverse comments of the vulgar. These rumors that rise tumultuously are soon destroyed by reason and give way to the opinions of the wise, which, finally recognized as true by the people themselves, establish a solid and lasting reputation upon a universal consensus. While waiting for the

world to be disabused of its errors, the testimony of our own conscience must be enough for us, so that as I sometimes reconsider
the retreat in question, far from being unhappy about it, I have
regarded it as the only action of this campaign in which I had truly
put my virtue to the test; for indeed, although the others may
perhaps have been more brilliant, if I have gained any acclaim, it
was only by following the usual motions of those in our capacity,
and if I have had some measure of success, fortune might claim
at least an equal part in it, whereas I owe the full benefit of this
only to doing violence to myself in scorning the foreseeable
comments.

In order to put a stop to the joy of the Spanish over this affair,
I immediately resolved to attack one of their biggest strongholds,
and I personally chose Lille. The enemy, who knew how important it was and how it would consolidate my other conquests if it
fell into my hands, assembled all their troops in order to reinforce
it. There were even some people in my camp in whom the size of
the city, its population, the strength of the garrison, and the extent of the lines that had to be guarded inspired some doubts of
success. And yet, my orders were executed with so much zeal that
the city was reduced to desperate straits before the Spanish could
even learn that it was in danger.

But their ignorance made me think of giving them another
setback by attacking them as soon as the city was mine. Therefore,
once it capitulated, I dispatched two of my lieutenant-generals,
Créqui and Bellefonds, by different routes, following close upon
them myself, stopping in the conquered city only long enough
to thank God for having placed it in my hands.

The enemy, who had finally learned what was happening, were
already withdrawing, but since our route crossed their line of
march, they were met by Créqui and by Bellefonds on the same
day, and although outnumbering them three to one, they still
fled before them on learning that I was coming with the entire
army. They lost around two thousand men, including dead,
prisoners, and those dispersed by flight; but my joy at their
defeat was mitigated by my vexation at having played such a
small part in the execution of an undertaking entirely of my own
planning.

I was actually well aware, of course, that I had made all possible haste in order to arrive there in time, to the point that those who wanted subtly to tax me with recklessness even said that at the first news of the enemy, I had rushed toward them with insufficient escort. The basis of this rumor was that I had indeed been among the first on horseback and had, moreover, ridden very fast, my reason being that there was a long passage at the exit from my quarter and that if my troops, which were then leaving the camp in all directions, had entered it before me, I would have lost too much time in getting out in front. But once beyond the passage, I put all my men in battle formation and had them marching in perfect order.

After this, I did not believe I should undertake any new siege, my reasons being that the enemy, who had not ventured out against me during the entire campaign and who were still weak from this battle, would thrust all their troops into their cities; that by endeavoring to camp in a bad season, I would lose so many men that not even the taking of the stronghold would compensate me for it; that with the approach of winter, my army would grow more fatigued and the Spanish more hopeful of discouraging us; and that, finally, having to consider the feelings of all my neighbors and to see to the necessary funds, men, and munitions for the completion of my undertaking, I would not find the time to think of so many things in the excitement of a campaign.

While I was carrying the war into Flanders, the peace under negotiation at Breda incurred a new delay, for the English seeing that they had by my intercession obtained almost everything they desired, it occurred to them to demand the return of the two ships whose capture by the Dutch had served as the pretext for the war, a demand over which tempers might have risen to a breaking point. But seeing the importance of this affair and the paltriness of the sum in question, which amounted to only one hundred thousand francs, I resolved to furnish half of it rather than leave the matter hanging. And yet, not wanting to disclose my interest in this openly, I had Le Tellier make the offer as if he had decided on his own to be of service to these two states.

But in the meanwhile, the Dutch fleet entered the Thames,[12] and having captured or burned many vessels, it threw the entire

12. The Battle of the Medway, June 10–12, 1667.

island into such great consternation that the English resolved to conclude the treaty immediately, without any need for my offer.

This agreement seemed, on the one hand, to increase my chances of bringing them over to my side; but since, moreover, they had been led to relent on their demands only by their humiliation, a misfortune they had suffered only because they had not dared to put their fleet out to sea lest mine join the Dutch, it appeared as if they would harbor some resentment against me for it; and I knew, furthermore, that the King of England was being courted by the Spanish and by the States of Holland themselves, who in spite of my recent aid to them, were working to unite all Europe against me.

Thus I believed that it would be desirable to send Ruvigny to him to get him either to declare for me, or at least to remain neutral, which seemed the natural thing for him to do, in view of the unpleasant novelties that were constantly arising in his state; for he had just recently been forced to banish his chancellor from his councils; and even though it was true that this minister had by his loftiness incurred a great deal of envy, there is reason to think, however, that the ill will of the English was not entirely limited to him personally, as neither his entire ouster nor his voluntary exile were sufficient to satisfy them, and they wanted to put him on trial for crimes that he seemed to share with his master.

From such a notable event, the ministers of kings should learn to restrain their ambition, because the higher they rise beyond their sphere, the greater is their peril of falling. But kings can also learn not to let their servants become too powerful, because after having raised them impulsively, they are almost always obliged either to abandon them feebly or to sustain them precariously, for it is usually kings who are not strongly supported or not very able who tolerate such monstrous advancements.

I don't say that we should not, for the sake of our own greatness, wish for some of it to encompass those in our good graces, but we must watch out that this does not go to extremes, and my counsel on how you can guard against this consists of three principal observations.

The first is that you know your affairs thoroughly, because a king who does not know them is always dependent on his servants and most often cannot avoid consenting to their wishes.

The second, that you divide your confidence among many, so that each one who shares in it being naturally opposed to the advancement of his rivals, the jealousy of one often serves as a brake to the ambition of the others.

And the third, that even though you can admit only a small number of people into your secret affairs or into your friendly or familiar conversations, let no one imagine, however, that those who have this advantage are in a position to give you, as they please, a good or bad impression of the others; but that, on the contrary, you purposely maintain a kind of contact with everyone who holds some important post in the state; that you give them all the same liberty to propose whatever they may believe to be for your service, that none of them should feel obliged to address himself for his needs to anyone but you, that they should think they have only your good graces to consider, and that, finally, the most remote as well as the most familiar should be convinced that they are entirely dependent on you.

For you must know that once this independence on which I insist so much is well established among servants, it enhances the authority of the master more than anything else, and that it alone shows that he is actually governing them instead of being governed by them; as on the contrary, once it stops, intrigues, connections, and private commitments inevitably enlarge the following of the influential and weaken the reputation of the prince.

But particularly if he is someone who by our preference or by his industry manages to distinguish himself from his peers, he is invariably thought to be the absolute master of our mind, he is immediately regarded as an official favorite, he is sometimes credited with things in which he has not had the slightest part, and he is rumored in the world to be infinitely more in favor than he actually is.

And yet this is not a case, my son, in which popular rumors can be disdained; on the contrary, they must be remedied wisely and promptly, because if this vain opinion lasts too long, it can harm your reputation and actually increase the influence of its object, for since each one strives for his friendship, he often finds a way of accomplishing through others what he would never have undertaken on his own, and because he is imagined to be all powerful, every effort is made to please him. Even those whom we allow the greatest familiarity with us try to strengthen themselves by his support. They make secret commitments to him that they occasionally cover with affected indifference, whereas in the things that he cares about, they inform him of everything that they see, they always speak to us with his opinions, they praise or blame whatever he wants, they protract whatever displeases him, they facilitate whatever he desires, so that we are almost miraculously drawn into all his opinions.

And this, my son, is all the more important, for this is how the power of favorites usually begins to establish itself and how most princes gradually come to be governed; for indeed, what is called being governed does not always mean having an official prime minister, to whom all decisions are openly referred: to the enlightened mind it is enough for there to be one or many persons, whatever their title, who can individually or collectively convince us of what they want, who know how to advance or postpone affairs according to their interest, and who can without our realizing it surround us with the people whom they favor or disenchant us with those whom they dislike.

After having maintained my navy until the month of October, I had dismissed it with the exception of a squadron that I sent beyond the Channel in order to harass the coasts of Spain.

In regard to my army, I had left it under the command of M. de Turenne, who soon after my departure marched to Alost, which the enemy had regarrisoned, took the stronghold, and dismantled it; after which, seeing that there was nothing else to do, he took—following my orders—the most extensive winter quarters he could for constricting the enemy all the more, and returning to my court, divided his troops among four lieutenant-generals who, each having his separate department, were, however, under orders to cooperate for my service.

Du Passage[13] commanded everything between the sea and the Lys. Duras had Tournai with all the advanced posts beyond the Scheldt. D'Humières[14] was in charge of Lille and the flatland between these two rivers. Bellefonds, detached from the others, guarded the strongholds between the Sambre and the Meuse,

13. Aimard de Poisieux (d. 1688), Count du Passage.
14. Louis de Crevant (1628–1694), Marquis, later Duke d'Humières, became Marshal of France in 1668.

where he accomplished a rather notable action upon his arrival, defeating with eight hundred horse fifteen hundred of the enemy, who had infantry and cavalry and were flanked by a wood.

I had most explicitly ordered all commanders of strongholds and all general officers to take good care of their men and to prevent any harm from coming to the inhabitants of the cities. But to contribute my share to this, I made sure that the troops received their full pay and even increased that of the junior officers by one third, so that they could live comfortably without being a burden upon the people of the country.

But I believed I should do still more for the good of the people as well as for the security of my conquests by building citadels in the largest strongholds, such as Lille and Tournai, because this dispensed me from having to maintain such strong garrisons there and delivered them from the fear of being taken and retaken in each campaign.

I was making every provision, of course, to relieve them of this fear; for far from letting the enemy think of retaking what I held, I was preparing to take a good part of what remained to them. My general plan was to put four armies in the field the following spring, one of which, under my brother, was to enter Catalonia in order to attack the Spanish in Spain itself, the second, under the Prince de Condé, was to advance up the Rhine so as to prevent any incursion from Germany, and the other two were to be in Flanders with only myself and M. de Turenne as generals, for I did not want to remain idle for a single moment, and I desired to have one army always fresh while the other rested.

In keeping with these plans, I was making new levies not merely in my domains, but in Germany, in Switzerland, and in England, where I even obtained many cavalrymen dismissed from the company of King's gendarmes because they were Catholics.

M. de Lorraine wanted his troops back at the end of the campaign, but I had the matter discussed with him in such a way that he was obliged to drop it and to let me keep them as long as I wanted.

In order to support such large forces, I took care to replenish my stores, which had been depleted during the past summer, and I made a detailed estimate of my collections and expenditures for the coming year.

But during all these preparations for war, there was still talk of peace. The Dutch, inspired by their own fear, were constantly pressing me to consent to it. While I was in Avesnes, Van Beuningen had arrived there for this purpose and even requested to accompany me to my camp, but I did not feel that I should permit this, because with so many people, there would hardly fail to be someone with a real or imaginary cause for complaint, and I did not want this to be observed unsympathetically.

Thus I sent him to Paris to deal with Lionne, and when I resumed this negotiation myself on my return, I finally resolved to show all Europe my moderation by offering to be satisfied with what I had taken in exchange for what I had inherited, unless they preferred to give me Franche-Comté or Luxembourg, with Aire, Saint-Omer, Douai, Cambrai, and Charleroi, consenting furthermore to letting the Spanish have three months to deliberate on this, during which time I would not attack any of their strongholds where cannon would have to be used.

The Pope was working very zealously to achieve this agreement, and his mediation having been accepted by me when his nephew saw me at Compiègne, the Spanish did not dare refuse it, but since they saw that this affair would not end without costing them something, they hesitated to conclude and resorted to various chicaneries on the time and on the place of meeting, in the hope that my neighbors would be jealous of my rise and would combine with them.

Meanwhile, my court was not all of one mind on this affair, and many, guided by their interests, found arguments for peace or for war, depending on which would enhance their functions and their influence. But since I knew their motives, their arguments made an impression on me only insofar as they furthered my affairs and never detracted from my impartiality; or at least, if I sometimes inclined ever so slightly toward war, this was not because of the favor or skill of those who might have an interest in it, but merely because it is undoubtedly the most brilliant way to acquire glory.

In regard to the German princes, I think that there were some who desired the continuation of the war, just as there were others who wanted peace, but generally speaking, they all dealt most honorably with me on this subject. I sent off to those who had recently engaged to defend the Rhine crossing against the Imperial troops in order to convince them to join forces with the Prince de Condé, whom I was sending for the same purpose.

As for the Emperor, I had informed him of my voyage to Flanders, and he had taken it better than I would have imagined, requesting merely that I be reasonable in my demands. And even when Count von Fürstenberg made some proposal to him concerning the ultimate treaty,[15] he indicated that his only objection to it was his hesitation to approach the ministers of Spain before the eventuality had occurred. But this did not prevent me from foreseeing that if my quarrel with the Spanish continued, this Prince would undoubtedly assist them, and counting on this, I sought to find ways of diverting his forces elsewhere.

My plan to give Poland a prince of my house having been obstructed by the death of the Queen,[16] on whom it was principally based, the Duke of Neuburg requested me to favor his claim, and the Prince de Condé, with whom I had this matter discussed, having replied most openly and submissively, I promised the Duke to do so, even supporting him by proposing the marriage of his daughter to the recently widowed King, whom I tried to dissuade from abdicating. But having subsequently heard that he had no inclination for this marriage and seeing that the Duke of Neuburg would not easily accomplish his plan, it occurred to me to put the situation to a different use. I immediately adjusted my conduct to this new plan, and I resolved to favor the abdication that I had been delaying, so that the ensuing disputes would attract the German armies while I established myself in Flanders.

As to the Swedes, I would certainly have desired to make sure of them before the war was declared, but seeing that the harder they were pressed, the further they withdrew, I wanted to try if treating them more coldly would have the opposite effect. And still later, seeing that this remedy was not working, and not wanting to stand on ceremony, I had this matter rediscussed with them, but it was all to no avail.

15. The Count proposed, on behalf of the Elector of Cologne, a treaty between Louis and the Emperor for the partitioning of the Spanish monarchy if Charles II died without direct heirs, but Fürstenberg was neither liked nor trusted in Vienna.

16. May 10, 1667.

I received some very courteous offers from the King of Denmark, but as he did not seem to be in a position to do anything of importance for me, I merely replied with equal courtesy.

I was more careful to maintain the good will of the Duke of Savoy, whom I had initially informed of my plan; and because he could be useful to me in Italy, I tried to attach him to my interests by making him whatever proposals I believed might please him.

The Dutch, who did not think, perhaps, that I knew of their intrigues against me, still spoke freely with me about their interests and tried to commit me not to conquer anything near their frontiers, but this is precisely what I refused them. And when the three months of grace that I had given to the Spanish at their intercession had expired around the end of December, I announced that I did not intend to extend it.

And indeed, already tired of remaining idle, I had everyone look around for something that could be executed suddenly. Among others, when the Prince de Condé went to hold the Estates of Burgundy, I charged him with looking into what might be done in Franche-Comté.

I had recently concluded a new treaty with the King of Portugal whereby he assumed the obligation not to make either peace or truce without my express consent, and I also promised him not to settle with Spain unless they accorded him the title of king that they had been refusing him. But toward the end of that year, my plans were entirely disrupted by a revolution in that state.

For the King, who was personally very disturbed, having rendered himself all the more unbearable by his morals, was ousted and made a prisoner in his own palace without any of his subjects or servants having lifted a finger to prevent such a heinous assault, an event so unique that past history has never seen anything like it.[17] But while the rest of mankind is content to wonder at this event, you should try to profit from it by observing its causes.

It must assuredly be agreed that as bad as a prince may be, the revolt of his subjects is always infinitely criminal. He who has given kings to men has wanted them to be respected as His

17. He was obliged to accept the regency of his brother Pedro, who later succeeded him on the throne.

lieutenants, reserving to Himself alone the right to examine their conduct. His will is that whoever is born a subject must obey without qualification; and this law, so explicit and universal, is not made in favor of princes alone, but is beneficial to the very people on whom it is imposed, who can never violate it without exposing themselves to much graver evils that those they claim to be guarding against. No maxim is more established by Christianity than this humble submission of subjects to those who are instituted over them; and indeed, those who would inquire into past times will easily see how rare, since the coming of Jesus Christ, have been those ghastly revolutions that occurred so often under paganism.

But it is not fair for the sovereigns who profess this holy doctrine to rely on the innocence that it inspires in their people in order to live, for their part, in greater indiscipline. They must sustain by their own example the religion whose support they desire and consider that their subjects, seeing them immersed in vice and in blood, can hardly render to their person the respect due their rank, nor recognize in them the living image of Him who is all-holy as well as all-powerful.

I am well aware that those who are born like yourself with virtuous inclinations never go to these scandalous extremes which openly offend the people, but you should know that in our high rank the smallest errors always have dangerous consequences. He who has committed them has the misfortune of never knowing their seriousness until it is too late to remedy them. Becoming accustomed to doing wrong makes him feel that it is increasingly more excusable and less known, while in the eyes of the public it appears more shameful and more obvious, for one of the greatest errors that a prince can make is to think that his faults remain hidden or that they are excused.

Kings, who are the sovereign arbiters of the fortunes and of the conduct of men, are themselves always the most severely judged and the most carefully scrutinized. With the many people who surround them, what escapes the notice of one is almost always discovered by the other. The slightest suspicion under which they fall immediately passes from ear to ear like a bit of good news. The speaker, always affecting to know more than the others, magnifies rather than minimizes things, and the listener, taking malicious pleasure in the depreciation of something that he feels is too far above him, is eager to believe what he hears.

The greater the merit and virtue of the prince who is being discussed, moreover, the harder the envious try to dim his brilliance, so that far from hiding his faults, he is sometimes even attributed some of which he is entirely innocent; from which you must conclude, my son, that a sovereign cannot live too wisely or too innocently, that in order to reign prosperously and gloriously, it is not enough to provide for general affairs if we do not also regulate our own morals, and that the only means to be truly independent and above the rest of mankind is to do nothing, either in public or in secret, that it could justly censure.

*

Before leaving, I sent an edict to the *Parlement*, by which I erected the estate of Vaujours into a duchy in favor of M[lle. de] L[a Vallière] [18] and acknowledged a daughter by her, for not going to the army with the intention of avoiding all peril, I believed that it was only fair to assure to this child the honor of its birth and to give the mother an establishment suitable to the affection that I had borne for her for six years.

I could undoubtedly have dispensed with discussing this unexemplary attachment with you, but after having drawn so many lessons by observing the failings of others, I have not wanted to deprive you of what you can learn from my own.

I should tell you first that since a prince should always be a perfect model of virtue, it would be desirable for him to be completely immune to the failings of the rest of mankind, all the more since he is sure that they could never be hidden; and yet, if we should happen to fall, in spite of ourselves, into one of these lapses, we must at least lessen their importance by taking two precautions that I have always found very practicable.

The first, that the time that we devote to our love never be taken away from our affairs, because our first object must always be the preservation of our glory and of our authority, which are

18. Louise-Françoise de La Baume Le Blanc (1644–1710), Duchess de La Vallière. The daughter was Marie-Anne de Bourbon (1666–1739), Mademoiselle de Blois.

absolutely impossible to maintain without great effort; for however possessed we may be, we must consider in the very interest
of our passion that by losing the favor of the public we would also
lose the esteem of the very person for whom we have trans-
gressed.

But the second consideration, which is the most delicate and
the most difficult to put into practice, is that while surrendering
our heart we remain the masters of our mind, that we keep the
affections of a lover separate from the decisions of a sovereign,
and that the beauty who gives us pleasure never has the liberty to
speak to us of our affairs or of our servants.

The heart of a prince is attacked like a stronghold. One begins
by occupying all the approaches. A skillful woman initially sets
about to eliminate whoever is not in her interests. She arouses
suspicion about some and disenchantment with others, so that
she and her friends alone will be favorably heard, and if we do
not guard against this, we must, in order to satisfy her alone,
dissatisfy everyone else.

Once you give a woman the liberty to speak to you of important
things, they are bound to make us fail. [sic] Our affection for them,
by making us relish their worst arguments, makes us gradually
fall in with them, and the weakness of their nature often making
them prefer trifling interests to more solid considerations, almost
always makes them take the wrong side. They are eloquent in
their expressions, insistent in their requests, stubborn in their
opinions; and all this is often based only on their aversion for
someone, on their intention to promote another, or on some
lightly made promise.

No secret is safe with them, for if they are of limited insight,
they can by their simplicity discover what should remain most
hidden, and if they have some intelligence, they are never without
their intrigues and their secret connections. There is always some
secret council for their advancement or for their preservation,
and they never fail to speak freely before it whenever they want
to consult it about their interests.

It is in these councils that they decide what side they must take
in each affair, what artifices they must use in achieving their
undertakings, how to get rid of those who are in their way, how
to establish their friends, by what skills to engage us more deeply

and hold us more permanently. Indeed, they sooner or later achieve all these things and we sooner or later give in to them without noticing that we are losing or disenchanting our best servants and that we are ruining our reputation; with the only way to guard against this being to give them the liberty to speak to you of nothing else but of simple pleasures and to make a studious effort not to believe them in anything that might concern our affairs or the persons of our servants.

I will confess to you that a prince who is deeply in love is so taken by his affection for his beloved that he would have difficulty in taking all these precautions. But it is in difficult things that we display our virtue; and moreover, it is certain that they are an absolute necessity, and it is from not having observed them that we see in history so many ghastly examples of houses extinct, of thrones overthrown, of provinces devastated, of empires destroyed.

1668

THE mediators, seeing the expiration at the beginning of the year of the three months that I had granted them in order to make the Queen of Spain decide on one of my two peace proposals, asked me for three more months; and in spite of my great reluctance, I could not refrain from according them, particularly upon the appeals of the Pope.

I was under strong pressure to grant an armistice for the same period, but my opposition to this was supported by the rashness of Castel-Rodrigo, whose cold reception of this proposal gave me a pretext for refusing it. Thus I continued to have everyone look around for something that could be executed hastily, calculating that whatever I might take would always be useful, either for improving my position if the war should last or for exhibiting my good faith further if I restored it by the peace.

I was proposed some undertakings against Ypres, against Namur, and against some other strongholds, but I liked my own idea concerning Burgundy[1] best of all, particularly after the Prince de Condé, who had been closer to it, had reported to me on its condition, for I considered that it was a large, fertile, and important province, which by its location, by its language, and by all rights should have been part of the kingdom, and which opened a new passage to Germany for me while at the same time closing the kingdom to my enemies.

I could see, furthermore, that by attacking it during this season, it would be hard to relieve, that the governor general of the Low Countries had limited forces and was very far away, that the Marquis d'Yenne,[2] the local governor, was a man of little intelligence and less reputation, that all the forces of the country consisted of some militia, which were not to be feared, and that the only authority then rested solely in the hands of the *Parlement*, which, as an assembly of mere bourgeois, would be easy to mislead

1. That is, Franche-Comté.
2. Philippe de La Baume (d. 1688), Marquis d'Yenne.

and to intimidate. The greatest difficulty in the undertaking lay in executing all the necessary preparations in secret.

But after thinking about it, I found a means of assembling eighteen thousand men without their even noticing it themselves, for some were commanded to go to Catalonia with my brother, the others to be at La Marche, where a minor rebellion had occurred, the others to wait for me in Metz, where I pretended to go myself. And their routes were so planned that they had to pass through Burgundy in order to reach their destination. I even arranged for M. le Prince to hold them there under the pretext of improper procedure, for as governor of the province, he refused to allow them to continue, pretending that he had not been informed of their route.

Only with my household troops was it necessary to do it differently, for I initially routed them to Troyes, where they received a second order to join the others, but by that time there was nothing more to hide.

Meanwhile, the cannon and the munitions, both of food and for artillery, were being brought in or were being prepared in the very province under various pretexts of one kind or another, while I entertained those who were the most concerned with proposals far removed from my intentions.

It just so happened that the Francs-Comtois, alarmed by the previous campaign, had recently made a request for the renewal of their neutrality, which they had often obtained, and I believed that this negotiation would be good for keeping them occupied while I made my preparations. But in order to derive the full benefit from it, I transferred it from Mouslier,[3] my resident in Switzerland, who had begun it, to the Prince de Condé, who could in this way innocently send back and forth into the country as often as was necessary for our plans; which was so well handled that between the Francs-Comtois coming to see him and he in turn sending off to them, he learned and arranged all that was necessary, always making it seem as if the conclusion of the negotiation was entirely up to them, so that they were not merely not alarmed, but even when they heard the truth in those vague rumors that cannot be prevented from preceding the most secret

3. François Mouslier.

things, they took them as an artifice specifically intended to make them increase their offers. Such was their assurance, that the Swiss, who had already become suspicious of these moves, were re-assured by the tranquillity of those who should have been most concerned by them.

Even Castel-Rodrigo, whom they kept informed of their negotiation, was for a long while fooled by it like them, along with all my other neighbors, although these could observe my conduct more closely through their ministers at my court. For even though it was impossible to prevent someone from guessing the truth, I gave so many indications to the contrary that even those who had been the first to suspect it sometimes had their doubts, and those who had been told of it could not believe it.

But finally, as I was about to depart, I wanted to inform the states of Europe myself of what I could no longer hide from them; and lest the most malicious take advantage of this undertaking to bring the others around to their sentiments, I declared that whatever its success, I would still keep my word.

I left accompanied by the entire nobility of my court. Only then were the Francs-Comtois finally aroused from their stupor, whether by the rumors of my voyage, or by the warnings of Castel-Rodrigo, or even by the declaration of the Prince de Condé, who, taking the opportunity of some difficulty that they were raising, suddenly broke with them.

They immediately asked for help from Flanders, offered great sums to the Swiss for troops, and mustered their own militia for February 8; but it was all too late, for I had ordered the Prince de Condé to invade the country on the fourteenth of the same month and to seize certain posts that would prevent both the junction of the militia and communication between the principal cities.

I had also resolved that Besançon and Salins should be attacked at the same time, so that they could both be taken before any relief could reach them; and I did not mind if this were done before my arrival, preferring the solid advantage of gaining time to the empty satisfaction of being present during these two attacks. These actually were, of course, two important strongholds, for Besançon, claiming to be an imperial city, recognized the King of Spain only as its protector and was considered to be the most populous in the country, as for that matter Salins was easily the richest, owing to the fountains that furnished it with salt; but after all, both these strongholds were then in hardly any condition to resist for long.

The Prince de Condé himself marched to Besançon, with only two thousand men at the most, and yet summoned it to surrender with so much assurance that the inhabitants, convinced that he was followed by my entire army, capitulated on the same day, while he sent the Duke de Luxembourg[4] to Salins, where amid similar consternation, the city and the two forts were surrendered to him without a fight.

This double news reached me during the same day at Auxonne, which I left the following day in order to attack Dôle, although it was actually no easy matter; for the plan of the stronghold showed me that it was equipped with seven large bastions, mostly built on rock, history taught me that it had twice resisted powerful armies, and the season gave me warning that I could not camp for long. But on the other hand, I also saw the small size of the garrison, the general consternation that gripped the entire country, the ardor that my people exhibited for this undertaking, and the good fortune that had accompanied all my others.

Thus I sent orders to M. le Prince to invest it from Besançon. I had [the Duke de Luxembourg] march from [Salins], and I marched myself from where I was.

I spent almost a day and one half in personally reconnoitering the stronghold, convinced that the time was not lost, for the success of a siege almost always depends on the proper choice of attacks. I finally resolved that there would be three and that, to save time, there would be a march right to the counterscarp. The guards and the Picardy regiment did as they were commanded in their two attacks, but the Lyonnais regiment, going beyond my orders, reached the covered way, undertook to scale the half moon, stormed it, and occupied it.

The inhabitants were incredibly terrified to see us thus posted at the foot of their walls on the first day, so that the Count de Gramont[5] having volunteered to go ask them to surrender, I believed that he might succeed in his purpose. He had some difficulty in reaching the city, but little in persuading the bourgeois,

4. François-Henri de Montmorency-Bouteville (1628–1695), Duke de Luxembourg, became Marshal of France in 1675.
5. Philibert (1621–1707), Count de Gramont.

from among whom he brought me some hostages, after which it capitulated.

Meanwhile, in order to leave the Spanish with no way of re-entering the province, I wanted to secure some of the cities and fortresses that still held out for them. I sent orders for this to Noisy,[6] Governor of Salins, who was able to exploit my reputation and the fright of the enemy so effectively that with a little more than one hundred and twenty men he took six strongholds in two days, some of which had undergone regular sieges. The fortresses of Sainte–Anne and Joux, especially, were considered to be impregnable in the country, and the Marquis d'Yenne, who had withdrawn into the latter, seemed to make it stronger by his presence. But whether from his dissatisfaction with Spain, or from despair of ever being relieved, or even from fear of being punished someday for having defended this province so badly, he agreed to surrender to me and to come to see me before Gray, where I had marched after having taken Dôle.

I joyfully accepted this gift of my good fortune, and to make the best possible use of it immediately, I desired for the Marquis d'Yenne to exert himself personally in effecting the surrender of Gray. The deputies of the *Parlement* of Dôle, whom I had already utilized for this purpose, had been very badly received there and the city seemed determined to resist. I had also, for my part, established quarters, personally reconnoitered the stronghold, and arranged everything in order to launch the attacks the following day. But to spare no effort that could save the lives of my men, it occurred to me to send the Marquis d'Yenne into the stronghold, believing that the inhabitants might perhaps be very pleased to be authorized by the governor of the province to do something that was in their interest. Indeed, I was requested that very day to suspend the attacks, and the capitulation taking place the following day, I entered Gray on February 19, thus completing in fifteen days of winter a conquest that, undertaken with less planning, might have occupied me for longer than one campaign.

Without bothering to visit the cities that had surrendered in my absence, I returned as quickly as I could to Saint-Germain, where I had important affairs to settle, but I permitted those who

6. Louis de Maupeau (d. 1669), Sieur de Noisy.

were with me to accompany me or to return at their convenience.

As the weather during this campaign was very bad, I had tried to relieve its discomforts for persons of quality by setting a good table for them, and because there is less time for paperwork in the country, I conversed more freely with everyone, both publicly and privately; but I nevertheless tried to profit as much as possible from these conversations, either for furthering my own work, or for getting to know more about the people to whom I was talking, or for delving into various other things.

It has been a warmly debated question among political thinkers whether a prince should confer with a few or with many people. Some say that since a king must know everything, he must confer with everyone. Others claim that by dividing the management of his affairs among a small number of councillors, he could find more relief in his work and less uncertainty in his councils. Some have even ventured to maintain that a monarch, whether for his own peace of mind or for his decisions to be firm, should confide only in a single minister.

But as for me, my son, I believe that all this advice can be reconciled by specifying the times and the persons to whom it would be given, for to begin with what appears to be the most dangerous, I would believe that in the case of a prince who, owing to his extreme youth, would not be capable of governing, he might with more reason be counseled to rely entirely on a single minister rather than on many, because if he had many and was not able either to limit their functions or to settle their disputes, they would be more interested in struggling against each other than in maintaining the greatness of his state, whereas if he turned everything over to a single person, his only problem would be to choose one whose capacity rendered him capable of such a great position and whose birth rendered him incapable of aspiring to anything more.

It would be quite different for a king who, naturally bright and vigorous, might be lacking merely in experience, for in such a case he would undoubtedly be both wiser and safer to divide his trust among a certain number of able people. But this number should be small, for since he would not yet be accustomed to the malicious artifices of men, he could not always, among so many differing reports, distinguish truth from probability, which would constantly produce uncertainty in his thinking, vacillation in his decisions, and concern in the minds of his most loyal servants, who would always fear that the malice of the court would destroy the merit of their services.

But finally, if there should be a prince who from natural intelligence, strength of character, and long experience in affairs knew how to be on his guard just as well as his most able councillors, who understood his most delicate interests at least as well as they, and who, taking their advice because it pleases him, could nevertheless decide wisely by himself whenever necessary, who would have enough restraint not to decide anything without sufficient reflection, and who would have enough control over his expression and over his statements to learn what everyone is thinking, without perhaps entirely revealing himself to anyone, I would counsel him differently. For he should not avoid, in his leisure time, whatever occasions might naturally arise to hear various people speak on all sorts of subjects, in the course of playing, hunting, chatting, or even in private audience.

One of the great men of antiquity,[7] taken by this thought, used to say that whoever governs a state must be prepared to listen to a great deal of nonsense; and his reason, in my opinion, is that the same man who tells us something useless today may tell us something very important tomorrow, and that even those who never say anything worthwhile still make those who deal with the greatest affairs more hesitant about lying, because they know in how many different ways we can learn the truth.

But another profit that a prince will undoubtedly derive from these different conversations is that he will gradually get to know for himself the most worthy people in his state, an advantage all the greater in that the principal function of a monarch is to place each person where he can be most useful to the public. We obviously cannot do everything, but we must provide for everything to be done well, and this depends primarily on whom we choose. In a great state, there is always someone proper to every task, and the only question is to know who they are and to put them where they belong. The maxim that in order to be wise it is enough to know oneself may be good for private individuals, but the able

7. Cicero (marginal note). Compare with *De Officiis*, Book I, Ch. XXV.

sovereign who wants to be served well is obliged to know every-one he sees around him; for indeed, those whose counsel we procure in everything else may reasonably be suspect to us on this score, because the more important the posts to be filled, the more their desire to fill them with their followers may either deceive them or tempt them to deceive us.

I am well aware, my son, that these observations are a little scrupulous and that few sovereigns go to the trouble of seeing to them, but there are also very few who entirely perform their duty. If you want to be an ordinary prince, satisfied to conduct yourself—or rather to let yourself be conducted—like the others, you have no need of these lessons, but if you should someday have, as I hope, the noble ambition of distinguishing yourself, and if you should want to avoid the shame not merely of being governed, but even of being suspected of it, you cannot be too careful about observing the principles I am furnishing you here and that you will continually find in the rest of this work.[8]

I had learned during this voyage that after long efforts, the Dutch had finally induced the English to conclude a treaty of alliance with them on January [23] at Brussels, whose principal provision was that they and any other states entering into this league would employ all their offices and persuasions until the month of May to bring about a peace between France and Spain, and that at the end of this period they resort to stronger measures; and I understood that although this agreement seemed to regard both crowns equally, it was nevertheless aimed directly at me, not merely because it had been concluded in enemy territory, but also because as things stood, the peace appeared to depend entirely on me.

The Swedes had not yet signed this treaty, but they were ex-pected to do so, and they engaged to furnish the Dutch Republic with ten thousand foot soldiers in return for a pension of seven hundred thousand *livres*.

I had no news of any German princes having as yet entered into this plot. But those obliged by treaty to defend the Rhine crossing for me had not yet replied definitely to my summons to join M. le

---

8. In 1668, when this text was prepared, Louis had every intention of continuing the *Mémoires*.

Prince. The Duke of Lüneburg was giving his troops to the States of Holland. The Bishop of Münster, whom I urged to some undertaking against the States General, had informed me that he lacked sufficient forces; and indeed I knew that he already feared the resentment of the Elector of Cologne, who, expecting to be appointed coadjutor of this bishopric, had been excluded by the Bishop of Paderborn.

The King of Denmark was outwardly most courteous, but he had close ties with the Dutch, and he was then arming a good number of ships.

Poland, still torn by its internal disputes, could assuredly give me no cause for alarm, but I also learned that I could not expect to create any diversion in that direction, because the King was still uncertain about abdicating, and the republic had not yet given its consent to this.

The Emperor appeared rather quiet, but he still had some old troops in service, and the Spanish were very impatiently pressing him to declare himself.

The Electors as a body had sent a delegation to offer me their impartial mediation; but actually they were not all of the same sentiment, and the Elector of Brandenburg had a sizable body of troops that he could give to my enemies.

From Italy, I heard only exhortations to peace, both from the Pope as the common father of all the Catholic princes, and from the Venetians, who expected to obtain some relief out of it for Crete; and the Duke of Savoy, whom I had incited by various proposals to try something on his own, had not been able to reach any decision.

As for the Swiss, I learned that they had been so displeased at my undertaking against Franche-Comté, which claimed to be under their protection, that they confiscated the property of the Swiss officers whom I had employed in the conquest.

It was rumored in Spain that Don Juan[9] was to cross over with six or seven thousand men and assume the governorship of the Low Countries, but I was informed that he had not yet left, and I was having him observed by the Duke de Beaufort, who was ready to dispute his passage.

9. Don Juan of Austria (1629–1679), illegitimate son of Philip IV and "dark horse" candidate for the Spanish succession.

Concerning the peace proposals, the Catholic King had empowered Castel-Rodrigo to accept one of my two alternatives, but after their various deceptions, I had a right to be skeptical; and indeed I was preparing to go to Flanders as soon as possible, for it was there ultimately that I intended to carry my major effort. I had even changed my mind about sending my brother to Catalonia, being content with leaving [someone][10] there with [a few thousand] men, in order to direct three large armies against the Low Countries. One, commanded by the Prince de Condé, was to go up to the Rhine, the other, led by my brother, toward the sea, and the third, to which I went myself, into the middle of the country, so that I could easily be on hand wherever I might be needed.

But toward the end of March, the Dutch, backed by a high delegation from the Electoral College, by the Pope, and by the King of England, came to ask me for a new postponement until the end of the month of May. They argued that the King of Spain had already done all that could be expected of him, that my terms had been met, and that I should not refuse to grant the time that was absolutely necessary for the remaining formalities. I could easily have replied to these protestations, but basically, it was a question of seeing whether it would be more advantageous and more proper for me to make peace on terms that I had set myself or to continue the war against the Spanish and against whoever might take their side.

The deliberation was assuredly difficult in itself, owing to the number and to the weight of the arguments on each side, but what made it particularly complicated for me was that I had to reach my decision purely on my own, there being no one whom I could consult with full confidence; for on the one hand, I had no doubt that those who were employed in the war would unconsciously favor its continuation, and moreover, it was easy to see that the people whom I employed in my other councils, finding it inconvenient to follow me to the armies and being jealous of those who did, would naturally be all for peace.

I did not fail, nevertheless, to hear both sides in order, at least,

10. Louis subsequently appointed the Count du Passage to command c. 5,000 troops in that area.

to compare their arguments before making a final decision. On one side, they portrayed to me the number and the vigor of my troops, the weakness of the Spanish, and the apathy that seemed to prevail in Germany. They protested to me that all my plans had already been made for the coming campaign, my troops being raised, my stores full, and a good deal spent; that the Dutch, who created so much commotion, had more ill will than power; that their English allies had neither the troops nor the money for any major effort; that the Swedes had not declared themselves outright and would probably think twice before leaving their old alliance with France in order to join with their former enemies, aside from their country being so far away that their troops could not arrive in time; but that, finally, all these powers combined would still not equal half my strength, without even considering, they said, my presence, my vigor, and my dedication, which they did not fail to emphasize strongly, so that I could regard the conquest of the Low Countries as inevitable by the end of the campaign.

But although these arguments were indeed appealing and capable of arousing my ambitions, I regretted to see that there were more pressing and more solid ones on the other side. Those who favored peace did not deny that I was stronger than the Spanish, but they maintained that it was much easier to defend oneself than to attack; that the more progress I made, the more my armies would be weakened by the large garrisons that would have to be left in the rear; that on the contrary, jealousy would increase the number of my enemies every day; that even if I made an important conquest, I would have to be prepared either to restore a good part of it by the peace or to sustain a perpetual war alone against all my neighbors; that having publicly declared from the first day of this quarrel that I was asking only for the equivalent of my rightful inheritance, I could not possibly refuse to be content with the value that I had set on it myself without alienating all the states to whom I had given my word; that the Emperor, who still appeared apathetic, would not lose such a fine opportunity to stem the decline of his house and to rally to his side as many of the states and princes of Germany as he could; that if the Swiss, already greatly ired at the conquest of Burgundy, saw me trying something new, they might either do something on their own or favor the designs of my enemies; that the Pope and all Christendom would reproach me if I immobilized all the forces of the Christian princes while Crete was left to fall into the hands of the Infidel; and that, finally, my people, deprived of my relief by the expenses of such a great war, could suspect me of preferring my personal glory to their welfare and tranquillity.

But aside from these arguments that might have occurred to anyone, there were others based entirely on my own secret ideas, for frankly, I wanted to profit not merely from the present circumstances but also from the future ones. With the great rise in fortune that may have been in store for me, nothing seemed more necessary for me than to establish a reputation for moderation and for honesty among my weakest neighbors that could allay their natural fright in the face of an overwhelming power, and I considered that there was no more brilliant way to display these virtues than by letting them see me, arms in hand, acceding to the request of my allies and contenting myself with a small compensation.

I noted, furthermore, that as small as this compensation appeared in contrast with what I might acquire by force of arms, it was nevertheless greater than it seemed, because the Spanish implicitly abandoned by a voluntary treaty the renunciations that were their only claim to exclude the Queen from her succession; that if I now insisted on war, the league that would wage it would subsequently remain as a perpetual impediment to my most legitimate claims, whereas by a quick settlement I would destroy it in its infancy and have the time to create enough problems for its members to prevent them from meddling in mine; that even if nothing happened, I could always find an occasion to break with Spain whenever I wanted; that I could restore Franche-Comté in such a condition that I could always become its master; and that once I consolidated my new conquests, they would give me better access to the rest of the Low Countries; that the peace would allow me each day to improve my finances, my navy, my contacts, and whatever else may be accomplished by a dedicated prince in a rich and powerful state; and that, finally, I would be more influential throughout Europe and more capable of gaining my ends with each individual state if they saw me without enemies than if there existed a party against me.

And indeed, shortly after having announced my decision to make peace, the Emperor, convinced of my good faith, entered into negotiations for the ultimate treaty that he had been rejecting; and the affair having been discussed by Count von Fürstenberg on my behalf [11] and by [the Prince von Auersperg] for the Emperor, it was concluded on [January 19, 1668], to the effect that in the given eventuality, the Emperor would receive [Spain and the West Indies,[12] Milan, the Italian *presidii*,[13] Sardinia, the Canary, and the Balearic Islands] and I [the Low Countries, including Franche-Comté, the Philippine Islands, Rosas, Navarre, the African possessions, Naples, and Sicily], which was another marvelous confirmation of the rights of the Queen and an explicit avowal of the nullity of her renunciations, an act all the more important since it was made by the very party who had the greatest interest in maintaining them.

11. Actually, Grémonville negotiated the Treaty with Johann Weikhart (1615–1677), Prince von Auersperg, Grand Chamberlain of the Emperor.

12. That is, the Spanish Empire in America.

13. Fortified ports.

INDEX

A

Africa, 198, 211, 261
Aire, 242
Aix-la-Chapelle, Treaty of, 16, 46
Alet, Bishop of. *See* Pavillon, Nicolas
Alexander of Macedon, 103, 220
Alexander VII, Pope, 74, 192
  assessment of, 28
  and Créqui affair, 1, 164*n*.
  death of, 226
  and Jansenism, 25*n*., 160–161, 211–212
  and monastic reform, 186–188, 222–223
  and papal infallibility, 8–9, 164
  relatives of, 212
  and Venetian-Turkish war, 225
Algiers, inhabitants of, 160, 173. *See also* Barbary Pirates
Aligre, Etienne d', 64
Alost, 234, 240
Alphonso VI, King of Portugal, 47
  marriage of, 116, 131, 148, 175
  Saint-Romain's mission to, 131, 156–157, 163, 214, 221, 244
  revolution against, 244
Alsace, 87, 97
  Landgrave of, 49
Amiens, 230
Amsterdam, 91
Andilly (d'). *See* Pomponne
Anglo-Dutch War, 4, 98*n*. 115, 118, 122–131, 132, 134–135, 145–146, 156, 157–158, 159–160, 167, 168, 170–172, 174–178, 180, 181–182, 189–190, 191, 194–196, 197–198, 202–203, 203–207, 209, 211, 213–214, 217–218, 221, 226–227, 228–230, 237–238
Anhalt, Prince of. *See* John George
Annat, François, S. J., 33
Anne of Austria, Queen of France

Anne of Austria [*cont.*]
  and childhood and youth of Louis, 3, 57, 92, 138
  evaluation of, 137–138, 143–144
  illness and death of, 5, 116 137–139, 143–144, 148, 178, 198
Armentières, 231
Artois, 13, 53, 232
Assembly of the Clergy
  of 1655 and of 1660, 25*n*.
  of 1660, 44
  of 1665, 139, 164–165
Ath, 233
Aubeville, Jean de Sève, Sieur d', 54
Auch, Archbishop of. *See* La Mothe-Houdancourt, Henri de
Augustinus, 25*n*.
Augustus, Roman Emperor, 80
Aumont, Antoine, Marshal d', 129
  governor of Paris, 104
  in war of Devolution, 230, 231, 232, 234
Auersperg, Johann Weikhart, Prince von, 261
Austria, house of, 14, 27, 52, 97, 98, 123, 133, 217, 226–227, 228
Auvergne
  Grands Jours of, 117, 142, 210
  regiment of, 154
Auxonne, 252
Avesnes, 242
Avocat-général. See Bignon, Jérôme II; Talon, Denis

B

Balearic Islands, 261
Baltic Sea, 27*n*, 128, 157, 177
Bamberg, 51
Barbary Pirates, 211. *See also* Algiers, Tunis
Barberini, Antonio, Cardinal, 54
Bastille, 54, 205
Bavaria, Duchess of, 133

F

DESIGN NOTE

THE DESIGN of this book observes the necessary conventions of the modern commercial book, but within these limitations it aims to give some real sense of the book Louis XIV's printers would have made for him. Modern convention dictates an octavo rather than a tall folio, dictates footnotes instead of side notes, and determines the structure of the front matter and the styling of the text. But proper to Louis are the type design, which is a modern adaptation of types used in his Imprimerie Royale; the decorations, which are from books associated with him; and the displayed matter, which follows XVIIth-century French style.

The book is set in English Monotype Garamond. Both the roman and italic of this typeface are derived from types used during its early years by the Imprimerie Royale, founded in 1640 by Richelieu and still existing today as the Imprimerie Nationale. The roman is an adaptation of the oldest roman types preserved at the Imprimerie Nationale, which formerly attributed them to Claude Garamond (d.1561), the most eminent French punch cutter of the XVIth century. They are now known to be copies of Garamond's types made between 1615 and 1620 by Jean Jannon (1580–1658), a Protestant typefounder and printer at Sedan. They were acquired by Richelieu for the Imprimerie Royale at the investiture of Sedan in 1642. The italic is a copy of the first italic used at the Imprimerie Royale in 1640; it was probably cut by Robert Granjon (fl.1545–1578). The Imprimerie Royale continued to print with these types until 1702, when they were displaced by the new *Romain du Roy*.

The frontispiece is a remarkably candid portrait of the young Louis, dated 1660, by two Flemish artists. It is reproduced from the engraving (F.D. 2203) by Pieter Louis Van Schuppen (1627–1702) after the portrait from life by Wallerant Vaillant (1623–1677). A portion of the border has been omitted.

The title-page ornament and tailpieces are reproduced from *Médailles sur les principaux Evénements du Regne de Louis le Grand* (Paris: De l'Imprimerie Royale, 1702). The engravings in this work were by Sébastien Le Clerc (1637–1714). The royal arms on the half titles are from the title page of *Ordonnance de Louis XIV . . . Donné à Saint Germain en Laye au Mois d'Avril 1667* (Paris, 1667); this version of them includes the collar of the Order of the Holy Spirit, referred to by Louis in the *Mémoires*. The headpiece to the two parts is reproduced from the headpiece of the dedication to the King in Du Cange's great edition of Geoffroy de Villehardouin's *Histoire de l'Empire de Constantinople* (Paris: De l'Imprimerie Royale, 1657). The decorative initials were engraved by the Flemish typefounder Jacques François Rosart (1714–1777) before 1760, when they were purchased by Enschedé en Zonen, Haarlem, where they are preserved. Properly speaking anachronistic, they are in XVIIth-century style and are more elegant than any of the contemporary stock initials available.

CHARLES FARRELL